Treasury of Crochet Techniques and Patterns

Treasury of Crochet Techniques and Patterns

Sedgewood™ Press

Published by Sedgewood™ Press

For Sedgewood™ Press
Editorial Director   Jane Ross
Managing Editor   Gail Kremer
Production Manager   Bill Rose

Produced for Sedgewood™ Press by
Marshall Cavendish Books Limited
58 Old Compton Street
London W1V 5PA

For Marshall Cavendish
House Editor Elizabeth Longley
Editor Eleanor Van Zandt
Designer   Heather Garioch

First printing 1984

ISBN 0-442-28198-6

Library of Congress Catalog Card Number 83-51238

Printed in the United States of America

Contents

Introduction

Crochet is one of the most popular needle-crafts. Its versatility and adaptability, plus the wide range of garments for everyone in the family and the numerous – and beautiful – items for the home that can be created, make crochet a skill that is widely practiced, and one that is loved by its practitioners.

The TREASURY OF CROCHET TECHNIQUES AND PATTERNS contains more than a simple selection of projects to execute. For each project in the book, there are a number of variations of the stitch, or technique, used to make that item, and directions for incorporating variations into that, or other, patterns to create a variety of totally different garments. It is a book for everyone who wants to improve their techniques and to explore lots of new ways of using crochet.

The TREASURY OF CROCHET TECHNIQUES AND PATTERNS is ideal for those who already enjoy crochet as well as those who are eager to learn. The main focus of the book is on the basic Techniques and Patterns in crochet. The first section deals with some of the textures, both simple and unusual, that can be created using crochet – from rice stitch and ridges to bobbles and shells, from Irish lace to extra-large patterns. Patterns and techniques using color – jacquards, stripes, "granny" squares, patchwork, and many more – make up the balance of Chapter One.

Each section of the chapter includes instructions for things to make using the skill described, plus ideas that can be adapted using the techniques learned. Each pattern, motif and variation is illustrated in full color, and charts are provided wherever they are needed.

Crochet PLUS is next – Crochet PLUS Appliqué, Crochet PLUS Embroidery and Crochet PLUS Quilting are all skills which can be practiced by a relative beginner, but which offer tremendous scope for creating beautiful things with great flair. Projects include an embroidered outfit for a baby, and jackets and vests for children.

One of the prettiest ways to use crochet is as a trim on both clothes and household linen. The TREASURY OF CROCHET TECHNIQUES AND PATTERNS devotes a chapter to the subject, offering a beautiful selection of dainty lace edgings, insertions and buttons.

In addition, there is a handy reference section of Know How, including the basic stitches and techniques required for the projects.

Tools and Materials

Very little equipment is required for crochet. The basic tool is the crochet hook, which comes in a wide range of sizes, suitable for different yarns and stitch patterns. There are several categories of hook, each with its own numbering system. The chart on p.168, which lists hooks in increasing order of size, includes equivalent metric sizes so that you can familiarize yourself with this numbering system.

For most crochet projects you will need regular or medium-sized hooks, which are made of aluminum or plastic. In this book these are designated by letter sizes (A, B and so on), but you will also see these hooks sized by number, from size 3 (the smallest) to 11. Fine steel hooks are used for delicate work, such as lacy edgings made of cotton thread. Jumbo and jiffy hooks, made of wood and plastic respectively, are used for working with bulky yarns and unusual materials such as fabric strips and twine. For different types of crochet you need other tools – such as afghan hooks and hairpin lace forks. But all the projects in this book use ordinary hooks.

Knitting needles are required for a few of the projects – for example, those with waistbands or cuffs of knitted ribbing. A tapestry needle in a fairly large size (15 to 13) is required for sewing seams. This type of needle has a blunt point, which will not snag the yarn, and a large eye for easy threading. It is also the type of needle to use for any embroidery you may wish to work on crochet.

Stainless steel pins, with round heads, are used for pinning work out when blocking it into shape and for joining sections for seaming.

A ruler and tape measure are necessary for checking gauge and for measuring the work.

A small pair of scissors is needed for cutting the yarn.

Yarns and threads

The range of materials suitable for crochet is enormous. In addition to the vast selection of knitting yarns, which include many different weights, fibers and styles – smooth, fluffy, silky and highly textured – you have a choice of numerous weights of crochet cotton, as well as linen and silk threads. Rug yarn and macramé cord can be used for household and personal accessories, from floor pillows to shopping bags. Ordinary parcel string, raffia, jute, and leather thonging are some of the unusual materials that can be used for crochet.

Yarns are classified in various ways – according to their weight, or thickness; their ply, or the number of strands used to form the yarn (for example, 3-ply or 4-ply); their fiber content; and their construction. Ply is relatively unimportant, as the strands themselves vary in thickness, so that a 3-ply can be as thick, or even thicker than a 4-ply. But you should understand the other factors and consider them when choosing yarn for a project.

Weight Listed below are the standard types of knitting yarn, in increasing order of thickness.

Fingering This is a lightweight yarn used for delicate garments, such as evening sweaters, scarves and lacy shawls.

Baby yarn (above) Slightly bulkier than fingering yarn, this is available in pastel shades.

Sport, or sport-weight yarn (below) A medium-weight yarn, this is used for many different items, including shawls, afghans and sweaters.

Knitting worsted Strictly speaking, this term refers to a heavyweight wool yarn, but it is also applied to synthetic yarns and blends of the same weight. It is used for any garment or accessory that needs to be fairly thick or warm.

Rug yarn and bulky yarns These are progressively heavier than knitting worsted. They are used for pillow covers and other household accessories and for some outer garments.

Fiber content Most knitting yarns today are spun either of wool, of a synthetic fiber such as acrylic, nylon or rayon, or of a blend of wool and synthetic fibers. Mohair is another natural fiber that is often used, either by itself or combined with wool or a synthetic; it comes from the Angora goat and has a fluffy texture. Angora yarn, which is even softer, is made from the fur of the Angora rabbit. Alpaca is another soft fiber, taken from a South American animal similar to a llama. It is often blended with wool. Cotton, silk and – less often – linen are other natural fibers used in knitting and crochet yarns.

Crochet cotton is a smooth yarn that comes in various types and thicknesses, graded by number, with the larger numbers designating finer threads. Among the types available are pearl cotton (size 5), a shiny 2-ply thread that comes in a wide range of colors, six-cord cotton (sizes 20 and 30), which comes in white and ecru; and the finest tatting-crochet cotton (size 70), which comes in various colors. These threads are sold by length, rather than weight. They are usually mercerized, a process that gives them greater strength and sheen; they may also be marked "boil-fast," which means that the color, if any, will not run.

Fiber content is an important consideration when buying yarn. Wool is the warmest and is the obvious choice for a garment intended for outdoor wear. It also has great resilience, holding its shape better than synthetics. Most wools can be hand-washed. Synthetic yarns, such as acrylics, are easy to care for – often machine-washable – which makes them the best choice for children's garments. The yarn label often includes information on the care, which should be followed carefully.

Construction Most yarns have a smooth texture, which may be loosely or tightly twisted. Some smooth yarns have a noticeable "cable" appearance; fisherman and rug yarns fall into this category. Others have a somewhat hard surface, which produces very clearly defined stitches. Still others, such as Shetland yarns, have a soft, slightly hairy texture. Smooth yarns are easy to handle and can be used for most projects.

Novelty yarns include a dazzling variety of textures that offer many possibilities for creating exciting fashions. Mohair is perhaps the most popular novelty yarn. It is often combined with wool or acrylic to produce a yarn that is less fuzzy than pure mohair. Bouclé is another popular yarn; its distinctive "bumpy" texture contrasts effectively with a smooth yarn in a harmonizing color. Cotton bouclé yarns make summer garments with an attractive "crunchy" look. Chenille yarn makes a velvety fabric. Metallic threads are popular for evening wear, and they may be combined with other threads to produce novelty yarns in which the glittery effect has an interesting random quality.

A visit to a good yarn shop will reveal more exciting textures. Many patterns, including some in this book, are designed for novelty yarns. And if a pattern specifies a smooth yarn, you can sometimes substitute a novelty yarn. However, if you want to do so, bear in mind this general rule: the more highly-textured the yarn, the simpler the stitch pattern should be; for these yarns tend to obscure the outlines of stitches. A mohair blend can often be used very successfully for bobbles or even some lace patterns, as it softens the outlines only slightly; however, a bouclé might ruin the effect. To make sure your choice of yarn is suitable, buy one ball to start with and make a sample of the stitch pattern. This will also enable you to see if you can achieve the correct gauge (see page 10) with the substitute yarn.

When buying any yarn, always buy enough for the whole project, making sure that all of the balls or skeins are from the same dye lot. This number is printed on the yarn label. Colors do vary slightly from one dye lot to another, and this variation would be apparent in the finished project.

Another point to remember is that the length of yarn may vary from one ball to another, depending on the color. Darker shades of dye add more weight to the yarn, so that one ounce of black yarn will contain fewer yards than an ounce of the same yarn in pink, for example.

Crochet Basics

From pages 12 to 138 you will find a selection of projects, along with alternative stitch patterns that can, in many cases, be substituted for the stitch pattern used in the project. Each project includes a special technique used in that design, which is explained and illustrated in detail.

Experienced crocheters will be able to follow the instructions for most projects with no further help. However, if you need help in other crochet techniques – including the most basic skills – you will find this in the special "Know How" section, from page 146 to 165. Beginners should turn to this section first and learn the basic crochet stitches and techniques, such as joining yarn, increasing and decreasing. The section also includes helpful tips for left-handed crocheters (page 162). Crochet patterns, like knitting patterns, are written in a kind of shorthand, which uses abbreviations and symbols to convey detailed information in relatively little space. Abbreviations are explained in the chart on this page.

Gauge

This term refers to the number of stitches – and sometimes also the number of rows – that must be worked in a given measurement in order to obtain a piece of crochet of the correct size. It is **vitally important** that you work to the same gauge as that established by the designer of the pattern; otherwise the measurements of the completed work will be either too large or too small. A difference of even half a stitch per inch will produce a considerable difference over a width of, say, 18 inches. People differ naturally in the tension with which they work – some hold the yarn and hook much more loosely than others, producing a more open fabric. If the gauge which you produce differs from the one given for the pattern, simply adjust it by using a different size crochet hook.

First, however, make a gauge swatch using the hook specified. Work a sample containing a few more stitches and rows than given; for example, if the gauge is 18 stitches and 20 rows to 4 inches, work about 22 stitches and 25 rows; this makes it easier to count the stitches. Lay the finished sample on a flat surface and mark off the specified number of stitches and rows with pins. Carefully measure the distances between the two sets of pins; the measurements should be the same as those stated. If it is less, your gauge is too small; change to a larger hook and work another sample. If it is more, change to a smaller hook. Make additional samples as necessary until you obtain the correct gauge. Sometimes you will find it difficult to obtain the correct gauge in both directions. Normally the stitch gauge is more important than the row gauge, particularly if little shaping is required. Concentrate on getting the stitch gauge right; if the row gauge is important (for example, on the top of a raglan sleeve, which contains a fixed number of rows), you should be able to adjust your method of working to correct it.

Finishing

You should devote as much care to finishing a crochet project as you give to working the stitches. "Finishing" generally includes: darning in the ends, blocking (sometimes pressing), and seaming.

To darn in ends, first thread them through a tapestry needle. Take the needle in and out of several stitches, either on the edge of the fabric or on the wrong side; work a backstitch once or twice as you go to anchor the thread. Trim the end.

To block a piece of crochet, pin it to the correct shape on a flat surface – an ironing board or several thicknesses of turkish towel placed over a plastic sheet on the floor. If the work is highly textured, place it right side up. Lay a damp cloth over the work and leave it to dry thoroughly. Or spray it with water.

Pressing is seldom required, except on flat-textured work made of wool or cotton. Use either a steam iron or a dry iron with a damp cloth. Hold the iron just above the work or so that it barely touches the surface – depending on the amount of texture. Do not slide the iron over the surface or let its weight rest on the work. Leave the crochet to dry thoroughly before unpinning it.

Different kinds of seams are used to join pieces of crochet, depending on the position of the seam and the type of work. A backstitch seam is often used on the underarm seam of a garment, for example, where a strong stitch is required. The edges are pinned together with right sides facing and the backstitch worked close to the edges, using a tapestry needle.

Other types of seam – both inconspicuous and decorative – are described on pages 86, 124, 162 and 165.

If a bulky or novelty yarn has been used, choose a lighter weight, smooth yarn in a matching color for the seaming to prevent excess bulk.

Abbreviations used in this book	
approx	approximately
beg	begin(ning)
ch	chain(s)
cont	continu(e)(ing)
dc	double crochet
dec	decreas(e)(ing)
dtr	double triple crochet
gr(s)	group(s)
hdc	half double crochet
in	inch(es)
inc	increas(e)(ing)
K	knit
LH	left hand
oz	ounce(s)
P	purl
pat	pattern
rem	remain(ing)
rep	repeat
RH	right hand
RS	right side
sc	single crochet
sl st	slip stitch
sp(s)	space(s)
st(s)	stitch(es)
tog	together
tr	triple crochet
tr tr	triple triple crochet
WS	wrong side
yo	yarn over hook

Additional abbreviations are explained within the pattern in which they are used.

Chapter 1
Techniques and Patterns

Afghan squares

Use up scraps of old yarn and at the same time make beautiful garments or accessories; they're easily made from afghan squares, such as the granny square used for this colorful afghan.

The basic afghan

Size
The afghan shown measures 43 x 33in.

Materials
Each square requires a small amount of sport yarn in main color A, and each of 5 contrasting colors: B, C, D, E and F. Size E crochet hook.

Gauge
Each square measures 5 x 5 in worked on a size E hook

To save time, take time to check gauge.

To make a square
Using B, make 6ch, sl st into first ch to form a ring.
1st round Ch 3, 3dc into ring, *ch 3, 4dc into ring, rep from * twice, ch 3, join with a sl st to 3rd of first 3ch. Fasten off.

2nd round Using C, join yarn to next 3ch sp, ch 3, 3dc, ch 3, 4dc all into 3ch sp, *ch 2, (4dc, ch 3, 4dc) into next 3ch sp, rep from * twice, ch 2, join with a sl st to 3rd of first 3ch. Fasten off.
3rd round Using D, join yarn to next 3ch sp, ch 3, 3dc, ch 3, 4dc all into 3ch sp, *ch 2, 4dc into 2ch sp, ch 2, (4dc, ch 3, 4dc) into next 3ch sp, rep from * twice, ch 2, 4dc into next 2ch sp, ch 2, join with a sl st to 3rd of first 3ch. Fasten off.
4th round Using E, join yarn to next 3ch sp, ch 3, 3dc, ch 3, 4dc all into next 3ch, sp, *(ch 2, 4dc into next 2ch sp) twice, ch 2, (4dc, ch 3, 4dc) into next 3ch sp, rep from * twice, (ch 2, 4dc into next 2ch sp) twice, ch 2, join with a sl st to 3rd of first 3ch. Fasten off.
5th round Using F, join yarn to next 3ch sp, ch 3, 3dc, ch 3, 4dc all into 3ch sp, *(ch 2, 4dc into next 2ch sp) 3 times, ch 2, (4dc, ch 3, 4dc) all into next 3ch sp, rep from * twice, (ch 2, 4dc into next 2ch sp) 3 times, ch 2, join with a sl st to 3rd of first 3ch. Fasten off.
6th round Using A, join yarn to next 3ch sp, ch 3, 3dc, ch 3, 4dc all into 3ch sp, *(ch 2, 4dc into next 2ch sp) 4 times, ch 2, (4dc, ch 3, 4dc) into next 3ch sp, rep from * twice, (ch 2, 4dc into next 2ch sp) 4 times, ch 2, join with a sl st to 3rd

of first 3ch. Fasten off. Make a total of 48 squares in the same way.

To finish
Darn in all ends neatly on the wrong side. Press lightly or block, according to yarn used. Using A and placing RS tog, join squares into 6 strips, each containing 8 squares. Catch-stitching corresponding loops on to last rounds of squares.
Sew long strips tog in the same way to form afghan.

Edging
Using A, work 3 rounds in dc, working 1dc into each st and working 3dc into each sp and 8dc into outer corners on first round. Work one round in sc. Fasten off.

SPECIAL TECHNIQUE
simple edging

1 When working a corner in the simple double and single crochet edging, on the first round work along the edge to the 3 chain space at the corner of the afghan. Work 8 stitches into the space. On subsequent rounds, work 1 stitch into each of the 8 stitches at the corner.

2 To join in rounds of crochet with a slip stitch, first work to the end of the round. Insert the hook into the top of the turning chain worked at the beginning of the round, take the yarn counter-clockwise over the hook and draw through all loops on the hook.

3 At the beginning of each round, work chains (3 chains for double crochet rounds, 1 chain for single crochet rounds) to count as the first stitch. Skip the first stitch and work double or single crochet into each of the remaining corner stitches.

Adapting the afghan

Each of these squares can be used to make an afghan, or you could work several in one design.

Planning

Before beginning, sort the yarns into "weights" – i.e. into knitting worsted, sport or fingering yarn. Mixing different yarns could cause the afghan to become distorted. Afghans can be carefully planned like fabric patchwork, so that colors are used in groups of light, medium and dark shades. Colors can also be used randomly to produce a multicolored fabric like the afghan on page 13, in which the final round of each square and the edging are worked in the main color.

Gauge

Gauge is generally less important than in making a garment, although you should use a hook that produces a firm, even fabric.

However, if you want the finished fabric to be a particular size – perhaps to cover a pillow form – you should check the gauge carefully. If the motif is slightly too small or too large, change your hook size. If the size difference is large, try omitting the last round or adding another one.

Pattern Library: Afghan patterns

Circled square (1)

This square is worked in 2 colors, A and B.

Using A, make 6ch, sl st into first ch to form a ring.

1st round Ch 3, 15dc into ring, join with a sl st to 3rd of first 3ch.

2nd round Ch 5, (1dc into next dc, ch 2) 15 times, join with a sl st to 3rd of 5ch.

3rd round Sl st into first sp, ch 3, 1dc into same sp, (ch 1, 2dc into next sp) 15 times, ch 1, join with a sl st to 3rd of 3ch.

4th round Sl st into next dc, sl st into next sp, 1sc into same sp, *(ch 3, 1sc into next sp) 3 times, ch 6, 1sc into next sp, rep from * 3 times omitting 1sc at end of last rep, join with a sl st to first sc. Fasten off.

5th round Join B to first 3ch sp of any side, ch 3, 2dc into same sp, *3dc into each 3ch sp to corner, (5dc, ch 2, 5dc) into corner 6ch sp, rep from * 3 times, join with a sl st to 3rd of first 3 ch. Fasten off.

Crossed square (2)

This square is worked in 4 colors, A, B, C and D.

Using A, make 6ch, sl st to first ch to form a ring.

1st round Ch 3, 3dc into ring, (ch 3, 4dc) 3 times into ring, ch 3, join with a sl st to 3rd of first 3ch. Fasten off and turn.

2nd round (RS) Join B to any 3ch sp, ch 3, 1dc into same sp, (1dc into each of next 4dc, 2dc into next 3ch sp, 1tr tr into beg ring between the 4dc groups, 2dc into same sp as last 2dc) 4 times, omitting 2dc at end of last rep, join with a sl st to 3rd of first 3ch. Fasten off and turn.

3rd round Join C to any tr tr, ch 3, (1dc into each of next 8dc, 1dc, ch 3, 1dc into next tr tr) 3 times, 1dc into each of last 8dc, 1dc into same place as joining, ch 3, sl st to 3rd of first 3ch. Fasten off and turn.

4th round Join D to any 3ch sp, ch 3, 1dc into same sp, (1dc into each of next 10dc, 2dc into next 3ch sp, 1tr tr around stem on tr tr worked on 2nd round, inserting hook from right to left from front of work, 2dc into same sp as last 2dc) 4 times, omitting 2dc at end of last rep, join with sl st to 3rd of first 3ch. Fasten off.

1

2

Five-color square (3)

This square is worked in 5 colors, A, B, C, D and E. Using A, make 4ch, sl st to first ch to form a ring.

1st round Ch 4, 3tr into ring, (ch 2, 4tr into ring) 3 times, ch 2, join with a sl st to 4th of first 4ch. Fasten off and turn.

2nd round (RS) Join B to any 2ch sp, 2sc into same sp, (1sc into each of next 4 sts, 2sc, ch 2, 2sc into corner 2ch sp) 3 times, 1sc into each of next 4 sts, 2sc into same sp as joining, ch 2, join with a sl st to first sc. Fasten off and turn.

3rd round Join C to first sc after a 2 ch sp, ch 3, 1dc into 2ch sp before joining, *(skip next sc, 1dc into next sc, 1dc into skipped sc) 3 times, skip 1sc, 1dc into next 2ch sp, 1dc into skipped sc, 1dc into next sc, 1dc into 2ch sp before last dc, rep from * 3 times omitting last 2dc at end of last rep, join with a sl st to 3rd of first 3ch. Fasten off and turn.

4th round Join D to same place as sl st of last round, ch 3, 2dc into same sp, (ch 1, 3dc into next dc, 1dc into each of next 8dc, 3dc into next dc) 4 times omitting 3dc at end of last rep, join with a sl st to 3rd of first 3ch. Fasten off and turn.

5th round Join E to first dc after any 1ch sp, 1sc into same place as joining, 1sc into next dc, *(1tr into next dc, then bending tr in half to form bobble on RS of square work 1sc into next dc, 1sc into next dc) 4 times, 3dc into corner 1ch sp, 1sc into each of next 2dc, rep from * 3 times omitting 2sc at end of last rep, join with a sl st to first sc. Fasten off and turn.

6th round Join A to first sc of any side, (1sc into each st to center dc of 3dc at corner, 3sc into corner dc) 4 times, 1sc in next dc, join with a sl st to first sc. Fasten off.

Sunburst square (4)

This square is worked in 3 colors: A, B and C. Using A, make 4ch, sl st to first ch to form a ring.

1st round Ch 4, 1tr into ring, ch 3, (leaving last loop of each tr on hook work 2tr into ring), yo and draw through all 3 loops, ch 3) 7 times, join with a sl st to 4th of first 4ch.

2nd round Sl st into first ch of next 3ch sp, (1sc into center ch of 3ch sp, ch 5) 8 times, join with a sl st into first sc. Fasten off.

3rd round Join B to the center ch of any 5ch sp, 1sc into same place as joining, *(1dtr, ch 1) 10 times, 1dtr all into next 5ch sp, 1sc into next 5ch sp, rep from * 3 times, omitting 1sc at end of last rep, join with a sl st to first sc. Fasten off.

4th round Join C to any 1ch sp, ch 2, 1dc into same sp, (ch 1, leaving last loop of each dc on hook work 2dc into next 1ch sp, yo and draw through all 3 loops) into each 1ch sp, ch 1, sl st to top of first dc. Fasten off.

Pinwheel square (5)

This square is worked in 2 colors: A and B.

Using A, make 6ch, join with a sl st into a ring.

1st round Ch 6, (1dc, ch 3 into ring) 7 times, join with a sl st to 3rd of first 6ch. Fasten off.

2nd round Join B to any 3ch sp, ch 3, 3dc, ch 2 into 3ch sp, (4dc, ch 2 into next 3ch sp) 7 times, join with a sl st to 3rd of first 3ch. Fasten off.

3rd round Rejoin A to any 2ch sp, ch 3, 5dc, ch 1 into 2ch sp, (6dc, ch 3 into next sp, 6dc, ch 1 into next sp) 3 times, 6dc, ch 3 into next 3ch sp, join with a sl st to 3rd of first 3ch. Fasten off.

4th round Rejoin B to any 3ch sp, ch 3, 1dc, ch 3, 2dc into 3ch sp, *ch 3, 1sc between 3rd and 4th dc of next group, ch 3, 1sc into 1ch sp, ch 3, 1sc between 3rd and 4th dc of next group, ch 3, (2dc, ch 3, 2dc) into next 3ch sp, rep from * twice, ch 3, 1sc between 3rd and 4th dc of next group, ch 3, 1sc into 1ch sp, ch 3, 1sc between 3rd and 4th dc of next group, ch 3, join with a sl st to 3rd of first 3ch. Fasten off.

5

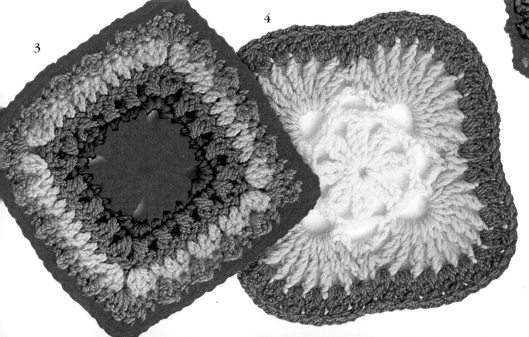

3

4

15

Single crochet variations

Basic single crochet can easily be varied to make firm, textured fabrics that are ideal for hard-wearing garments such as these children's vests.

The basic single crochet vest

Sizes
C-7 [C-8:C-10:C-12]
Length 17 [19:21:22] in including border
Note: *Length is adjustable. Instructions for larger sizes are in brackets [ ]; where there is only one set of figures it applies to all sizes.*

Materials
9 [11:14:16] oz of a bulky yarn, A
2 [2:4:4] oz of a knitting worsted, B
Size F crochet hook
Size K crochet hook

Gauge
10sc and 14 rows to 4in in pattern using A, worked on size K hook

To save time, take time to check gauge.

Body (worked in one piece to armholes)
Using larger hook and A, make 65 [71:77:83] ch.
Base row 1sc into 3rd ch from hook, 1sc into each ch to end. Turn.
Pattern row Ch 2, working into back loop only of each st, work 1sc into each sc to end. Turn.
64 [70:76:82] sts.
Rep pat row until work measures 10½ [11½::12½:13½] in, ending with a WS row.
Divide for armholes
Next row Work in pat across first 13 [14:15:16] sts, turn.
Cont in pat for a further 10 [12:14:15] rows on these sts (until armhole measures 4¼ [5½:6¼:7½] in), ending at armhole edge.
Next row Work in pat across first 6 [7:7:8] sts, turn.
Leave 6 [7:7:8] sts unworked for neck. Work 6 [6:7:7] more rows on these 6 [7:7:8] sts. Fasten off.

Back
Return to rem sts at armhole. With RS of work facing, leave 6 [7:8:9] sts

unworked at armhole. Rejoin yarn to 7th [8th:9th:10th] st, ch 2, work in pat across first 25 [27:29:31] sts, turn and leave rem sts unworked. Work 16 [18:21:22] more rows on these sts. Fasten off.

Front
Return to rem sts at armhole. With RS of work facing, leave next 6 [7:8:9] sts unworked, rejoin yarn to 7th [8th:9th:10th] st, ch 2, work in pat across next 12 [13:14:15] sts. Turn. Work a further 10 [12:14:15] rows in pat on these sts so that armhole measures 4¼ [5½:6¼:7½] in, ending at neck edge.
Shape neck
Next row Sl st over first 8 [8:8:9] sts, 2ch, pat to end.
Work in pat on rem 6 [7:7:8] sts for 6 [6:7:7] more rows. Fasten off.

To finish
Join shoulder seams.
Front, neck and lower borders
With RS of work facing and using

smaller hook and B, rejoin yarn to center back neck. Work all around edge in sc, working 4sc for every 3 sts on main body at back neck, 1sc into each row end down front edges, 1sc into each st at front neck, 6sc for every 5 foundation sts along lower edge, and 3sc into each right-angled corner. Join with a sl st to center back. Work 4 more rounds sc on these sts, working 1 turning ch at beg of each round and remembering to work 3sc into each corner sc and dec 1sc at inner front neck corner shaping.
Next round Work in crab st (see Special Technique page 18) so that sc is worked from left to right rather than right to left. Join with a sl st. Fasten off.

Armhole borders
Work as for front, neck and lower edging, working 1sc into each sc at underarm and dec one st at underarm corners on each row. Work 1 round in in crab st as before. Fasten off.

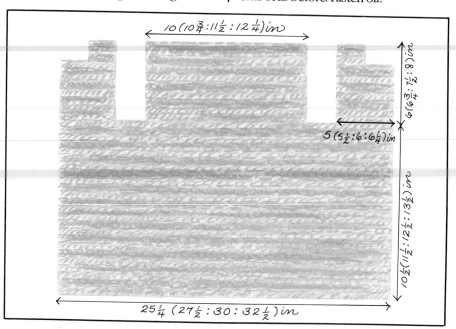

10 (10¾ : 11½ : 12¼) in

6 (6 : 3¾ : 7½ : 8) in

5 (5½ : 6 : 6¼) in

10¾ (11½ : 12½ : 13½) in

25¼ (27½ : 30 : 32½) in

working a crab stitch edging

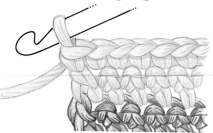

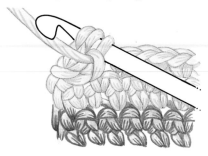

1 Crab stitch is achieved by working single crochet from left to right instead of from right to left, usually on one or more foundation rows of single crochet, depending on how deep you would like the edging to be. End with the right side of the work facing.

2 Do not turn the work once the foundation rows have been completed. Keeping the yarn at left of work, work from left to right. Make one chain, then insert the hook from front to back into the next stitch. Hold the hook over the yarn before drawing yarn through from back to front.

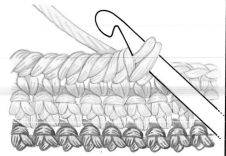

3 Complete the single crochet in the usual way. Continue to work each stitch in the same way, working from left to right instead of from right to left to the end of the row.

Adapting the vest

Any of the stitches on the following pages could be substituted for the ridge stitch used in the vest to create a different texture.

Substituting a pattern
In order to substitute one of the alternative patterns you must first make a gauge swatch in the pattern and yarn of your choice. If the gauge obtained is the same as that given in the instructions you can proceed at once to make the garment from the original instructions. If, however, the gauge is not the same, a certain amount of calculation will be needed before you can start.

Calculating from a gauge swatch
In order to determine the number of stitches you will need to start your pattern, you must make a gauge swatch approximately 4in square in the yarn and stitch pattern of your choice, and then count the number of stitches and rows obtained in your sample. You will

Pattern Library: Single crochet variations

Double grain stitch (1)
Make a multiple of 2 plus 1 ch with 3 extra ch.
Base row Insert hook into 4th ch from hook, yo and draw through a loop, yo and draw through 2 loops on hook – called 1 exsc –, *1ch, skip 1ch, 1exsc into next ch, rep from * to end. Turn.
Pattern row Ch 2, *1exsc into next 1ch sp of previous row, ch 1, rep from * to end, 1 exsc into turning ch. Turn.
Rep pat row throughout.

1

see on the pattern diagram given with the instructions the width needed for your garment, and from your gauge swatch you can calculate the number of stitches needed to obtain this measurement. For example, if the total width is 28in and you obtain 12 stitches to 4in (or 3 stitches to 1in), you will need 84 stitches to obtain the correct width. Row gauge is not so important on a simple pattern.

Fitting in a pattern
Remember that when you calculate the number of stitches needed for the width of your garment, you must make allowances for the number of stitches needed to accommodate your stitch pattern. If, for example, your stitch pattern is divisible by 4, the number of stitches across the garment must either also be divisible by 4 or include edge stitches, to keep the pattern correct.

Shaping
If the shape of the garment is quite simple, requiring very little shaping at the armhole or neck – as in the vest – it should be quite easy to calculate how many stitches need to be decreased, increased, or left unworked, using your gauge swatch and measurement diagram once more. By working from the original instructions and gauge you will see how many inches must be decreased to shape the armhole and can then calculate from your own sample the number of stitches you will need to decrease at that point, using your own pattern.

For a garment entailing more complicated shaping or stitch patterns, more detailed calculations would be necessary, and you should work out the shape precisely on graph paper.

Albania stitch (2)
Make any number of ch.
Base row 1sc into 3rd ch from hook, 1sc into each ch to end. Turn.
Pattern row Ch 1 to count as first st, inserting hook into front loop only of each st work 1sc into each sc to end, 1sc into turning ch. Turn.
Rep pat row throughout.

Crochet bobble stitch (3)
Make a multiple of 4 ch plus 3 extra.
Base row 1sc into 3rd ch from hook, 1sc into each ch to end. Turn.
1st row (RS) Ch 1 to count as first sc, *ch 4, 1sc into each of next 4sc, rep from * ending ch 4, 1sc into turning ch. Turn.
2nd row Holding 4ch at back (RS) of work, work ch 1 to count as first sc, 1sc into each sc to end, 1sc into turning ch. Turn.
3rd row Ch 1 to count as first sc, 1sc into each of next 2sc, *4ch, 1sc into each of next 4sc, rep from * to end, ending with 4ch, 1sc into each of last 2sc, 1sc into turning ch. Turn.
4th row As 2nd.
Rep first-4th rows throughout.

4

Daisy stitch (4)
Make an even number of ch plus 1.
Base row 1sc into 3rd ch from hook (1sc, ch 1, 1sc) into next ch – called 1sc group –, *skip 1ch, 1sc group into next ch, rep from * to last ch, 1sc into last ch. Turn.
Pattern row Ch 2, *1sc group into center 1ch sp of next 1sc group worked in previous row, rep from * to end, 1sc into top of turning ch. Turn.
Rep pat row throughout.

2

3

Half-double variations

Half double is one of the basic crochet stitches. By itself it produces a firm, fairly dense fabric; varied and combined with other basic stitches, it can form a surprising variety of stitch patterns, as shown in this cotton cardigan.

The basic half-double cardigan

Sizes
Misses' sizes 8 [12]
Length (including waistband) 21½ [22¼]in
Sleeve seam 7½ [8]in
Note: *Instructions for larger size are in brackets* [ ] ; where there is only one set of figures it applies to both sizes.

Materials
975 [1110]yd of size 3 cotton in main color A
140 [280]yd in contrasting colour B
140 [140]yd in contrasting color C
Size E crochet hook
Size F crochet hook
Pair of size 2 knitting needles
6 buttons

Gauge
13 sts to 4in in pattern worked on size F hook

To save time, take time to check gauge.

Back and fronts (worked in one piece to armholes)
Using A and larger hook, make 100 [112] ch *loosely.*
Base row 1sc into 3rd ch from hook, 1sc into each ch to end. Turn. 99 [111] sts.
1st row Ch 2, yo, insert hook into first st, yo and draw through a loop, yo, insert hook into next st, yo and draw through a loop, yo and draw through all 5 loops on hook, ch 1, * yo, insert hook into same st as 2nd loop of previous st, yo and draw through a loop, yo, insert a hook into next st, yo and draw through a loop, yo, and draw through all 5 loops on hook – double half double or dhdc worked –, ch 1, rep from * to turning ch, 1hdc into turning ch. Turn.
2nd row (RS) Ch 1, skip first st, 1sc into each 1ch sp to end, 1sc into top of turning ch. Turn.
First and 2nd rows form one pat rep.

Work 2 more pats in A. Cont in stripe sequence as follows: one rep in B, 3 reps in A, one rep in C.
Cont in pat, working stripe sequence as set until 17 pats in all have been worked.
Shape neck
Next row Ch 2, skip first sc, work in dhdc to last 2 sts, 1dhdc into last sc. Turn. 2dhdc dec.
Next row As 2nd row of pat.
Divide for armholes
Next row Ch 2, work in dhdc across 15 [19] sc. Turn.
Left front
Next row As 2nd row of pat.
Next row Ch 2, skip first sc, work in dhdc to end. 14 [17] dhdc.
Next row As 2nd row of pat.
Next row As first row of pat.
Next row As 2nd row of pat.
Next row As previous shaping row. 13 [16] dhdc.
Cont to dec one st at neck edge on alternate dhdc rows until 9 [12] dhdc rem. Work even until work measures 19½ [20¼]in, ending with a 2nd row. Fasten off.

Back
With WS facing, skip next 10sc and rejoin yarn to next st, ch 2, work in dhdc across 46 [52] sc. Turn.
Cont in pat, until work measures same as left front to shoulder, ending with a 2nd row.
Next row Ch 2, work in dhdc across 15 [17] sc, sl st across 16[18] sc, work in dhdc to end. Fasten off.

Right front
With WS facing, skip next 10sc and rejoin yarn to next st, ch 2, work in dhdc across rem 16[19] sc.
Next row As 2nd row of pat.
Next row Ch 2, work in dhdc to last st. Turn. 15[18] dhdc.

Next row As 2nd row of pat.
Next row As first row of pat.
Next row As previous shaping row. 14[17] dhdc.
Complete to match left front.

Sleeves (both alike)
Using A and larger hook, make 45 [49] ch *loosely.*
Base row 1sc into 3rd ch from hook, 1sc into each ch to end. Turn. 43[47] sts.
Work 2 pat reps in A, one in C, 2[3] in A.
Cont to work in stripe sequence as for back and fronts and at the same time:
Shape top
Next row Sl st into first 7 sts, ch 2, work in dhdc to last 7sc, 1dhdc into next sc. Turn.
Next row As 2nd row of pat.
Next row Ch 2, skip first sc, work in dhdc to last 2 sts, 1dhdc in last st. Turn. 2dhdc dec.
Next row As 2nd row of pat.
Next row As first row of pat.
Next row As 2nd row of pat.
Rep last 4 rows twice more. 31 [35] sts.
Next row Ch 2, skip first sc, dhdc to last 2 sts, 1dhdc into last st. Turn.
Next row As 2nd row of pat.
Rep last 2 rows 4 [5] times more. 21 [23] sts.
Next row Ch 2, skip first sc, work in dhdc to last 2 sts, 1dhdc in last st. Turn.
Next row Sl st into first 2 sts, ch 1, skip first st, work in sc to last 2 dhdc, turn.
Next row Sl st into first 2 sts, ch 2, work in dhdc to last 2sc, sl st into next sc. Fasten off.

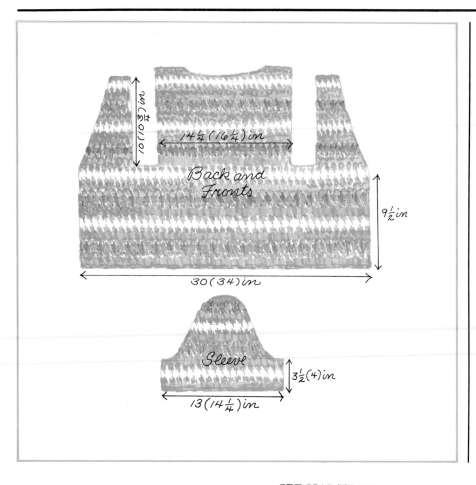

14¼ (16¼) in

10 (10¾) in

Back and Fronts

9½ in

30 (34) in

Sleeve

3½ (4) in

13 (14¼) in

Waistband

Using A, knitting needles and with RS facing, pick up and K sts from free edge of foundation ch as follows: one st from first ch, * 2 sts from next ch, one st from next ch, rep from * to end. 148 [166] sts. Work 2in in K2, P2 ribbing. Bind off in ribbing.

Cuffs (both alike)

Using A, knitting needles and with RS facing, pick up and K sts from free edge of foundation ch as for waistband. 64 [70] sts. Work 4in in K2, P2 ribbing. Bind off in ribbing.

To finish

Join shoulder seams.

Front border

Using A, smaller hook and with RS facing, beg at lower edge of center front and work into front edge as follows: 1sc into each row end on right front, working 2sc into angle at beg of neck shaping, 1sc into each st across back neck, 1sc into each row end on left front, working 2sc as before. Turn.

Next row As for first row of pat rep.
Next row As 2nd row of pat. Rep last 2 rows once more.

SPECIAL TECHNIQUE
working double half double

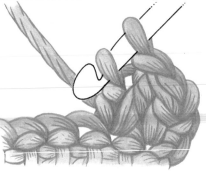

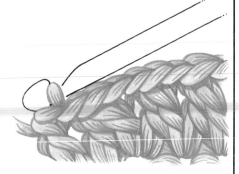

1 Make two chains to begin the double half double row. Take the yarn over the hook and insert the hook into the first stitch. * Yarn over and draw through a loop, yarn over and insert the hook into the next stitch, yarn over and draw through a loop.

2 Take the yarn over the hook and draw through all five loops on the hook * to form the first double half double. Work one chain. To work the next double half double, take the yarn over the hook and insert the hook into the same stitch as the second loop of the previous stitch. Work from * to * Work one chain.

3 Continue to work double half double and one chain alternately to the turning chain. Work one half double into the last stitch. On the next row begin with one chain, skip the first stitch and work one single crochet into each one-chain space to the end, ending with one single crochet into the turning chain.

Next row As first row of pat. On right front border, mark positions of 6 buttonholes, one ½in from lower edge and one at beg of neck shaping and rem 4 spaced equally between.

Buttonhole row Using B, ch 1, 1sc into first 1ch sp, * ch 2, skip next 1ch sp – buttonhole worked,* cont as for 2nd row of pat, working from * to * at markers until 6 buttonholes in all have been worked, then cont in sc to end. Turn.

Next row As for first row of pat, working 2dhdc into each 2ch sp. Turn.

Next row As for 2nd row of pat. Fasten off.

Join sleeve seams.

Set in sleeves, matching stripes.

Steam press work on WS, omitting ribbing. Sew on buttons to correspond with buttonholes.

Adapting the basic cardigan

Use simple half-double variations to create a variety of textured, firm and openwork fabrics.

Because of the gauge of the double half double pattern used for the basic cardigan – in which the first and second pattern rows are of different depths – it is not possible to use any of the following half-double variations as an alternative. These patterns do, however, show the range of effects that can be produced using the half-double stitch in different combinations. To vary the cardigan, you could change the stripe sequence. Wider, narrower and random stripes are just three of the possibilities.

Matching stripes

The back and fronts of the cardigan on page 21 are worked in one piece to the armholes, so there is no difficulty in matching stripes at the side seams. However, whether you are working the basic cardigan or a variation of your own, take care to match stripes carefully at the armholes.

To do this, simply make sure that the shaping on both the body and the sleeves begins on the same row in the stripe sequence. For example, on the basic cardigan the armhole shaping begins on the third pattern worked in the main color. When setting in the sleeves, ease the sleeve top so that the stripes match those on the body.

Pattern Library: Half-double samples

Rug stitch (1)

Make a multiple of 2ch plus 3 extra.

Base row (RS) 1hdc into 3rd ch from hook, 1hdc into side or previous hdc, * skip next ch, 1hdc next ch, 1hdc into side of previous hdc, rep from * to last 2ch, 1hdc into last ch. Turn.

1st row Ch 1, skip first st, 1sc into each st to end. Turn.

2nd row Ch 2 to count as first hdc, skip first st, * 1hdc into next st, 1hdc into edge of previous hdc, skip next st, rep from * to turning ch, 1hdc into top of turning ch. Turn.

Rep first and 2nd rows throughout.

Tulip stitch (2)

Use 2 colors, A and B. Using A, make a multiple of 3ch plus 3.

Base row (RS) (1hdc, ch 1, 1hdc) into 3rd ch from hook, * skip 2ch, (1hdc, ch 1, 1hdc) into next ch, rep from * to last 2ch, 1hdc into last ch. Turn.

1st row Ch 2 to count as first hdc, * (1hdc, ch 1, 1hdc) into next 1ch sp, rep from * to end, ending 1hdc into top of turning ch. Turn.

2nd row Using B, ch 2 to count as first hdc, * 3hdc into next 1ch sp, rep from * to end, ending 1hdc into top of turning ch. Return to beg of row.

3rd row Using A, ch 2, 1sc between turning ch and first group of 3hdc, * ch 3, 1sc between next two groups of 3hdc, rep from * to end, ending ch 3, 1sc into top of last st.

4th row Ch 2 to count as first hdc, * (1hdc, ch 1, 1hdc) into next 3ch sp, rep from * to end, ending 1hdc into top of turning ch. Turn.

Rep first-4th rows throughout.

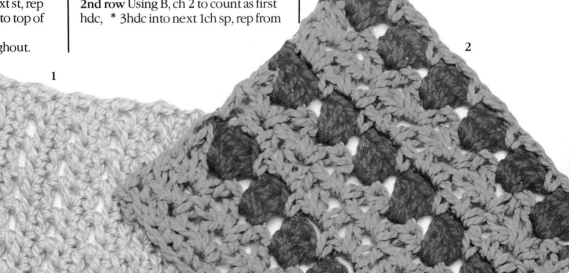

1

2

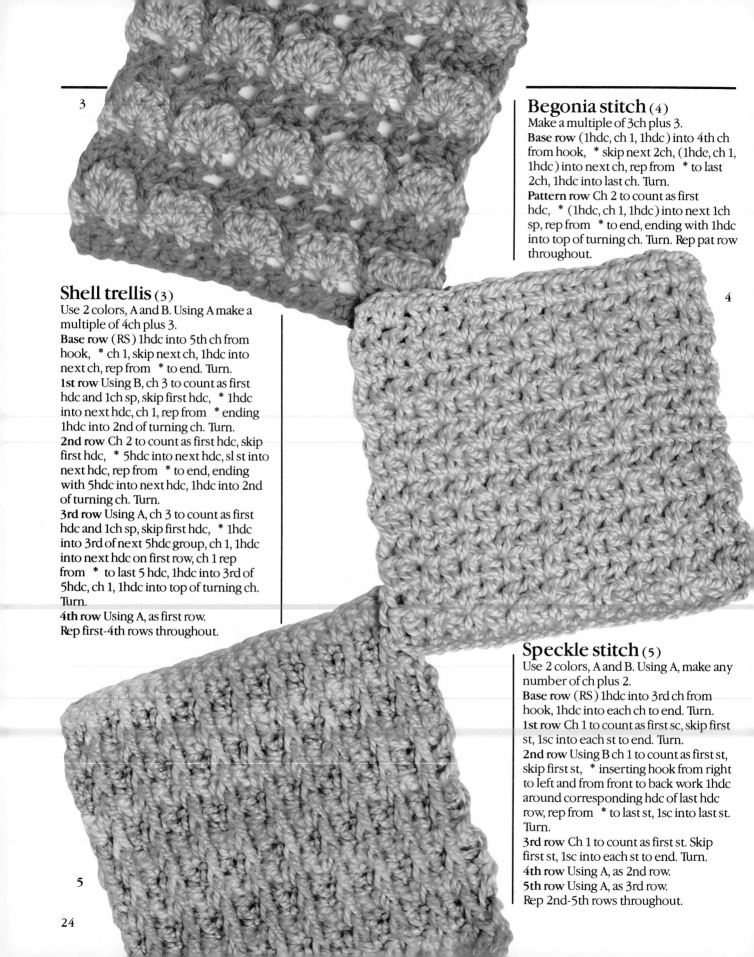

3

Begonia stitch (4)

Make a multiple of 3ch plus 3.
Base row (1hdc, ch 1, 1hdc) into 4th ch
from hook, * skip next 2ch, (1hdc, ch 1,
1hdc) into next ch, rep from * to last
2ch, 1hdc into last ch. Turn.
Pattern row Ch 2 to count as first
hdc, * (1hdc, ch 1, 1hdc) into next 1ch
sp, rep from * to end, ending with 1hdc
into top of turning ch. Turn. Rep pat row
throughout.

Shell trellis (3)

Use 2 colors, A and B. Using A make a
multiple of 4ch plus 3.
Base row (RS) 1hdc into 5th ch from
hook, * ch 1, skip next ch, 1hdc into
next ch, rep from * to end. Turn.
1st row Using B, ch 3 to count as first
hdc and 1ch sp, skip first hdc, * 1hdc
into next hdc, ch 1, rep from * ending
1hdc into 2nd of turning ch. Turn.
2nd row Ch 2 to count as first hdc, skip
first hdc, * 5hdc into next hdc, sl st into
next hdc, rep from * to end, ending
with 5hdc into next hdc, 1hdc into 2nd
of turning ch. Turn.
3rd row Using A, ch 3 to count as first
hdc and 1ch sp, skip first hdc, * 1hdc
into 3rd of next 5hdc group, ch 1, 1hdc
into next hdc on first row, ch 1 rep
from * to last 5 hdc, 1hdc into 3rd of
5hdc, ch 1, 1hdc into top of turning ch.
Turn.
4th row Using A, as first row.
Rep first-4th rows throughout.

4

Speckle stitch (5)

Use 2 colors, A and B. Using A, make any
number of ch plus 2.
Base row (RS) 1hdc into 3rd ch from
hook, 1hdc into each ch to end. Turn.
1st row Ch 1 to count as first sc, skip first
st, 1sc into each st to end. Turn.
2nd row Using B ch 1 to count as first st,
skip first st, * inserting hook from right
to left and from front to back work 1hdc
around corresponding hdc of last hdc
row, rep from * to last st, 1sc into last st.
Turn.
3rd row Ch 1 to count as first st. Skip
first st, 1sc into each st to end. Turn.
4th row Using A, as 2nd row.
5th row Using A, as 3rd row.
Rep 2nd-5th rows throughout.

5

Ridged patterns

Three-dimensional ridges form beautifully tactile fabrics, especially when alternated with plain crochet stitches. Use these extremely versatile stitches as allover patterns – as in this handsome jacket – or to highlight particular features of a garment.

The basic ridged jacket

Sizes

Men's sizes 38 [40:42] in
Length 27½in
Sleeve seam 19in
Note: *Instructions for larger sizes are in brackets [ ]; where there is only one set of figures it applies to all sizes.*

Materials

30 [32:34] oz of a Shetland-type knitting worsted in main color A
11 [13:15] oz in contrasting color B
Sizes C and E crochet hooks
8 buttons

Gauge

16dc to 4in worked on size E crochet hook

To save time, take time to check gauge.

Back and fronts (worked in one piece to armholes)

Using smaller hook and A, make 48ch.
Base row 1sc into 2nd ch from hook, 1sc into each ch to end. Turn. 47sc.
Waistband ribbing row Ch 1 to count as first sc, skip first st, 1sc into back loop only of each st to end. Turn.

Rep waistband ribbing row until 160 [168:176] rows have been worked from beg.
Fasten off.
Change to larger hook.
Fold waistband in half lengthwise so that row ends meet.
Next row Using A, work a row of sc through both thickness of waistband row ends. Turn.
160 [168:176] sts.
Inc row Work in sc and inc 8 sts evenly across row. 168 [176:184] sts.
Beg pat
** Next row (WS) Using A, ch 2, skip first st, 1hdc into front loop only of each st to turning ch, 1hdc into top of turning ch. Turn.
Next row Ch 2, skip first st, 1hdc into each st to end, inserting hook under both loops of each st as usual.
Fasten off and do not turn.
Return to loops unworked 2 rows previously and join A to free loop of first st.
Next row (RS) Ch 3, skip first st, 1dc into each free loop to end. Turn.
Next row Ch 3, skip first st, 1dc into each st to end. Turn.

Next row As last row. Turn. Fasten off.
With WS facing, insert hook into first hdc and dc of the 2 layers. Join in B.
Next row Using B, ch 2, skip first st, inserting hook into corresponding hdc and dc work in hdc to end. Turn.
Next row Ch 2, skip first st, 1hdc into each st to end. Turn.
Rep last row 3 times more.
Change to A.
Next row Using A, ch 1 to count as first sc, skip first st, 1sc into each st to end. Turn.**
Rep from ** to ** until 8th ridge in A has been completed and work measures approx 20½in, ending with a WS row.
Divide for back and fronts
Next row Pat 37 [39:41] sts, sl st across next 10 sts, pat 74 [78:82] sts, sl st across next 10 sts, pat last 37 [39:41] sts. Turn.

Left front

Working on last set of sts, work even in pat until work measures 26in, ending at front edge.
Shape neck
Next row Sl st across first 5 sts, pat to

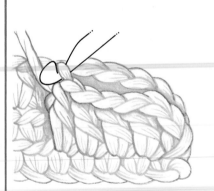
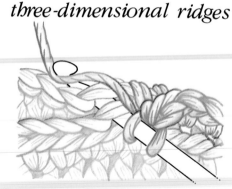
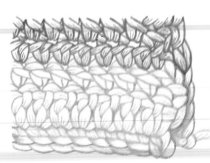

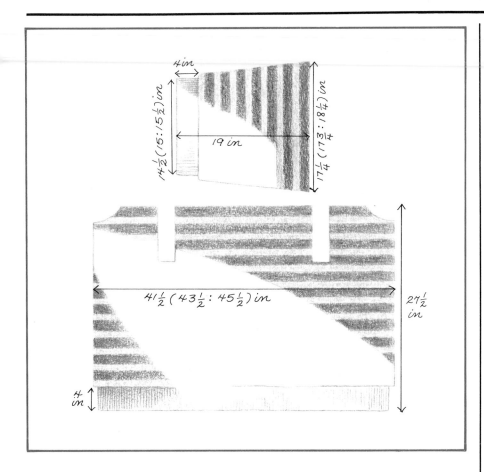

4 in

14½ (15:15½) in

19 in

17¼ (17¾:18¼) in

41½ (43½ : 45½) in

27½ in

4 in

Right front band
Using smaller hook and A, make 19ch.
Base row 1sc into 2nd ch from hook, 1sc into each ch to end. Turn. 18sc.
Next row Ch 1 to count as first sc, skip first st, 1sc into each st to end. Turn.
Rep last row until band, when slightly stretched, fits up right front from lower edge of waistband to beg of neck shaping. Fasten off.

Left front band
Mark position of 7 buttonholes on left front, the first 1½in from lower edge, the last 1¼in from neck shaping and the rem 5 evenly spaced in between.
Work left front band as for right front band, working buttonholes as follows:
Next row Ch 1 to count as first sc, skip first st, 1sc into next st, ch 3, skip next 3 sts, 1sc into each of next 8 sts, ch 3, skip next 3 sts, 1sc into each of last 2 sts. Turn.
Next row Ch 1 to count as first sc, skip first st, 1sc into next st, 3sc into next 3ch sp, 1sc into each of next 8 sts, 3sc into next 3ch sp, 1sc into each of last 2 sts. Turn.

To finish
Finish all side edges with a row of sc, using colors to match ridge pat (see Special Technique, page 26). Fold right front band in half lengthwise so that row ends meet and sew neatly to right front.
Using smaller hook and A, work a row of sc through both thicknesses at lower edge.
Attach left front band in the same way and work buttonhole stitch over edges of buttonholes.
Join shoulder seams.

Neckband
Using smaller hook and A and with RS facing, join A to first st on right front band and work 87 [89:91] sc evenly all around neck edge, ending at front edge of left front band. Turn. Work in sc as for right front band for 2in, ending at right front edge.
Buttonhole row Work in sc to last 6 sts, ch 3, skip next 3 sts, 1sc into each of last

end. Turn. 33 [35:37] sts.
Dec one st at neck edge on next 2 rows and every following alternate row until 18 [18:20] sts rem.
Work even until work measures 27in, ending at armhole edge.
Shape shoulder
Next row Sl st across first 9 [9:1] sts, pat to end. Turn.
Next row Pat to end. Fasten off.

Back
With WS facing, return to sts left at armholes, skip 10 slipped sts and keeping pat correct, join yarn to next st.
Next row Pat to end. Turn.
74 [78:82] sts.
Work even in pat until work measures same as back to beg of shoulder shaping.
Shape shoulders
Next row Sl st across first 9 [9:10] sts, pat to last 9 [9:10] sts, turn.
Next row As last row. Fasten off.

Right front
With WS facing, return to sts left at armholes, skip 10 sl st and keeping pat correct, join yarn to next st.
Next row Pat to end. Turn.
37 [39:41] sts. Complete to match left front, reversing all shaping.

Sleeves (alike)
Using smaller hook and A, make 30ch.
Work base row and waistband ribbing row as for waistband until 51 [53:55] rows have been worked from beg.
Work next row and inc row as for waistband. 59 [61:63] sts.
Using larger hook, rep from ** to ** as for back and fronts until work measures 4¼in, ending with a WS row.
Shape sleeve
Inc one st at each end of next and every following 6th row until there are 71 [73:75] sts.
Work even until work measures 19in. Fasten off.

3 sts. Turn.
Next row Ch 1 to count as first sc, skip first st, 1sc into each st to 3ch sp, 3sc into next 3ch sp, 1sc into each st to end. Turn.
Work in sc for another 2in and then make a second buttonhole in the same way.
Work in sc for another 2in.
Fasten off.
Fold neckband in half so that first and last rows meet and sew neatly in place on WS using matching yarn and an overcast seam.
Finish neckband buttonhole as before.
Work a row of sc through both thicknesses to close row ends of neckband.
Set in sleeves, matching centre of sleeve top to shoulder seam.
Join side and underarm seams.
Sew on buttons to correspond with buttonholes.

Adapting the basic ridged jacket

Use these variations from the Pattern Library to work several versions of the basic jacket. Whatever variation you choose, it's sure to please.

On the jacket the ridges are separated by four rows of half doubles, worked in a contrasting color. The ridges could easily be spaced differently by working more or fewer rows in between.
An interesting, and more difficult, variation would be to work broken ridges. These could be left plain, or you could thread contrasting yarn through the tubes to accentuate them.

Altering the jacket
Men sometimes find sleeves restricting, and if you prefer you could easily use the jacket pattern to make a vest instead. Work the back and fronts as instructed on pages 26-27. Omit the sleeves and substitute armbands, worked in the same way as the right front band.
The jacket can easily be made longer or shorter by working more ridged patterns on the back and fronts before dividing the stitches at the armholes. Sleeves could also be lenthened or shortened by working more rows in pattern. Remember always to end on a right or wrong side row as instructed.

Pattern Library: Ridged patterns

Crab stitch ridges (1)
Make any number of ch.
Base row 1sc into 2nd ch from hook, 1sc into each ch to end. Do not turn.
1st row (RS) Ch 1, working into front loop only and working from left to right work 1sc into each st to end. Do not turn.
2nd row Ch 1, 1sc into each unworked loop on first row. Turn.
3rd row Ch 1 to count as first sc, skip first st, 1sc into each st to end. Turn.
4th row As 3rd row. Do not turn. Rep first-4th rows throughout.

Cabled ridges (2)
Make a multiple of 3ch plus 3 extra.
Base row 1sc into 2nd ch from hook, 1sc into each ch to end. Turn.
1st row Ch 1 to count as first sc, skip first st, 1sc into each st to end. Turn.
2nd row (RS) Ch 1, 1sc into first st, * ch 3, skip next 2 sts, 1sc into next st, turn, 1sc into each of 3ch just worked, turn, inserting hook behind 3ch work 1sc into each of 2 skipped sts, rep from * to last st, 1sc into last st.
3rd row Ch 1, 1sc into first st, *2sc into next st behind cable, 1sc into next st behind cable, skip sc where 3ch were attached on last row, rep from * to last st, 1sc into last st.
4th row As first row.
Rep first-4th rows throughout.

4

3

5

6

Single crochet ridges (3)

Make any number of ch.

Base row 1sc into 2nd ch from hook, 1sc into each ch to end. Turn.

1st row (RS) Ch 1 to count as first sc, skip first st, 1sc into front loop only of each st to end. Turn.

2nd row Ch 1 to count as first sc, skip first st, 1sc into each unworked loop of 2nd row to end. Turn.

3rd row Ch 1 to count as first sc, skip first st, 1sc into each st to end. Turn.

4th row As 3rd row.

Rep first–4th rows throughout.

Popcorn ridges (4)

Make a multiple of 6ch plus 3.

Base row (RS) 1dc into 4th ch from hook, 1dc into each ch to end. Turn.

1st row Ch 1, 1sc into first st, * ch 1 skip next st, 1sc into next st, rep from * to end. Turn.

2nd row Ch 3, skip first st, *skip next 1ch sp, (5dc into next 1ch sp, remove hook from loop, insert into top of first of 5dc just worked and into loop just left, yo and draw through all loops on hook – popcorn formed –, ch 1, 1dc, ch 1, popcorn) into next 1ch sp, skip next 1ch sp, 1dc into next sc, rep from * to end. Turn.

3rd row Ch 1, 1sc into first st, *(ch 1, 1sc into next 1ch sp) twice, ch 1, 1sc into next dc, rep from * to end, ending with 1sc into top of turning ch. Turn.

4th row Ch 3, skip first st, *1dc into next 1ch sp, 1dc into next sc, rep from * to end. Turn.

Rep first–4th rows throughout.

Puff stitch ridges (5)

Make a multiple of 2ch plus 3 extra. Use 2 colors alternately.

Base row 1dc into 4th ch from hook, 1dc into each ch to end. Turn.

1st row (WS) Ch 3, skip first st, * (yo, insert hook into next st, draw through a loop) 4 times, yo and draw through all 9 loops on hook – puff st formed –, 1dc into next st, rep from * to end. Turn.

2nd row Ch 3, skip first st, 1dc into each unworked loop of first row to end. Turn.

Rep first and 2nd rows throughout.

Multicolor ridges (6)

Work as for the basic jacket, omitting two of the half-double rows worked between the ridges and using a different color for edge ridge.

Extra-large patterns

Extra-large stitches are shown off to their best when worked over a large area. The structure of each stitch produces a large-scale texture that is most striking worked in one color, as in this attractive cover for a big floor pillow.

The basic textured pillow

Size
To fit a pillow form 36in square

Materials
A bulky yarn
18oz for back
25oz for front
Pillow form 36in square
Size H crochet hook

Gauge
11sts and 8 rows to 4in measured over pattern of back using size H hook

To save time, take time to check gauge.

Back
Make 103ch.
Base row 1sc into 2nd ch from hook, 1sc into each ch to end. Turn.
1st row Ch 3, skip first st, 1dc into each st to end. Turn.
2nd row (RS) Ch 1, 1sc into first dc, 1sc into each dc ending 1sc into top of turning ch. Turn.
Rep first and 2nd rows 43 times. Fasten off.
With RS facing, work 112 sc evenly along row ends of each side edge.

Front
Note: *The measurement given in parentheses at the end of each section of pat refers only to that section and not to the complete piece.*
Make 113 ch.
Base row 1sc into 2nd ch from hook, 1sc into each ch to end. Turn.
1st row Ch 2, skip first st, 1dc into each st to end. Turn.

Raised double boxes
1st row (RS) Ch 2, skip first dc, 1dc into next dc, *inserting hook from front of work, from right to left, work 1dc around stem of next dc – 1dc front

worked –, 1dc into each of next 2 dc, rep from * to last 2 sts, 1dc front around stem of next dc, 1dc into top of turning ch. Turn.
2nd row Ch 2, skip first dc, *1dc into next dc, 1dc front around stem of each of next 2dc, rep from * to last 3 sts, 1dc into next dc, 1dc front around stem of next st, 1dc into top of turning ch. Rep last 2 rows 3 times, then first row again. (3⅛in)
Next row Ch 2, skip first dc, 1dc front around stem of each dc to last st, 1dc into top of turning ch. Turn.
Next row Ch 2, skip first dc, inserting hook from back of work, from right to left work 1dc around stem of each dc to last st, 1dc into top of turning ch. Turn.

Raised crosses
1st row Ch 2, skip first st, 1dc into each st to end, 1dc into top of turning ch. Turn.
2nd row (RS) Ch 1, 1sc into first st, 1sc into next st, *skip next 2dc, 1tr front around stem of next dc, working behind tr work 1sc into each of 2 skipped sts, skip next st, 1sc into each of next 2 sts, 1tr front around stem of skipped st, rep from * to last 2 sts, 1sc into next st, 1sc into top of turning ch. Turn.
3rd row As first row.
4th row Ch 1, 1sc into first dc, 1sc into next dc, *skip next dc, 1sc into each of next 2 dc, 1tr front around stem of skipped dc, skip next 2dc, 1tr front around stem of next dc, working behind tr work 1sc into each of 2 skipped dc, rep from * to last 2 sts, 1sc into next st, 1sc into top of turning ch. Turn.
Rep last 4 rows twice. (4¾in)
Next row Ch 2, skip first sc, 1dc into each st to end. Turn.
Next row Ch 2, skip first dc, 1dc back

around stem of each dc, 1dc into top of turning ch. Turn.
Next row Ch 2, skip first dc, 1dc front around stem of each dc, 1dc into top of turning ch. Turn.

Basket stitch
1st row (RS) Ch 2, skip first dc, 1dc front around stem of each of next 3 dc, *1dc back around stem of each of next 4dc, 1dc front around stem of each of next 4dc, rep from * to last 4 sts, 1dc back around stem of each of next 3dc, 1dc into top of turning ch. Turn.
2nd to 4th rows Rep first row 3 times.
5th row Ch 2, skip first dc, 1dc back around stem of each of next 3dc, *1dc front around stem of each of next 4 dc, 1dc back around stem of each of next 4dc, rep from * to last 4 sts, 1dc front around stem of each of next 3 dc, 1dc into top of turning ch. Turn.
6th to 8th rows Rep 5th row 3 times. Rep first–4th rows once. (4¼in)
Next row Ch 2, skip first dc, 1dc back around stem of each dc to end, 1dc into top of turning ch. Turn.
Next row Ch 2, skip first dc, 1dc front around stem of each dc to end, 1dc into top of turning ch. Turn.

Large diamond pattern
1st row (RS) Ch 1, 1sc into first dc, 1sc into each dc to end, 1sc into top of turning ch. Turn.
2nd row Ch 2, skip first st, 1dc into each of next 7 sts, *leaving last loop of each st on hook work 4dc into next st, yo and draw through all 5 loops – cluster worked –, 1dc into each of next 15 sts,

rep from * omitting 8dc at end of last rep. Turn.

3rd row Ch 1, 1sc into first st, 1sc into each of next 4 sts, **1dtr front around stem of st 3 rows below and 2 sts to the left, skip next st of last row, 1sc into next st, inserting hook from front of work, from right to left, work 1sc around top of cluster – 1sc front worked –, 1sc into next st, 1dtr front around same st as last dtr, skip next st, 1sc into each of next 4 sts*, 1dtr front around stem of st 3 rows below and 1 st to left, skip next st, 1sc into next st, 1dtr front around same st as last dtr, skip next st, 1sc into each of next 4 sts **, rep from ** to ** to last 11 sts, rep from ** to *, 1sc into next st, 1sc into top of turning ch. Turn.

4th row Ch 2, skip first st, 1dc into each of next 5 sts, *cluster into next st, 1dc into each of next 3 sts, cluster into next st, 1dc into each of next 11 sts, rep from * to end omitting 6dc at end of last rep. Turn.

5th row Ch 1, 1sc into first st, 1sc into each of next 2 sts, **1dtr front around stem of next dtr 2 rows below, skip next st, 1sc into next st, 1sc front around top of next cluster, 1sc into each of next 3 sts, 1sc front around top of next cluster, 1sc into next st, 1dtr front around stem of next dtr 2 rows below, skip next st, 1sc into each of next 3 sts *, leaving last loop of each st on hook work 1dtr front around stem of each of next 2dtr 2 rows below, yo and draw through all 3 loops, skip next st, 1sc into each of next 3 sts **, rep from ** to ** to last 13 sts, rep from ** to *, 1sc into top of turning ch. Turn.

6th row Ch 2, skip first sc, 1dc into each of next 3sts, *(cluster into next st, 1dc into each of next 3sts) twice, cluster into next st, 1dc into each of next 7sts, rep from * to end omitting 4dc at end of last rep. Turn.

7th row Ch 1, 1sc into first st, *1dtr front around stem of next dtr 2 rows below, skip next st of last row, 1sc into next st, (1sc front around top of next cluster, 1sc into each of next 3 sts) twice, 1sc front around top of next cluster, 1sc into next sc, 1dtr front around stem of next dtr 2 rows below, skip next st, 1sc into each of next 3 sts, rep from * to end omitting 1sc at end of last rep and working last sc into top of turning ch. Turn.

8th row As 4th row.

9th row Ch 1, 1sc into first st, 1sc into each of next 2 sts, *1dtr front around dtr to right 2 rows below, skip next st, 1sc into next st, 1sc front around top of next cluster, 1sc into each of next 3 sts, 1sc front around top of next cluster, 1sc into next st, 1dtr front around stem of next dtr to left 2 rows below, skip next st, 1sc into each of next 7 sts, rep from * to end omitting 3sc at end of last rep and working last sc into top of turning ch. Turn.

10th row As 2nd row.

11th row Ch 1, 1sc into first sc, 1sc into each of next 4 sts, **1dtr front around dtr to right 2 rows below, skip next st, 1sc into next st, 1sc front around top of cluster, 1sc into next st, 1dtr front around dtr to left 2 rows below, skip next st, 1sc into each of next 4 sts*, 1dtr front around stem of dc 1 st to left 3 rows below, skip next st, 1sc into next st, 1dtr front around same dc as last dtr, skip next st, 1sc into each of next 4 sts**, rep from ** to ** to last 11 sts, rep from ** to *, 1sc into next st, 1sc into top of turning ch. Turn.

12th row Ch 2, skip first st, 1dc into each st to end. Turn.

SPECIAL TECHNIQUE
horizontal ridges

1 Articles made up of panels of different stitches look most effective when the patterns and textures are divided by horizontal ridges. The double ridges on the pillow on page 31 are formed from doubles worked around the stem.

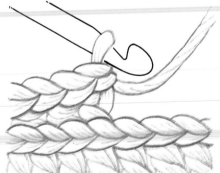

2 Work the first ridge row with the wrong side facing. Make two chains to count as the first stitch. Inserting the hook from the front of the work, work one double around the stem of the next and every following double to the last stitch. Work one double into the turning chain. Turn.

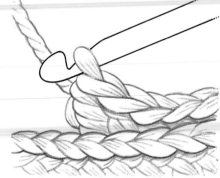

3 Begin and end the following, right side row as in step 2, but when working the double around the stem of each stitch, insert the hook from the back of the work. As before, this forms a ridge on the right side. (See page 159 for more on working around the stem of a stitch.)

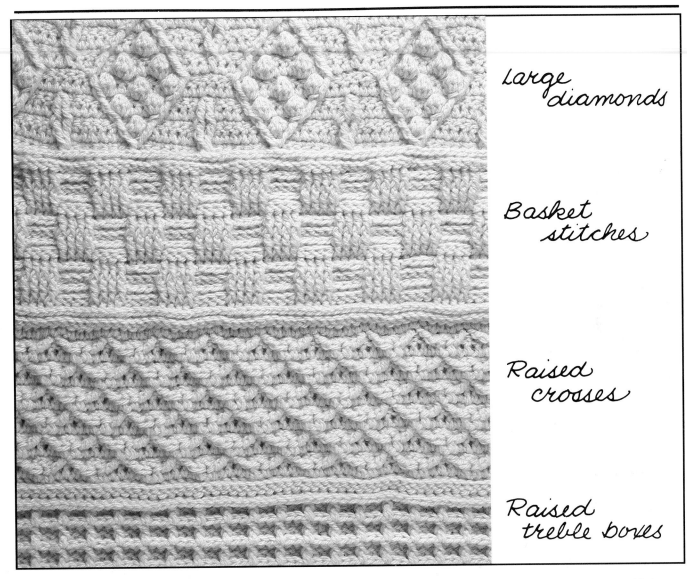

Large diamonds

Basket stitches

Raised crosses

Raised treble boxes

13th row Ch 1, 1sc into first st, 1sc into each of next 6 sts, *leaving last loop of each st on hook work 1dtr front around each of next 2dtr 2 rows below, yo and draw through all 3 loops, skip next st, 1sc into each of next 7 sts, rep from * to last st, 1sc into top of turning ch. Turn.
14th row As 12th row.
Next row Ch 2, skip first st, 1dc back around stem of each st to end working 1dc into top of turning ch. Turn.
Next row Ch 2, skip first st, 1dc front around stem of each st to last sc, 1dc into top of turning ch. Turn.
Work the 12 rows of basket stitch section.
Next row Ch 2, skip first st, 1dc back

around stem of each st to last st, 1dc into top of turning ch. Turn.
Next row Ch 2, skip first st, 1dc front around stem of each st to last st, 1dc into top of turning ch. Turn.
Next row Ch 1, 1sc into first st, 1sc into each st, 1sc into top of turning ch. Turn.
Work the 12 rows of raised crosses section.
Next row Ch 2, skip first st, 1dc into each st to end. Turn.
Next row Ch 2, skip first st, 1dc back around stem of each st to last st, 1dc into top of turning ch. Turn.
Next row Ch 2, skip first st, 1dc front around stem of each st to last st. 1dc into top of turning ch. Turn.

Work the 9 rows of raised double box section.
Next row Ch 1, 1sc into first st, 1sc into each st to end. Fasten off.
With RS facing work 102 sc evenly along row ends of each side.

To finish
With WS tog place front on top of back with the row ends of the front at the beg ch and last row of back. (Placing the pieces at a right-angle to each other helps to maintain shape.) Leaving an opening to insert pillow form, join back and front with sc, working 2sc at each corner. Insert pillow form and join opening edges.

Adapting the textured pillow

Crochet a multi-textured pillow to display your repertoire of stitch patterns.

Most of these extra-large patterns could be crocheted in a bulky yarn to make a textured pillow, but for successful results some calculations are necessary.

Checking gauge

First, carefully measure your pillow form. The finished cover should be slightly smaller than the pillow to ensure a neat fit, so subtract ¾in from both the height and width of the pillow.

The result will be the measurements of the finished cover. Work a gauge swatch, using your yarn and the stitch you intend to use for the back of the cover. Count the number of stitches in 4in of your sample. Multiply this number by the finished width of the cover. Then divide by 4 to obtain the number of stitches required to go across the width of the cover.

The pattern repeat

Make sure that each extra-large pattern can be worked *exactly* on the number of stitches across the width of the pillow. Count the stitches between the first asterisk (*) in the pattern rows and the words "rep from . . ."; this will give you the number of stitches in the pattern repeat. Count the stitches at each side of the repeat; these are the edge stitches.

Divide the total number of stitches by the pattern repeat. For the pattern to fit exactly, the result should be a whole number, plus the number of edge stitches. Because of this, you may need to alter slightly the total number of stitches to accommodate the pattern repeat and edge stitches.

Pattern Library: Extra-large patterns

1

Alternating raised doubles (1)

Make an odd number of ch.
Base row 1dc into 4th ch from hook, 1dc into each ch to end. Turn.
1st row Ch 1, 1sc into first dc, 1sc into each st to end, working last sc into top of turning ch. Turn.
2nd row (RS) Ch 3, skip first sc, *skip next sc of last row and inserting hook from front of work, from right to left, work 1tr around stem of corresponding dc on row below – 1tr front worked –, 1dc into next sc, rep from * to end. Turn.
3rd row As first row.
4th row Ch 3, skip first sc, *1dc into next sc, skip next sc of last row and work 1tr front around stem of corresponding dc on row below, rep from * to last 2sc, 1dc into each of last 2sc. Turn.
Rep first-4th rows throughout.

2

3

Raised double cables (2)

Make 19ch.

Base row 1dc into 4th ch from hook, 1dc into each ch to end. Turn.

1st and every alternate row Ch 1, 1sc into first st, 1sc into each st to end working last sc into top of turning ch. Turn.

2nd row (RS) Ch 3, skip first sc, *(skip next sc of last row and inserting hook from front of work, from right to left, work 1tr around stem of corresponding st of row below – 1tr below worked) 4 times *, 1dc into each of next 7sc, rep from * to * once, 1dc into last sc. Turn.

4th row Ch 3, skip first sc, 1dc into next sc, rep from * to * of 2nd row, 1dc into each of next 5sc, rep from * to * of 2nd row, 1dc into each of last 2sc. Turn.

6th row Ch 3, skip first sc, 1dc into each of next 2sc, rep from * to * of 2nd row, 1dc into each of next 3sc, rep from * to * of 2nd row, 1dc into each of last 3sc. Turn.

8th row Ch 3, skip first sc, 1dc into each of next 3sc, rep from * to * of 2nd row, 1dc into next sc, rep from * to * of 2nd row, 1dc into each of last 4sc. Turn.

10th row As 6th row.

12th row As 4th row.

14th row As 2nd row.

15th row As first row.

Rep 14th-15th rows throughout.

Basket stitch (3)

Make a multiple of 8ch plus 4 extra.

Base row 1dc into 4th ch from hook, 1dc into each ch to end. Turn.

1st row Ch 2, skip first dc, *(inserting hook from front of work, from right to left, work 1dc around stem of next dc – 1dc front worked) twice, (inserting hook from back of work, from right to left, work 1dc around stem of next dc – 1dc back worked) 4 times, 1dc front around stem of each of next 2dc, rep from * to last st, 1dc into top of turning ch. Turn.

2nd row Ch 2, skip first dc, *1dc back around stem of each of next 2dc, 1dc front around stem of each of next 4 dc, 1dc back around stem of each of next 2dc, rep from * to last st, 1dc into top of turning ch.

3rd row As first row.

4th row As 2nd row.

5th row As 2nd row.

6th row As 2nd row.

7th row As 2nd row.

8th row As 2nd row.

Rep first-8th rows throughout.

Bobbles

Bobbles are fun to work and look great on most kinds of garment, so either make our dazzling sweater or use one of our bobble patterns to create your own original design.

The basic bobble sweater

Sizes
Misses' sizes 10 [12:14:16]
Length 22½ [23¼:24:24¾] in
Sleeve seam 18½ [19¼:19¾:20½] in
Note: *Instructions for larger sizes are in brackets [ ]; where there is only one set of figures it applies to all sizes.*

Materials
8 [9:9:11] oz of a medium-weight wool/mohair blend in main color A
8 [8:9:9] oz in contrasting color B
Sizes G and I crochet hooks

Gauge
7dc and 3 rows to 2in worked on size I hook.

To save time, take time to check gauge.

Back and front (alike)
Note: *Work the 2 sts at each end of every row with a slightly looser tension to keep work flat.*
Using larger hook and A, make 4ch.
Base row 4dc into 4th ch from hook. Turn.
1st inc row Ch 3, 2dc into first dc, 1dc into each of next 3dc, 3dc into top of turning ch. Turn. 9 sts.
2nd inc row Ch 3, 2dc into first dc, 1dc into each st to last st, 3dc into top of turning ch. Turn. 4 sts inc.
Rep last row 17 [18:19:20] times. 81 [85:89:93] sts.
Next row (RS) Ch 3, 2dc into first dc, 1dc into next dc, change to B, 5dc into next dc, remove loop from hook, insert hook from front to back in top of first dc,

replace loop on hook and draw through the dc – 1 bobble formed on RS of work –, *change to A, 1dc into each of next 3dc, change to B, 1 bobble into next dc, rep from * to last 2 sts, 1dc into next dc, 3dc into top of turning ch. Turn. Fasten off B. Rep 2nd inc row once. 89 [93:97:101] sts. Fasten off A. Join in B.
1st dec row Ch 3, skip first dc, leaving last loop of each st on hook work 1dc into each of next 3 sts, yo and draw through all 4 loops – 2dc dec –, 1dc into each st to within last 4 sts, dec 2dc over next 3 sts, 1dc into top of turning ch. Turn. 4 sts dec.
2nd dec row (WS) Ch 3, skip first dc, dec 2dc over next 3 sts, *change to A, work 1 bobble in next dc but insert hook from back to front in top of first of 5dc to make the bobble at the back (RS) of work, change to B, 1dc into each of next 3dc, rep from * to last 5 sts, 1 bobble in next dc, dec 2dc over next 3 sts, 1dc into top of turning ch. Turn. Fasten off A.
Rep first dec row until 5 sts rem.
Next row Ch 3, skip first dc, leaving last loop of each st on hook work 1dc into each of next 3dc, 1dc into top of turning ch, yo and draw through all 5 loops. Fasten off.

Sleeves
Make one sleeve in A and one sleeve in B.
Using larger hook make 52 [56:60:64] ch.
Base row 1dc into 4th ch from hook, 1dc into each ch to end. Turn. 50 [54:58:62] sts.

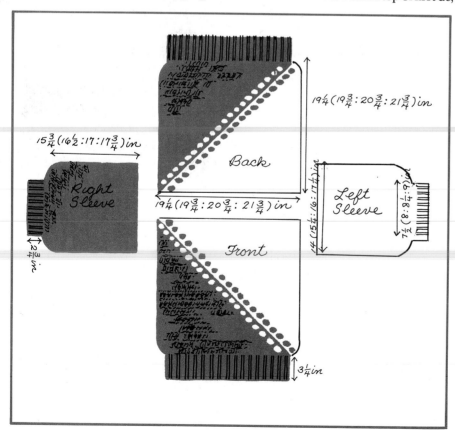

15¾ (16½:17:17¾) in

Right Sleeve

2¾ in

Back

19¼ (19¾:20¾:21¾) in

19¼ (19¾:20¾:21¾) in

Front

3¼ in

Left Sleeve

7½ (15¼:16:17¼) in

14 (15¼:16:17¼) in

8:8:9

crochet ribbing

1 A crochet rib with "knit" and "purl" stitches can be formed by working around the stems of the stitches on the previous row. Work the turning chain. Take the yarn over the hook and insert the hook from front to back between the stems of the first and second doubles. Bring the hook to the front between the second and third doubles. Complete the double as usual.

2 To form the "purl" stitches of the rib, take the yarn over the hook and insert the hook from back to front between the stems of the second and third doubles. Then bring the hook from front to back between the stems of the third and fourth doubles. Complete the double.

3 Continue in this way along the row, working the last stitch around the stem of the turning chain. On following rows, keep the ribbing correct by working from front to back around the stems of the doubles that form the "knit" ribs and from back to front around the stems of the "purl" doubles.

1st row Ch 3, skip first dc, 1dc into each st, ending 1dc into top of turning ch. Turn.
Rep first row 20 [21:22:23] times.
Dec row Ch 3, skip first dc, *leaving last loop of each st on hook work 1dc into each of next 2dc, yo and draw through all 3 loops, rep from * to last st, 1dc into top of turning ch.
Turn. 26 [28:30:32] sts.
Rep first row once more.

Cuff
Change to smaller hook.
Next row Ch 2, skip first dc, *work 1dc around stem of next dc inserting hook from front from right to left – 1dc front worked –, work 1dc around stem of next dc inserting hook from back, from right to left – 1dc back worked –, rep from * to end, ending 1dc front around stem of turning ch. Turn.
Rep last row 6 times. Fasten off.

Waistband
With wrong sides facing place back and front tog with A sections tog and with B sections tog. Join side seams for 13 rows and shoulder seams for 7 rows. With smaller hook join A to side seam, work 104 [108:112:116] sc evenly around lower edge, sl st to first sc.
Next round Ch 3, skip first sc, 1dc into each sc to end, sl st to top of 3ch.
Next round Ch 2, * 1dc front around next dc, 1dc back around next dc, rep from * ending 1dc front around last dc, sl st to top of 2ch.
Rep last round 6 times. Fasten off.

To finish
Join sleeve seams. Matching colors, set in sleeves. Using smaller hook and B, work 1 round of sc evenly around neck, sl st to first sc.
Fasten off.

Adapting the basic sweater pattern

Vary the basic sweater shown here, or add bobbles to your favorite simple crochet pattern.

The front and back of the sweater on page 37 are worked on the diagonal, beginning and ending at a corner, with the colors changing at the widest point. The bobbles are in contrasting colors to emphasize the diagonal styling.

Varying the pattern
The basic sweater could easily be crocheted in one background color, with bobbles worked every few rows, either in the same or in a contrasting color and placed on the sleeves, as well as on the front and back, to produce a highly-textured fabric. Randomly-scattered bobbles, crocheted along with the main fabric or added to the background after it has been completed, could be worked in contrasting colors; or the diagonal lines could be emphasized by working the fabric, including the bobbles, in narrow or broad bands.
More experienced workers could, after working a gauge swatch, use the measurement diagram as a guide to the basic shape and work the back and front vertically, in the usual way, beginning at the lower edge and including bands of horizontally-placed bobbles.

Adding bobbles
It is easy to add bobbles to a pattern worked in double or single crochet.
Use the smaller, triple bobbles with a single crochet fabric and the larger, double crochet bobbles with doubles.
Large bobbles, like those in the basic sweater pattern, can be added to other stitch patterns after the main fabric is completed by working into the free loops at the top of the stitches on the right side of the fabric.

Buying yarn
Both large- and small-bobbled fabrics need more yarn than plain fabrics, so if you add more bobbles to the basic sweater or to any other crochet pattern, remember to buy more yarn than quoted by the pattern, so that you have enough to complete the garment.

Pattern Library: Bobble patterns

Tufted bobbles (1)

Note: This pattern can be used to make the sweater on page 37. Use three colors, A, B and C.

Background Using A make any number of ch.

Base row 1dc into 4th ch from hook, 1dc into each ch to end. Turn.

1st row (RS) Ch 3, skip first dc, working into back loops only work 1dc into each dc, 1dc into top of turning ch. Turn.

2nd row Ch 3, skip first dc, working into front loops only work 1dc into each dc, 1dc into top of turning ch.
Turn.

Rep first and 2nd rows throughout.

Bobbles Join B to any free loop on RS of work, ch 3, 4dc into same place as joining, remove loop from hook, insert hook through the top of the 3ch, replace loop on hook and draw loop through the ch, sl st to corresponding loop of row above.

Fasten off. Secure ends on WS.

Using 3 strands of C tog, knot a small tassel into the base of each bobble.

Scattered bobbles (2)

Note: This pattern can be used to make the sweater on page 37. Work the bobbles in assorted short lengths of yarn.

Background Make any number of ch.

Base row 1dc into 4th ch from hook, 1dc into each ch to end. Turn.

1st row (RS) Ch 3, skip first dc, working into back loops only work 1dc into each dc, 1dc into top of turning ch. Turn.

2nd row Ch 3, skip first dc, working into front loops only work 1dc into each dc, 1dc into top of turning ch. Turn.

Rep first and 2nd rows throughout.

Bobbles Join yarn to any free loop on RS of work, ch 3, 4dc into same place as joining, remove loop from hook, insert hook through the top of the 3ch, replace loop on hook and draw loop through the ch, sl st to corresponding loop of row above. Fasten off. Secure ends on WS.

Large bobble pattern (3)

Note: This pattern can be used to make the sweater on page 37.

Make a multiple of 4ch plus 1 extra.

Base row (RS) 5dc into 4th ch from hook, remove loop from hook, insert hook in top of first of 5dc, replace loop on hook and draw loop through dc – 1 bobble worked –, *1dc into each of next 3ch, 1 bobble in next ch, rep from * to end, ending 1dc into last ch. Turn.

1st row Ch 1, 1sc into first dc, 1sc into each st to end. Turn.

2nd row Ch 3, skip first sc, 1dc into each of next 2sc, *1 bobble into next sc, 1dc into each of next 3 sc, rep from * to end. Turn.

3rd row As first row.

4th row Ch 3, skip first sc, *1 bobble into next sc, 1dc into each of next 3sc, rep from * to end, ending 1 bobble into next sc, 1dc into last sc. Turn.

Rep first-4th throughout.

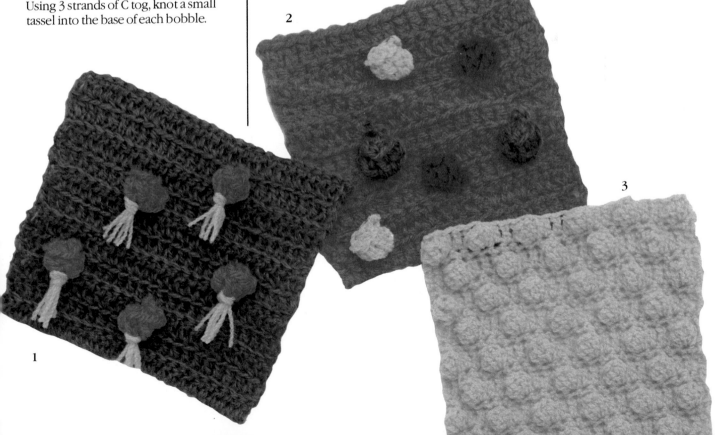

1

2

3

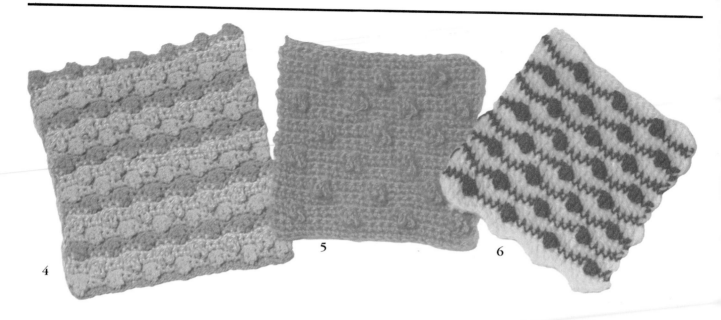

4

5

6

Three-color alternating bobbles (4)

Use 3 colors, A, B and C.

Using A make a multiple of 4ch.

Base row (RS) With A, 1sc into 2nd ch from hook, 1sc into each ch to end. Turn.

1st row With B, ch 1, skip first sc, 1sc into first sc, *leaving last loop of each st on hook, work 2tr into next sc, yo and draw through all 3 loops, bend the 2tr in half to back (RS) of work, 1sc into each of next 3sc*, rep from * to * to end, omitting 2sc at end of last rep. Turn.

2nd row With B, ch 1, 1sc into first sc, 1sc into each st to end. Turn.

3rd row With C, ch 1, 1sc into first sc, 1sc into each of next 2sc, rep from * to * of first row to end. Turn.

4th row With C, as 2nd row.

5th row With A, as first row.

6th row With A, as 2nd row.

7th row With B, as 3rd row.

8th row As 2nd row.

9th row With C, as first row.

10th row With C, as 2nd row.

11th row With A, as 3rd row.

12th row With A, as 2nd row. Rep first-12th throughout.

Bobbles on single crochet (5)

Make a multiple of 6ch.

Base row (RS) 1sc into 2nd ch from hook, 1sc into each ch to end. Turn.

1st row Ch 1, 1sc into first sc, 1sc into each sc to end. Turn.

2nd row As first row.

3rd row Ch 1, 1sc into first sc, 1sc into next sc, *leaving last loop of each st on hook work 3tr into next sc, yo and draw through all 4 loops, bend the 3tr to back (RS) of work to form a bobble, 1sc into each of next 5sc*, rep from * to * to end, omitting 3sc at end of last rep. Turn.

4th row Ch 1, 1sc into first sc, 1sc into each st to end. Turn.

5th and 6th rows As first row.

7th row Ch 1, 1sc into first sc, 1sc into each of next 4sc, work from * to * of 3rd row to end. Turn.

8th row As 4th row.

Rep first-8th rows throughout.

Wavy bobbles (6)

Use 2 colors, A and B.

With A make a multiple of 6ch plus 2 extra.

Base row (RS) With A, 1sc into 2nd ch from hook, *1hdc into next ch, 1dc into next ch, 1tr into next ch, 1dc into next ch, 1hdc into next ch, 1sc into next ch, rep from * to end. Turn.

1st row With B, ch 1, 1sc into first sc, 1sc into each of next 2 sts, *1tr into next st, bend tr in half to back (RS) of work, 1sc into each of next 5 sts, rep from * to end, omitting 2sc at end of last rep. Turn.

2nd row With A, ch 4, skip first sc, *1dc into next st, 1hdc into next st, 1sc into next st, 1hdc into next st, 1dc into next st, 1tr into next st, rep from * to end. Turn.

3rd row With B, ch 1, 1sc into first tr, *1sc into each of next 5 sts, 1tr into next st, bend tr in half to back (RS) of work, rep from * to last 6 sts, 1sc into each of last 5 sts, 1sc into top of turning ch. Turn.

4th row With A, ch 1, 1sc into first sc, *1hdc into next st, 1dc into next st, 1tr into next st, 1dc into next st, 1hdc into next st, 1sc into next st, rep from * to end. Turn.

Rep first-4th rows throughout.

Graduated patterns

Graduated patterns are made by working stitches of different heights in the same row – as illustrated by this ice-cream color top.

The basic graduated-stitch top

Size
Misses sizes 10-12.
Length 18½in, including edging
Sleeve seam 2¾in, including edging

Materials
3oz of a sport-weight cotton yarn in main color A
3oz in contrasting color B
4oz in contrasting color C
3oz in contrasting color D
Size G crochet hook
Note: *Introduce new color while working last stitch in old color.*

Gauge
12 tr and 5 rows to 4in worked on size G hook

To save time, take time to check gauge.

Back
Using A, make 53ch.
Base row (RS) 1tr into 5th ch from hook, 1tr into each ch to end. Turn. 50 sts.

1st row Ch 1 to count as first sc, skip first st, 1sc into each of next 13 sts, 1dc into each of next 7 sts, 1tr into each of next 29 sts. Turn.
2nd row Ch 4, skip first st, 1tr into each of next 15 sts, 1dc into each of next 9 sts, sl st into each of next 25 sts. Turn.
3rd row Using B, ch 4, skip first st, 1tr into each of next 20 sts, 1dc into each of next 5 sts, 1sc into each of next 24 sts. Turn.
4th row Ch 2, skip first st, 1hdc into each of next 21 sts, 1dc into each of next 13 sts, 1tr into each of next 15 sts. Turn.
5th row Ch 4, skip first st, 1tr into each of next 23 sts, 1dc into each of next 6 sts, 1hdc into next st, sl st into each of next 19 sts. Turn.
6th row Ch 1 to count as first sc, skip first st, 1sc into each of next 21 sts, 1hdc into each of next 6 sts, 1dc into each of next 4 sts, 1tr into each of next 18 sts. Turn.
7th row Using C, ch 1 to count as first sc, skip first st, 1sc into each of next 16 sts, 1hdc into each of next 6 sts, 1dc into each of next 7 sts, 1tr into each of next 20 sts. Turn.
8th row Ch 4, skip first st, 1tr into each

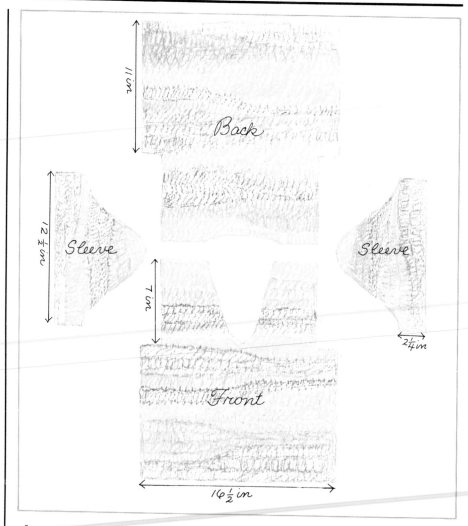

of next 19 sts, 1dc into each of next 6 sts, 1hdc into each of next 24 sts. Turn.
9th row Ch 1 to count as first sc, skip first sc, 1sc into each of next 17 sts, 1hdc into each of next 7 sts, 1dc into each of next 6 sts, 1tr into each of next 19 sts. Turn.
10th row Ch 4, skip first st, 1tr into each of next 19 sts, 1dc into each of next 6 sts, 1hdc into each of next 24 sts. Turn.
11th row Ch 1 to count as first sc, skip first st, 1sc into each of next 17 sts, 1dc into each of next 6 sts, 1tr into each of next 26 sts. Turn.
12th row Using D, ch 1 to count as first sc, skip first st, 1sc into each of next 14 sts, 1hdc into each of next 3 sts, 1dc into each of next 8 sts, 1tr into each of next 24 sts. Turn.
13th row Using B, ch 4, skip first st, 1tr

into each of next 12 sts, 1dc into each of next 4 sts, 1hdc into each of next 4 sts, 1sc into each of next 29 sts. Turn.
14th row Using A, ch 1 to count as first sc, skip first st, 1sc into each of next 15 sts, 1hdc into each of next 15 sts, 1dc into each of next 7 sts, 1tr into each of next 12 sts. Turn.
15th row Ch 4, skip first st, 1tr into each of next 16 sts, 1dc into each of next 8 sts, 1hdc into each of next 25 sts. Turn.
16th row Ch 2, skip first st, 1hdc into each of next 22 sts, 1dc into each of next 11 sts, 1tr into each of next 16 sts.
Shape armholes
17th row Join C to 5th st from beg, ch 1 to count as first sc, skip first st, 1sc into each of next 12 sts, 1hdc into each of next 4 sts, 1dc into each of next 4 sts, 1tr into each of next 25 sts. Turn.

18th row Sl st into first 5 sts, ch 4, skip first st, 1tr into each of next 20 sts, 1dc into each of next 3 sts, 1hdc into each of next 18 sts. Turn. 42 sts.

19th row Ch 3, skip first st, 1dc into each of next 19 sts, 1tr into each of next 22 sts. Turn.

20th row Using A, ch 4, skip first st, 1tr into each of next 18 sts, 1dc into each of next 3 sts, 1hdc into each of next 2 sts, 1sc into each of next 18 sts. Turn.

21st row Using D, ch 4, skip first st, 1tr into each of next 16 sts, 1dc into each of next 8 sts, 1hdc into each of next 17 sts. Turn.

22nd row Ch 2, skip first st, 1hdc into each of next 16 sts, 1dc into each of next 8 sts, 1tr into each of next 17 sts. Turn.

23rd row Ch 4, skip first st, 1tr into each of next 16 sts, 1dc into each of next 2 sts, 1hdc into each of next 23 sts. Turn.

24th row Using B, ch 4, skip first st, 1tr into each of next 16 sts, 1dc into each of next 7 sts, 1hdc into each of next 18 sts. Turn.

25th row Ch 2, skip first st, 1hdc into each of next 19 sts, 1dc into each of next 3 sts, 1tr into each of next 19 sts. Turn.

26th row Ch 4, skip first st, 1tr into each of next 16 sts, 1dc into each of next 4 sts, 1hdc into each of next 6 sts, 1sc into each of next 15 sts. Turn.

27th row Ch 2, skip first st, 1hdc into

each of next 18 sts, 1dc into each of next 7 sts, 1tr into each of next 16 sts. Turn.

28th row Using C, ch 1 to count as first sc, skip first st, 1sc into each of next 16 sts, 1hdc into each of next 5 sts, 1dc into each of next 2 sts, 1tr into each of next 18 sts. Turn.

29th row Ch 4, skip first st, 1tr into each of next 18 sts, 1dc into next st, 1hdc into next st, 1sc into each of next 21 sts. Turn.

Shape neck

30th row Ch 3, skip first st, 1dc into each of next 10 sts. Fasten off.
Skip next 20 sts and rejoin C to next st, ch 3, skip first st, 1dc into each of next 10 sts. Fasten off.

Front

Using A, make 53ch.
Base row 1tr into 5th ch from hook, 1tr into each ch to end. Turn. 50 sts.
Cont as for back, but match side seams by reversing pat thus:
1st row Ch 4 to count as first tr, skip first st, 1tr into each of next 28 sts, 1dc into each of next 7 sts, 1sc into each of next 14 sts. Cont reversing pat in this way to the end of 16th row.

Shape right armhole

17th row Using C, ch 4, skip first st, 1tr into each of next 24 sts, 1dc into each of next 4 sts, 1hdc into each of next 4 sts,

1sc into each of next 12 sts, turn. 46 sts.

Shape right neck

18th row Ch 2, skip first st, 1hdc into each of next 11 sts, 1dc into each of next 4 sts, 1hdc into next st, 1sc into next st, turn. 18 sts.

19th row Ch 1 to count as first sc, skip first st, work 2sc tog, 1hdc into each of next 2 sts, 1dc into each of next 4 sts, 1hdc into each of next 9 sts. Turn. 17 sts.

20th row Using A, ch 1 to count as first sc, skip first st, 1sc into each of next 8 sts, 1hdc into each of next 4 sts, 1dc into each of next 2 sts, work 2hdc tog. Turn. 16 sts.

21st row Using D, ch 4, skip first st, work 2tr tog, 1tr into each of next 13 sts. Turn. 15 sts.

22nd row Ch 4, skip first st, 1tr into each of next 12 sts, work 2tr tog. Turn. 14 sts.

23rd row Ch 4, skip first st, work 2tr tog, 1tr into each of next 10 sts, 1dc into next st. Turn. 13 sts.

24th row Using B, ch 1 to count as first sc, skip first st, 1sc into each of next 10 sts, work 2sc tog. Turn. 12 sts.

25th row Ch 1 to count as first sc, skip first st, work 2sc tog, 1sc into each of next 9sc. Turn. 11 sts.

26th row Ch 2, skip first st, 1hdc into each st to end. Turn.

27th row Ch 3, skip first st, 1dc into each

working a graduated edging

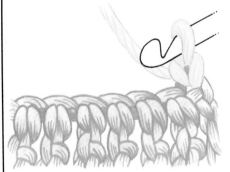

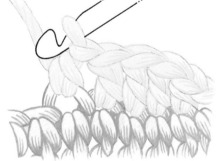

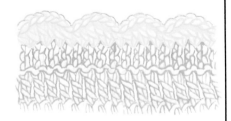

1 *Graduated stitches can be used to form a curved edging. With right side facing, join the yarn to the first stitch on the free side of the foundation chain. Make one chain to count as the first stitch.*

2 *Work a slip stitch into the next stitch, one half double into the next stitch, one double into each of the next three stitches, and one half double into the next stitch.*

3 *Repeat the six stitches in step 2 to the end of the foundation chain. Work one slip stitch into the last stitch and fasten off.*

st to end. Turn.
28th row Using C, ch 4, skip first st, 1tr into each st to end. Turn.
29th-30th rows As 28th row.
Fasten off.
Shape left armhole and neck
18th row With WS facing, skip next 6 sts at center front and rejoin C to next st, ch 2, skip first st, 1dc into each of next 3dc, 1tr into each of next 14 sts. Turn. 18 sts.
19th row Ch 3, skip first st, 1tr into each of next 14 sts, 1dc into next dc, work 2hdc tog. Turn. 17 sts.
20th row Using A, ch 3, skip first st, work 2dc tog, 1tr into each of next 14 sts. Turn. 16 sts.
21st row Using D, ch 2, skip first st, 1hdc into each of next 11 sts, 1dc into each of next 2 sts, work 2dc tog. Turn. 15 sts.
22nd row Ch 2, skip first st, work 2hdc tog, 1hdc into each of next 8 sts, 1dc into each of next 4 sts. Turn. 14 sts.
23rd row Ch 1 to count as first sc, skip first st, 1sc into each of next 11 sts, work 2sc tog. Turn. 13 sts.
24th row Using B, ch 4, skip first st, work 2tr tog, 1tr into each of next 10 sts. Turn. 12 sts.
25th row Ch 4, skip first st, work 2tr tog, 1tr into each of next 9 sts. Turn. 11 sts.
26th row Ch 4, skip first st, 1tr into each st to end. Turn.
27th row As 26th row.
28th row Using C, ch 1 to count as first st, skip first st, 1sc into each st to end.
29th row As 28th row.
30th row Ch 2, skip first st, 1hdc into each st to end. Turn. Fasten off.

Sleeves (alike)
Using A, make 41ch.
Base row 1tr into 5th ch from hook, 1tr into each ch to end. 38 sts.
1st row Ch 4, skip first st, 1tr into each of next 6 sts, 1dc into each of next 2 sts, 1hdc into each of next 9 sts, 1sc into each of next 20sc. Turn.
2nd row Ch 1 to count as first sc, skip first st, 1sc into each of next 13 sts, 1hdc into each of next 4 sts, 1dc into each of next 3 sts, 1tr into each of next 17 sts. Turn.
3rd row Using C, ch 1 to count as first sc, skip first st, 1sc into each of next 16 sts,

1hdc into each of next 4 sts, 1dc into each of next 3 sts, 1tr into each of next 14 sts. Turn.
Shape sleeve top
4th row Sl st into first 3 sts, ch 4, skip first st, 1tr into each of next 12 sts, 1dc into each of next 5 sts, 1hdc into each of next 16 sts. Turn. 34 sts.
5th row Ch 2, skip first st, 1hdc into each of next 15 sts, 1dc into each of next 4 sts, 1tr into each of next 11 sts, 1dc into next st. Turn. 32 sts.
6th row Using A, ch 4, skip first st, 1tr into each of next 11 sts, 1dc into each of next 3 sts, 1hdc into each of next 6 sts, 1sc into each of next 11 sts. Turn. 32 sts.
7th row Using D, ch 4, skip first st, 1tr into each of next 12 sts, 1dc into each of next 5 sts, 1hdc into each of next 14 sts. Turn. 32 sts.
8th row Sl st into each of first 2 sts, ch 2, skip first st, 1hdc into each of next 12 sts, 1dc into each of next 7 sts, 1tr into each of next 8 sts, 1dc into each of next 2 sts. Turn. 30 sts.
9th row Sl st into each of first 2 sts, ch 4, skip first st, 1tr into each of next 10 sts, 1dc into each of next 4 sts, 1hdc into each of next 13 sts. Turn. 28 sts.
10th row Using B, ch 4, skip first st, 1tr into each of next 13 sts, 1dc into each of next 5 sts, 1hdc into each of next 9 sts. Turn.
11th row Sl st into first 2 sts, ch 1 to count as first sc, skip first st, 1sc into each of next 8 sts, 1hdc into each of next 4 sts, 1dc into each of next 3dc, 1tr into each of next 10 sts. Turn.
12th row Sl st into first 3 sts, ch 4, skip first st, 1tr into each of next 5 sts, 1dc into each of next 4 sts, 1hdc into each of

next 5 sts, 1sc into each of next 7 sts. Turn. 22 sts.
13th row Sl st into first 2 sts, ch 3, skip first st, 1dc into each of next 11 sts, 1tr into each of next 4 sts, 1dc into each of next 2 sts, 1hdc into next st, 1sc into next st. Turn. 20 sts.
14th row Using C, sl st into first 3 sts, ch 1 to count as first sc, skip first st, 1sc into each of next 5 sts, 1hdc into each of next 3 sts, 1dc into each of next 4 sts, 1tr into each of next 2 sts, 1dc into next st. Turn. 16 sts.
15th row Sl st into first 2 sts, ch 3, skip first st, 1dc into each of next 5 sts, 1hdc into each of next 8 sts. Turn. 14 sts.
16th row Sl st into each of first 5 sts, ch 2, skip first st, 1hdc into each of next 5 sts. Fasten off.

To finish
Join shoulder seams.
Work in sc all around neck opening, working 1 st in sc and hdc row ends, 2 sts into dc row ends and 3 sts into tr row ends.
Work 1 round of hdc. Fasten off.
Set in sleeves, easing sleeve top to fit, and matching pat with front.
Sleeve edging
With RS facing, join yarn to lower edge of sleeve, ch 1, skip first st, *sl st into next st, 1hdc into next st, 1dc into each of next 3 sts, 1hdc into next st, rep from * to last st, sl st into last st. Fasten off.
Lower edging
With RS facing, join yarn to lower edge and work as for sleeve edging. Join side and sleeve seams. Press seams lightly under a damp cloth.

Adapting the graduated top

Graduated patterns are fascinating to work and look good when used for either lightweight or bulky garments.

Because the pattern for the top on page 41 is fairly complex, it is not possible to substitute another stitch pattern for the one used. However, different effects could be obtained by the clever use of

different yarn or colors.
Yarn manufacturers often produce both smooth and textured yarns of the same weight. You could combine two such yarns – of a sport weight – and perhaps add others to create intriguing variations in texture and appearance.
If you prefer to use only one yarn, using a different color for each row would produce a marvelously marbled effect.

Designing

Of course, when substituting yarn, you must check your gauge very carefully before you begin and change your hook size as necessary to obtain the specified gauge.

Gauge is especially important when creating your own design; unless you are very experienced, avoid shaping if at all possible and work with simple T-shaped patterns.

Pattern Library: Graduated patterns

Millstone stitch (2)

Use 2 colors, A and B. Using A, make a multiple of 10ch plus 2 extra.
Base row 1sc into 2nd ch from hook, 1sc into each ch to end. Turn.

1st row (RS) Using B, ch 1, skip first st, *1sc into next st, 1hdc into next st, 1dc into each of next 5 sts, 1hdc into next st, 1sc into next st, ch 1, skip next st, rep from * to end, omitting 1ch at end of last rep and working 1sc into last st. Turn.
2nd row As first row.
3rd row Using A, ch 1, skip first st, *1sc into each of next 9 sts, 1dc into skipped st of 2 rows below, rep from * to end, omitting 1dc at end of last rep and working 1sc into last st.
4th row Ch 1, skip first st, 1sc into each st to end. Turn.
5th row Using B, ch 3, skip first st, *1dc into each of next 2 sts, 1hdc into next st, 1sc into next st, ch 1, skip next st, 1sc into next st, 1hdc into next st, 1dc into each of next 3 sts, rep from * to end. Turn.
6th row As 5th row.
7th row Using A, ch 1, skip first st, *1sc into each of next 4 sts, 1dc into skipped st on 3rd row, 1sc into each of next 5 sts, rep from * to end. Turn.
8th row Ch 1, skip first st, 1sc into each st to end. Turn.
Rep first-8th rows throughout.

2

Diamond pattern (1)

Use 2 colors, A and B. Using A, make a multiple of 6ch plus 2 extra.
Base row (RS) 1sc into 2nd ch from hook, 1sc into each ch to end. Turn.
1st row Ch 4, skip first st, 1dc into next st, 1hdc into next st, 1sc into next st, *1hdc into next st, 1dc into next st, 1tr into next st, 1dc into next st, 1hdc into next st, 1sc into next st, rep from * to last 3 sts, 1hdc into next st, 1dc into next st, 1tr into last st. Turn.
2nd row Using B, ch 1, skip first st, 1hdc into next st, 1dc into next st, *1tr into next st, 1dc into next st, 1hdc into next st, 1sc into next st, 1hdc into next st, 1dc into next st, rep from * to last 4 sts, 1tr into next st, 1dc into next st, 1hdc into

next st, 1sc into top of turning ch.
3rd row As 2nd row.
4th row Using A, as first row.
Rep first-4th rows throughout.

1

Jacquard patterns

Jacquard patterns can easily be crocheted using bright colors and simple stitches. Work small, repeating patterns for a "Fair Isle" effect, as on this boy's pullover, or scatter individual motifs as your fancy takes you.

The basic jacquard pattern

Sizes
C-10 [C-12:C-14:C-16]
Length 22½ [23:24:24½] in
Sleeve seam 16 [16:17:17] in
Note: *Instructions for larger sizes are in brackets [ ]; where there is only one set of figures it applies to all sizes.*

Materials
6 [6:8:8] oz of a sport yarn in main color A
4oz in each of contrasting colors B, C and D
2oz in each of contrasting colors E and F
Size C crochet hook
Pair of size 2 knitting needles
Set of 4 size 2 double-pointed knitting needles
Note: *Strand yarn not in use loosely on the wrong side of the work.*

Gauge
24 sts and 30 rows to 4 in in jacquard pat worked on size C hook

To save time, take time to check gauge.

Back
Using pair of knitting needles and A, cast on 99 [103:107:111] sts.
Work in K1, P1 ribbing beg alternate rows P1, K1, until work measures 2in from beg. Bind off in ribbing until one loop rem.
Transfer loop to crochet hook.
Next row (RS) Ch 1 to count as first sc, skip first st, 1sc into top of each bound-off st to end. Turn. 99 [103:107:111] sts.
Next row Ch 1 to count as first sc, skip first st, 1sc into each st to end.
Cont to work in sc, beg jacquard pat from chart.
Work 36 rows of jacquard pat 3 times in all.

3rd and 4th sizes only
Work 5 more rows in jacquard pat.

All sizes
Fasten off at end of last row.

Shape armholes
Keeping jacquard pat correct, skip first 7 sts and rejoin yarn to next st.
Next row Ch 1 to count as first sc, skip first st, pat to last 7 sts, turn. 85 [89:93:97] sts.
Next row Ch 1 to count as first sc, skip first st, work next 2sc tog, pat to last 3 sts, work 2sc tog, 1sc into last st. Turn.
Next row Ch 1 to count as first sc, skip first sc, 1sc into each st to end. Turn.
Rep last 2 rows until 75 [79:83:87] sts rem.
Work even until 18th [18th:24th:24th] row of jacquard pat is complete.
Break off yarn. Join in B.
Next 2 rows Using B, ch 1 to count as first sc, skip first st, 1sc into each st to end. Turn.
Break off B. Join in A.

Yoke
Using A only, work in sc for 29

SPECIAL TECHNIQUE
working into knitted ribbing

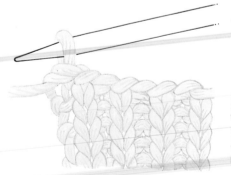

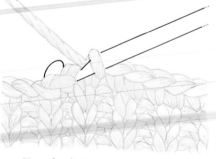

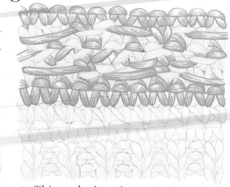

1 Being more elastic, knitted ribbing is often preferable to crocheted ribbing, especially if the garment will receive hard wear. The knitting can be worked after the crochet is completed, or, as in the basic sweater, the crochet can be worked into the top of the knitting. Bind off in ribbing until only one loop remains on the needle.

2 Transfer the loop to a crochet hook. Work one chain to count as the first single crochet and skip the first stitch. Inserting the hook under both horizontal loops, work one single crochet into each bound-off stitch to the end of the row. Work following rows in single crochet as usual.

3 This method can be used whenever you want knitted ribbing on a crochet garment. It not only prevents a hard ridge on the wrong side (as shown above), but also avoids the need to work into the other side of the foundation chain, which can be difficult, especially when using textured yarns.

[32:29:32] rows.

Shape neck and shoulders
Next row Ch 1 to count as first sc, skip first sc, 1sc into each of next 17 [19:20:22] sts, turn.
Next row Ch 1 to count as first sc, skip first sc, work next 2sc tog, 1sc into each st to end. Turn.

Next row Sl st over first 5 [6:6:7] sts, ch 1 to count as first sc, skip first st, 1sc into each st to end. Turn.
Next row Ch 1 to count as first sc, skip first st, 1sc into each of next 5 [6:6:6] sts. Fasten off.
Skip next 39 [39:41:41] sts on back neck and rejoin A to next st.
Next row Ch 1 to count as first sc, skip

first st, 1sc into each st to end. Turn.
Next row Ch 1 to count as first sc, skip first st, 1sc into each st to last 3 sts, work next 2sc tog, 1sc into last st. Turn.
Next row Ch 1 to count as first sc, skip first st, 1sc into each of next 11 [12:13:13] sts, turn.
Next row Sl st across first 5 [6:7:7] sts, ch 1 to count as first sc, skip first st, 1sc

into each st to end. Fasten off.

Front

Work as for back until 21 [24:21:24] rows of yoke have been completed.

Shape left neck

Next row Ch 1 to count as first sc, skip first st, 1sc into each of next 22 [24:25:27] sts, turn.

Next row Sl st across first 4 sts, ch 1 to count as first sc, skip first st, 1sc into each st to end. Turn.

Next row Ch 1 to count as first sc, skip first st, 1sc into each of next 16 [18:19:20] sts, turn.

Work even for 7 more rows.

Shape left shoulder

Next row Sl st across first 5 [6:6:7] sts, ch 1 to count as first sc, skip first st, 1sc into each st to end. Turn.

Next row Ch 1 to count as first sc, skip first st, 1sc into each of next 5 [6:6:7] sts. Fasten off.

Skip next 29 [29:31:31] sts on front neck and rejoin A to next st.

Complete right neck and shoulder to match left side, reversing all shaping.

Sleeves (both alike)

Using knitting needles and A, cast on 67 [67:75:75] sts.

Work in K1, P1 ribbing as for back until work measures 2in. Bind off in ribbing until one loop rem. Transfer loop to crochet hook.

Next row (RS) Ch 1 to count as first sc, skip first st, 1sc into top of each bound-off st to end. Turn. 67 [67:75:75] sts.

Next row Ch 1 to count as first sc, skip first st, 1sc into each st to end. Turn. Cont to work in sc, work first 9 rows of jacquard pat from chart.

Next row Ch 1 to count as first sc, skip first st, 2sc into next st, 1sc into each st to last 2 sts, 2sc into next st, 1sc into last st. Turn.

Keeping jacquard pat correct, cont to inc one st at each end of every following 10th row 6 [6:4:4] times in all. 79 [79:83:83] sts.

Work even in pat until 3 reps of jacquard pat have been worked. Work 1 [1:5:5] more rows in pat. Fasten off.

Shape top

Keeping jacquard pat correct, skip first 6 sts and rejoin yarn to next st.

Next row Ch 1 to count as first sc, skip first st, pat to last 6 sts, turn.

Next row Ch 1 to count as first sc, skip first st, work next 2sc tog, pat to last 3 sts, work next 2sc tog, 1sc into last st. Turn.

Keeping jacquard pat correct, cont to dec one st at each end of every following alternate row until 43 [43:47:47] sts rem.

Cont to dec one st at each end of next 12 rows. 19 [19:23:23] sts.

Break off yarn. Join in B.

Next row Using B only, sl st across first 4 [4:5:5] sts, ch 1 to count as first sc, skip first st, 1sc into each of next 10 [10:12:12] sts, turn.

Next row Sl st across first 4 sts, ch 1 to count as first sc, skip first st, 1sc into each of next 3 [3:5:5] sts. Fasten off.

To finish

Press or block, according to yarn used. Join shoulder seams. Join side and sleeve seams.

Armhole borders (both alike)

Using crochet hook and with RS facing, join B to underarm seam. Work 80 [84:86:90] sc evenly around armhole, joining last st to first st with a sl st. Work one more round in sc, ending with a sl st to first st.

Fasten off.

Set in sleeves.

Neckband

Using A and set of 4 double-pointed knitting needles, pick up and K 112 [112:120:120] sts evenly around neck.

Work in rounds of K1, P1 ribbing for 2in. Bind off.

Turn ribbing to WS and sew to base of ribbing on WS to form a crew neck.

Press all seams.

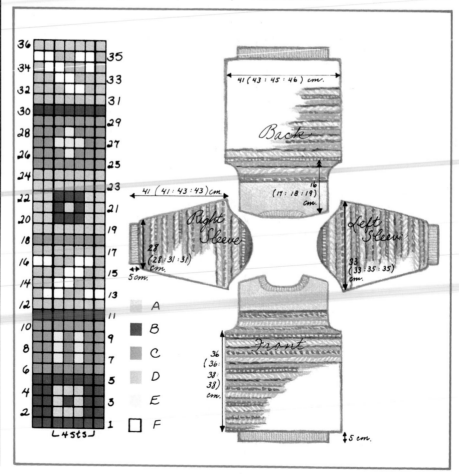

Adapting the basic jacquard sweater

Jacquard is fun to do and the results are very impressive.

The simple pattern repeat on the teenager's sweater on page 47 is worked by stranding the yarn not in use loosely across the back of the work.

The pattern is a simple repeat of four stitches plus three edge stitches; a number of the single crochet patterns on this page and on page 51 can be substituted for the original one.

Using large motifs

The repeating "Fair Isle" pattern could be omitted and the basic shape of the sweater could provide a plain background for a large motif. When working larger motifs, you should not, of course, strand the yarn but use separate balls of yarn for each section of color in the design.

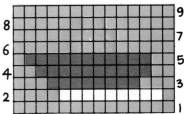

Pattern Library: Jacquard patterns

Seascape

These single crochet charts can be used either for repeating patterns, as here, or for separate motifs. Use a separate ball of yarn for each section of color.

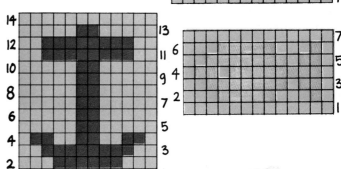

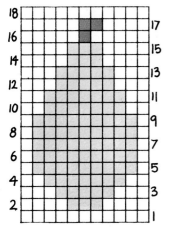

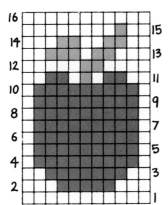

Fruit salad

Work these charts in single crochet, using a separate ball of yarn for each color. Use the motifs individually or in a repeating pattern.

Child's jacquard sweater

Two basic shapes – one for the back and front and the other for the sleeves – make this warm, bright-colored sweater.

Size C-7
Length 17in
Sleeve seam 11½in

Gauge
18 sts and 10 rows to 4in in pattern on size F hook

To save time, take time to check gauge.

Materials
8oz of a knitting worsted in color A
2oz in each of contrasting colors B, C, D and E
Sizes E and F crochet hook

Front and Back (alike)
Using smaller hook and A, make 64ch.
Base row 1dc into 4th ch from hook, 1dc into each ch to end. Turn. 62 sts.
1st row (RS) Using larger hook, work from checks chart (page 51) to end.
Cont in pat for 38 more rows.
40th row Using A only, ch 3, 1dc into next 17 sts, turn.
41st row Ch 3, 1dc into each st to end. Fasten off.
Return to 39th row. Skip next 27 sts across neck and rejoin A with sl st to next st.
Next row As 40th row.
Next row As 41st row. Fasten off.

Sleeves (both alike)
Using A and smaller hook, make 52ch.
Work as for back until 27 rows have been completed. Fasten off.

To finish
Press or block, according to yarn used.
Join shoulder and sleeve seams. Join side seams leaving 2in unjoined at lower edge. Set in sleeves. With RS facing, using smaller hook, join A with sl st to neck edge of shoulder seam. Work 3 rows sc all around neck edge. Fasten off. Using smaller hook, join A with sl st to lower edge of sweater. Work 1 row sc all around edge including unsewn sides. Fasten off. Using larger hook, join A with a sl st to sleeve seam and work 8 rows sc all around sleeve. Fasten off. Turn up cuffs.

Squares   Diamonds

Dazzling doubles

Doubles are best suited to simple repeating patterns, as shown here, in which the yarn is stranded loosely on the wrong side of the work.

Dots   Arrows

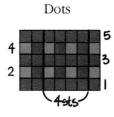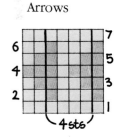

Squares   Fences

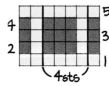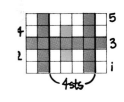

Super single crochet

All these repeating patterns, in which the yarn is stranded on the wrong side of the work, could be used in the basic sweater on page 45.

Checks   Zigzags

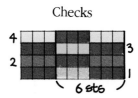

Crosses

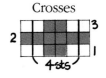

Picture jacquard

Picture sweaters worked in crochet are fascinating to make and are always great fun to wear. Either make the winter or spring sweaters shown here or choose your own subject, collect yarns in beautiful colors and start to create your own work of art.

The basic picture sweaters

Sizes
To fit 34-36 [38-40] in Bust/Chest
Length 24½ [26] in

Long sleeve seam 16 [18] in
Short sleeve seam 10 [11½] in

Note: *Instructions for the larger size are in brackets [ ]; where there is only one set of figures it applies to both sizes.*

Materials
Winter sweater
16 [18] oz of a knitting worsted in main color A
4oz in contrasting color B
2oz in each of contrasting colors C, D, E

52

and F
4oz in contrasting color G
Spring sweater
15 [16] oz in main color A
4oz in contrasting color B
2oz in each of contrasting colors C, D, E
and F
2 [4] oz in contrasting color G
2oz in contrasting color H
Sizes E and F crochet hooks

Gauge
18sc and 19 rows to 4in worked on size
F hook
18hdc and 14 rows to 4in worked on a
size F hook
To save time, take time to check gauge.

Winter sweater
Back
Using larger hook and A, make 84 [93]
ch.
Base row 1hdc into 3rd ch from hook,
1hdc into each ch to end. Turn. 83 [92]
sts.
Pattern row 2ch to count as first hdc,
skip first st, 1hdc into each st to end.
Turn.
Rep pat row 74 [78] more times.
Shape neck
Next row Ch 2 to count as first hdc, skip
first st, 1hdc into each of next 24 [27]
hdc, work next 3hdc tog, turn. 26 [29]
sts.
Next row Ch 2 to count as first hdc, skip
first st, work next 3hdc tog, 1hdc into
each st to end. Turn. 24 [27] sts.
Next row Ch 2 to count as first hdc, skip
first st, 1hdc into each hdc to last 3 sts,
work last 3 sts tog. Turn.
22 [25] sts. Fasten off.
Return to sts left at beg of neck shaping,
skip next 27 [30] sts and rejoin A to
next st.
Next row Ch 2 to count as first hdc, skip
first st, work next 3hdc tog, 1hdc into
each st to end. Turn. 27 [29] sts.
Complete to match other side of neck.

Sleeves (both alike)
Using smaller hook and A, make 38 [44]
ch.
Base row 1dc into 4th ch from hook, 1dc
into each ch to end. Turn. 36 [42] sts.
Ribbing row Ch 3 to count as first dc,
skip first st, *inserting hook from front
to back work 1dc around stem of next
dc – 1dc front worked –, inserting hook
from back to front work 1dc around
stem of next dc – 1dc back worked –,
rep from * to turning ch, 1dc into top of
turning ch. Turn.
Rep ribbing row 8 more times.
Change to larger hook.
Inc row Ch 2 to count as first hdc, skip
first st, *2hdc into next st, 1hdc into

next st, rep from * to turning ch, 1hdc into top of turning ch. Turn. 53 [62] sts.
Work 5 more rows of hdc.

Shape sleeve

Inc row Ch 2 to count as first hdc, skip first st, 2hdc into next st, 1hdc into each st to last 2 sts, 2hdc into next st, 1hdc into last st. Turn. 55 [64] sts.
Work 6 more rows of hdc.
Work one inc row. 57 [66] sts.
Rep last 7 rows 5 [6] more times, ending with an inc row. 67 [78] sts.
Fasten off.

Note: *Use new color to complete last st in old color and use small separate balls of yarn for each area of color. (See Special Technique, below.)*

Front

Using larger hook and B, make 84 [93] ch.

Base row (RS) 1sc into 2nd ch from hook, 1sc into each ch to end. Turn. 83 [92] sc.

1st row Ch 1 to count as first sc, skip first st, 1sc into each st to end. Turn. Cont in sc and follow "winter" chart, beg at appropriate arrow on RH edge and working rem 89 rows of chart.
Using A, work 10 [14] more rows of sc.

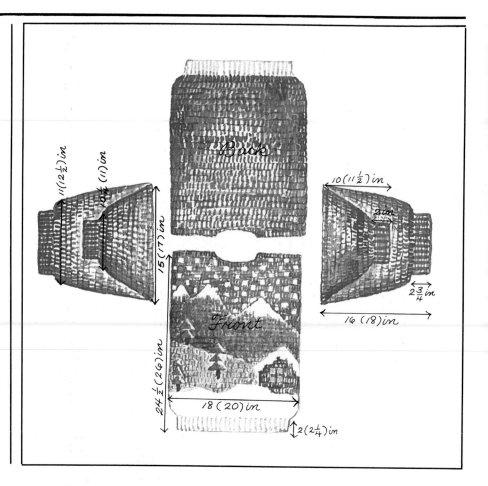

---

working picture jacquard

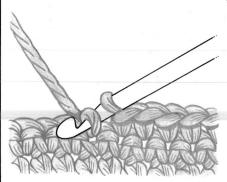

1 *When changing color, always introduce the new color when completing the last stitch in the old color. When working single crochet, insert the hook into the last stitch, wind the old color around the hook and draw through a loop.*

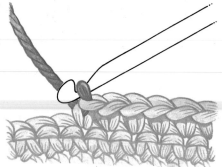

2 *Drop the old color and wind the new color around the hook. Draw the new color through both loops on the hook to complete the stitch. Continue as appropriate in the new color.*

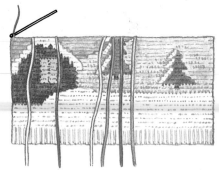

3 *Stranding yarn across the back of the work would be very wasteful in picture jacquard, so use separate balls of yarn for each color, and leave them on the wrong side of the work when not in use. Either wind small amounts of yarn onto bobbins or use long, loose strands.*

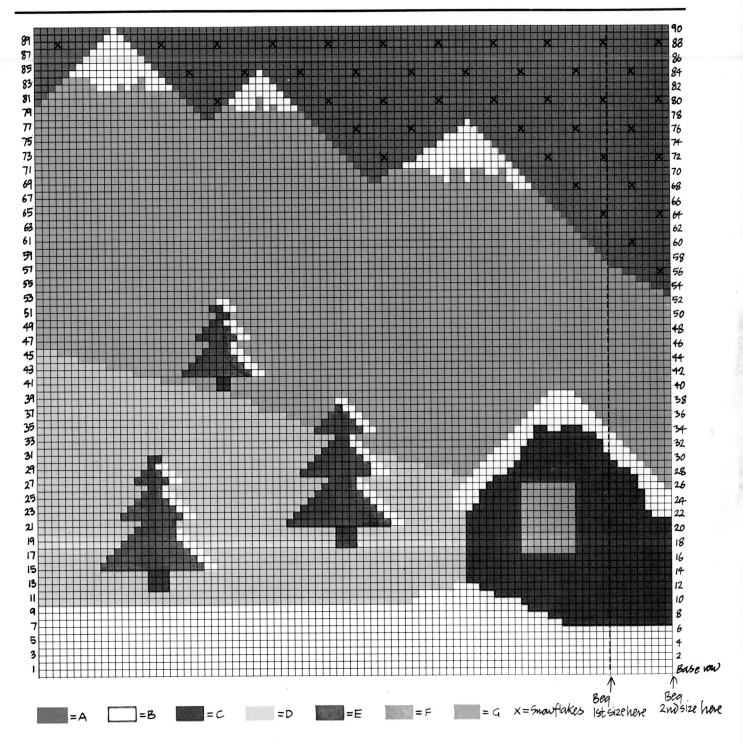

=A =B =C =D =E =F =G x=Snowflakes Beg 1st size here Beg 2nd size here

Shape neck

Next row Ch 1 to count as first sc, skip first st, 1sc into each of next 26 [29] sc, work next 2sc tog, turn. 28 [31] sts.

Next row Ch 1, skip first st, work next 2sc tog, 1sc into each st to end. Turn. 27

[30] sts. Turn.

Rep last 2 rows until 22 [25] sts rem. Fasten off.

Return to sts left at beg of neck shaping, skip next 25 [28] sts and rejoin A to next st.

Next row Ch 1 to count as first sc, skip first st, work next 2sc tog, 1sc into each st to end. Turn. 28 [31] sts. Complete to match first side of neck.

To finish

Using B and following "winter" chart,

55

embroider snowflakes on front using French knots.
Using C, embroider window frame on cottage in chain stitch.

Neckband
Join shoulder seams.
With RS facing and using smaller hook, join A to left shoulder seam and work 10dc down left front, 25 [28] dc across front neck, 10dc up right front and 27 [30] dc across back neck, sl st to first st. 72 [78] sts.
Ribbing round Ch 3 to count as first dc, skip first st, *1dc front into next st, 1dc back into next st, rep from * to last st, 1dc front into last st, sl st to top of first 3ch. Rep ribbing round once more.
Fasten off.
Set in sleeves, matching center of sleeve top with shoulder seam.
Join side and sleeve seams.

56

Waistband

With RS facing and using smaller hook, join A to left side seam and work 166 [184] dc into lower edge of front and back.

Rep ribbing round as for neckband 5[6] more times. Fasten off.

Spring sweater

Back

Work as for back of Winter Sweater.

Sleeves (both alike)

Using smaller hook and A, make 44 [48] ch.

Base row 1dc into 4th ch from hook, 1dc into each ch to end. 42 [46] sts. Work ribbing row as for winter sweater sleeve 7 times in all.

Change to larger hook.

Shape sleeve

Inc row Ch 2 to count as first hdc, skip first st, 2hdc, into next st, 1hdc, into each st to last 2 sts, 2hdc into next st, 1hdc into top of turning ch. Turn. 44 [48] sts.

Rep inc row twice more. 48 [52] sts.

Next row Work in hdc.

Next row Work inc row. 50 [54] sts. Rep last 2 rows 10 [12] more times. 70 [78] sts.

Work even for 3 [5] more rows of hdc. Fasten off.

Front

Working in sc and following "spring" chart (see page 56) work as for Winter Sweater.

To finish

Using H, embroider window frame on cottage, using chain stitch.

Complete as for Winter Sweater, omitting snowflakes.

Adapting the basic picture sweaters

Create your own original design by adapting one of these sweaters.

The basic sweaters can easily be varied if you use equivalent textured yarns instead of smooth yarns. For example, the snow could be worked in white mohair or the trees could be worked in green bouclé yarn to suggest leaves.

The Pattern Library gives motifs which could also be added to the sweaters. Draw the motif on the appropriate chart on page 55 or 56 and use suitable colors to work the motif as part of the picture.

Pattern Library: Picture jacquard patterns

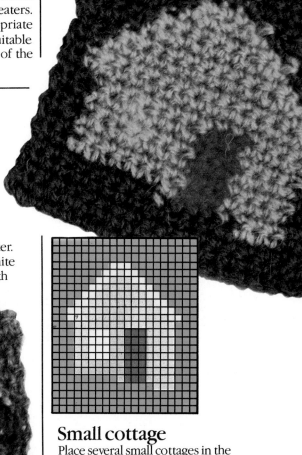

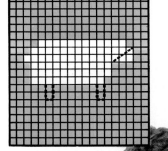

Sheep

Use this motif on the spring sweater. Work the body of the sheep in white bouclé yarn and the legs in smooth black yarn.

Small cottage

Place several small cottages in the background of either sweater. Change the background color, as appropriate, for the seasons.

Random jacquard

Random jacquard is a fascinating technique which presents the ideal opportunity to use your own imagination to work multi-colored fabrics. Here, the technique is used for a charming outfit for a baby.

The basic random jacquard outfit
Jacket and overalls

Size
Baby's size B-2
Jacket length 9½in
Sleeve seam 7in
Overalls
Length from waist to ankle 17¼in
Inside leg to ankle 8¼in

Materials
Jacket 3oz of a baby yarn in main color A
1oz in each of 3 contrasting colors B, C and D
3 small toggles
Overalls 5oz in main color A

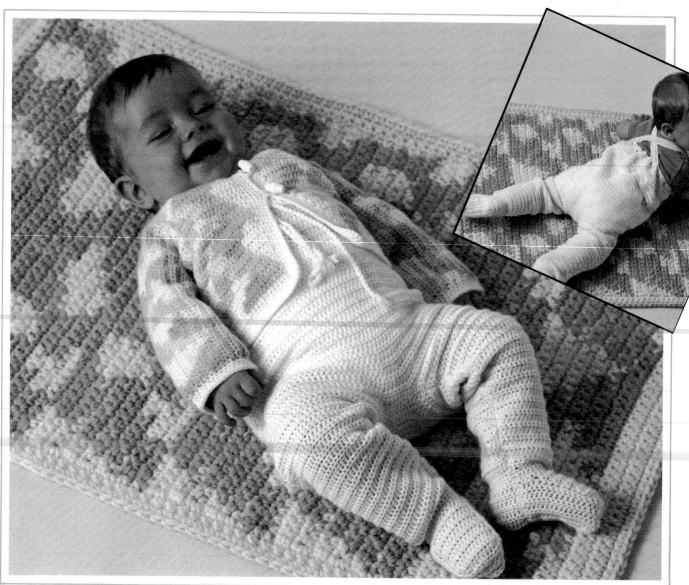

2 small buttons
Size C crochet hook

Gauge
22hdc and 18 rows to 4in worked on
size C hook

To save time, take time to check gauge.

Note: *When working jacquard pattern
on the jacket and blanket, use a small
ball of yarn for each area of color.*

Jacket
Note: *Jacket is worked in one piece,
beg at lower back edge.*
Using A, make 63ch.
Base row (WS) Using A, 1hdc into 3rd
ch from hook, 1hdc into each ch to end.
Turn. 62 sts.
1st row Using A, ch 2 to count as first
hdc, skip first st, following chart on page
61, work 1hdc into each st to end. Turn.
Cont in hdc, working jacquard pat from
chart until work measures approx 5½in
and 12th row of chart has been
completed.
Shape sleeve
Using 2nd ball of A, make 41 ch. Fasten
off.
Return to main piece, join in A at beg of
next row and make 41ch.
Next row Using D, 1hdc into 3rd ch
from hook, skip first st, 1hdc into each of
next 5 sts, using B 1hdc into each of
next 3 sts, work 13th row of chart across
next 30 sts and across first 41 sts of back,
using B, yo, insert hook into last st of
back and into first of separate 41ch, yo
and draw through first ch and last st of
back, yo and draw through 3 loops on
hook – left-sleeve sts joined to back –,
pat across rem 40ch. Turn. 142 sts.
Cont in jacquard pat until work
measures 9½in, ending with a WS row.

Shape right neck
Next row Ch 2, skip first st, pat across
next 60 sts, turn. 61 sts.
Work even in pat for 2 more rows.
Keeping jacquard pat correct, inc one st
at neck edge on following 4 rows,
ending at neck edge. 65 sts.
Next row Using A, make 5ch, keeping

jacquard pat correct work 1hdc into 3rd
ch from hook, 1hdc into each of next
2ch, pat to end. 69 sts.
Shape right front
Work even in jacquard pat until sleeve
measures 8in from underarm, ending at
center-front edge.
Next row Ch 2, skip first st, pat across
next 28 sts, turn. 29 sts.
Cont in jacquard pat on these sts until
work measures 19in.
Using A, work one row of hdc.
Fasten off.
Shape left neck and front
With RS facing, return to back neck sts,
skip next 20 sts, keeping jacquard pat
correct rejoin yarn to next st.
Next row Ch 2, skip first st, pat to end.
61 sts.
Complete to match other side of neck
and front, reversing all shaping.

To finish
Press or block, according to yarn used.
Join underarm and side seams.
Outer edging
With RS facing, join A to lower edge at
right side seam.
Work a round of sc along right front, up
right front edge, around neck, down left
front edge, along left front and back,
working 1sc into each st and row end
and 3sc into corners. Work 3 more
rounds of sc.
Fasten off.
Sleeve edging (both alike)
With RS facing, join A to sleeve seam.
Work a round of sc, working 1sc into
each st.
Work 3 more rounds of sc.
Fasten off.

Button loops (make 3)
Sew toggles in place on left front (for
girls) or right front (for boys) placing
one toggle ½in from neck edge, one 5in
from lower edge and one evenly spaced
in between.
Make button loop on opposite front
edge as follows:
With RS facing, join A to edge st directly
opposite toggle, sl st into same place as
joining, ch 8, sl st into same place as
joining.
Fasten off.

Overalls
Front
Beg at waist, make 62ch.
Base row (RS) 1hdc into 3rd ch from
hook, 1hdc into each ch to end. Turn. 61
sts.
Next row Ch 2 to count as first hdc, skip
first st, 1hdc into each st to end. Turn.
Cont in hdc until work measures 8in,
ending with a WS row.
Shape crotch
1st row Ch 2, skip first st, 1hdc into each
of next 28 sts, 2hdc into next st, 1hdc
into next st, 2hdc into next st, 1hdc into
each of last 29 sts. Turn. 63 sts.
2nd, 4th and 6th rows Working in hdc.
3rd row Ch 2, skip first st, 1hdc into
each of next 28 sts, 2hdc into next st,
1hdc into each of next 3 sts, 2hdc into
each of last 29 sts. Turn. 65 sts.
5th row Ch 2, skip first st, 1hdc into each
of next 28hdc, 2hdc into next st, 1hdc
into each of next 5 sts, 2hdc into next st,
1hdc into each of last 29hdc. Turn. 67
sts.
** Divide for legs
Next row Ch 2, skip first st, 1hdc into
each of next 28 sts, turn. 29 sts.
Work in hdc on these sts for 3 more
rows.
Dec one st at inside leg edge on next
and every following 6th row until 23 sts
rem.
Work even in hdc until work measures
17½in.
Fasten off.
With RS facing, return to skipped sts on
front, skip next 9 sts, rejoin yarn to next
st.
Next row Ch 2, skip first st, 1hdc into
each st to end. 29 sts.
Complete as for first leg, reversing all
shaping.**

Back
Work base row and 9 rows of hdc as for
back, ending with a WS row.
Shape back
Next row Ch 2, skip first st, 1hdc into
each of next 53 sts, turn.
Next row Ch 2, skip first st, 1hdc into
each of next 46 sts, turn.
Next row Ch 2, skip first st, 1hdc into
each of next 39 sts, turn.
Next row Ch 2, skip first st, 1hdc into

each of next 32 sts, turn.

Next row Ch 2, skip first st, 1hdc into each of next 32 sts just worked, 1hdc into 14 sts skipped at side edge. Turn.

Next row Ch 2, skip first st, 1hdc into each of next 46 sts, 1hdc into 14 sts skipped at side edge. Turn. 61 sts. Cont working even in hdc until back measures same as front at side edges. Work from ** to ** as for front.

Feet

Press or block, according to yarn used. Join outside leg seams.

With RS facing, rejoin yarn to first st on left leg.

Next row Ch 1 to count as first sc, skip first st, *1sc into each of next 2 sts, work next 2sc tog, rep from * to last st, 1sc into last st. 35 sts.

Work even in sc for 3 more rows.

Next row Sl st across first 4sc, ch 2 skip sl st at base of 2ch, 1hdc into each of next 11 sts, turn. 12 sts.

Work even in hdc for 10 more rows. Fasten off.

With RS facing, rejoin yarn to first sl st.

Next row Ch 2, skip first st, 1hdc into each of next 2 sl st, 1hdc into each of next 10 row ends, 1hdc into each of next 12 sts, 1hdc into each of next 10 row ends, 1 hdc into each of next 20 sts. Turn. 55 sts.

Next row Ch 2, skip first st, 1hdc into each of next 29 sts, (work next 2hdc tog) 4 times, 1hdc into each of next 15 sts. Turn. 51 sts.

Work even in hdc for 4 more rows.

Next row Ch 2, skip first st, 1hdc into each of next 15 sts, (work next 2hdc tog) twice, 1hdc into each of next 21 sts, (work next 2hdc tog) twice, 1hdc into each of next 6 sts. Turn. 47 sts.

Next row Ch 2, skip first st, 1hdc into each of next 5 sts, (work next 2hdc tog) twice, 1hdc into each of next 19 sts, (work next 2hdc tog) twice, 1hdc into each of next 14 sts. 43 sts. Fasten off.

Work 2nd foot in the same way reversing all shaping.

Front bib

** With RS facing rejoin yarn to first st on front.

Next row Ch 1 to count as first sc, skip first 2 sts, 1sc into each st to last 2 sts, work last 2sc tog. Turn. 59 sts. Work even in dc for 4 more rows.

Next row Ch 3, skip first st, 1dc into each of next 2 sts, * ch 1, skip next st, 1dc into each of next 3 sts, rep from * to end. Turn.

Next row Ch 1 to count as first sc, skip first st, 1sc into each of next 2 sts, *1sc into next 1ch sp, 1sc into each of next 3 sts, rep from * to end. Work one more row in sc.

Fasten off.**

With RS facing, skip first 12 sts on bib and rejoin yarn to next st.

Next row Ch 2, skip first st, 1hdc into each of next 34 sts, turn. 35 sts. Work one more row of hdc.

Cont in hdc, dec one st at each end of next and every following 3rd row until 25 sts rem.

Work one more row in hdc.

Work 2 rows of sc.

Buttonhole row Ch 1 to count as first sc, skip first st, 1sc into next st, ch 3, skip next 3 sts, 1sc into each of next 15 sts, ch 3, skip next 3 sts, 1sc into each of last 2 sts. Turn.

---

increasing for the sleeves

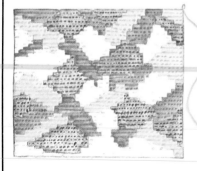  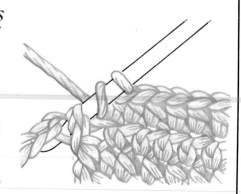

1 The basic jacket is worked in one piece, beginning at the lower back edge, and so stitches must be increased to form the sleeves. Work as given until the back is the required length to the underarms, ending with a wrong side row. Remove the hook from the loop on the back. Using another ball of main color, chain 41 and fasten off.

2 Return to the loop on the back that was left in step 1. Join in the main color at the beginning of the row and chain 41. Pattern across these in single crochet — 40 sleeve stitches. Pattern across the first 61 stitches of the back.

3 To join the 41 chains worked separately (which will form the left sleeve stiches), wind the yarn over the hook and insert the hook into the last stitch on the back and into the first of the 41 chains. Wind the yarn over the hook and draw a loop through the chain and last stitch. Wind the yarn over the hook and draw through the remaining three loops on the hook. Pat the next 40 stitches — 142 stitches have been worked.

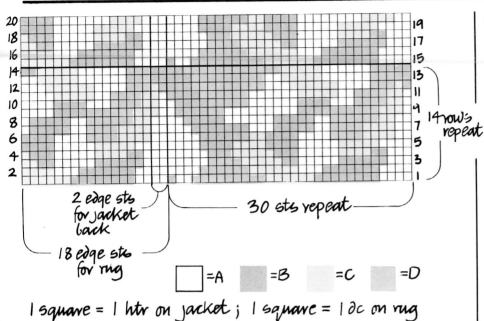

20
18
16
14
12
10
8
6
4
2

19
17
15
13
11
9
7
5
3
1

14 rows repeat

2 edge sts for jacket back

18 edge sts for rug

30 sts repeat

☐ =A   ▨ =B   ▧ =C   ▨ =D

1 square = 1 htr on jacket ; 1 square = 1 dc on rug

Next row Ch 1 to count as first sc, skip first st, 1sc into next st, 3sc into next 3ch sp, 1sc into each of next 15 sts, 3sc into next 3ch sp, 1sc into each of last 2 sts. Turn.
Fasten off.
With RS facing rejoin yarn to first row end of bib and work 1sc into each row end up left side, into each st across top and into each row end down right side. Fasten off.

Back bib
Work from ** to ** as for front bib.

Straps (make 2)
Make 61ch.
Base row 1hdc into 3rd ch from hook, 1hdc into each ch to end. Turn. 60 sts.
Work 3 more rows of hdc.
Fasten off.

To finish
Press or block, according to yarn used. Join inside-leg and foot seams. Sew straps in place at back and sew buttons to straps as required to correspond with buttonholes. Make a twisted cord (see page 164) 40in long and thread it through eyelet holes with ends in front.

Blanket

Size
Blanket measures approx 36 x 24in

Materials
23oz of a bulky yarn in main color A
9oz in each of 3 contrasting colors: B, C and D.
Size K crochet hook

Gauge
9sc and 9 rows to 4in worked on size K hook

To make
Using A, make 49ch.
Base row (WS) 1sc into 2nd ch from hook, 1sc into each ch to end. Turn. 48 sts.
1st row Using A ch 1 to count as first sc, skip first st, following chart shown above, work 1sc into each st to end. Turn.
Cont in sc, working jacquard pat from chart until work measures 32½in. Using A, work one row of hdc. Fasten off.

Edging
Press or block, according to yarn used.
With RS facing rejoin A to first st on foundation ch.
1st round Ch 1 to count as first sc, skip first st, (1sc into each st to corner st, 3sc into corner st, 1sc into each row end to corner st, 3sc into corner st) twice, ending last rep with 2sc, sl st to first ch. Rep last round twice more. Fasten off.

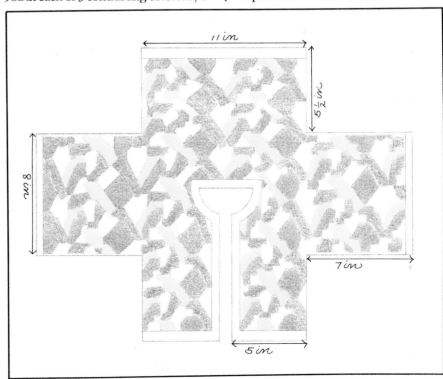

Adapting the jacquard outfit

Use the Pattern Library to make an original outfit for a baby.

Many of the Pattern Library samples can be used to make the basic jacket and blanket, since, unlike conventional jacquard patterns, random jacquard does not have obvious pattern repeats. There is therefore no need to worry about balancing the pattern at the side edges. You can either work a totally random pattern, inventing the design as you go, or work a random-style repeating pattern as on the basic jacket.

Work the stitch repeat as often as possible within the stitches for the garment. Then work as much of the repeat as required for the remaining stitches. For example, on the chart shown on page 61, the 18 edge stitches on the blanket are the last 18 stitches of the stitch repeat, whereas the jacket uses only the last two stitches of the repeat (the first two at the right) as edge stitches.

Pattern Library: Random jacquard patterns

Stairways (3)
In this sample, which could also be used to make the basic jacket and blanket, stairs of double crochet have been worked in four colors.

Random doubles (1)
In this sample, which could be used on the baby's jacket and blanket on page 58, blocks of three doubles have been placed at random. The blocks have been worked in a combination of five colors, introduced at random to give a pleasing effect.

Morse (2)
In this half-double sample, which could be used to make the basic jacket and blanket, colorful dots and dashes have been placed at random on every alternate row on a dark background to create a striking effect.

Triangles (4)
A number of different-sized triangles have been worked in this single crochet sample.

Puffs and popcorns

Puffs and popcorns are two kinds of large crochet bobble that can be worked either by themselves or in combination with other stitches. Use them to make highly textured fabrics, as for this attractive pullover and cardigan, or scatter them on a plain background.

The basic textured pullover and cardigan

Sizes

To fit 34-36 [38-40]in bust/chest
Length 20½ [23]in excluding knitted ribbing waistband
Sleeve seam 18 [19¾]in excluding knitted ribbing cuffs

Note: *Instructions for larger size are in brackets [ ]; where there is only one set of figures it applies to both sizes.*

Materials

Pullover or cardigan
1850 [2350]yd of knitting-worsted weight cotton
Size G crochet hook
Pair of size 3 knitting needles
Cardigan only size E crochet hook

Gauge

14 sts and 10 rows to 4in in pattern worked on size G hook

To save time, take time to check gauge.

Special abbreviations

Br – berry st: (yo, insert hook into st and draw through a loose loop, yo and draw through first loop on hook) twice, yo and draw through first 4 loops on hook, yo and draw through rem 2 loops on hook.

Cb – cluster bobble: leaving last loop of each st on hook work 4dc into next st, yo and draw through first 4 loops on hook, yo and draw through rem 2 loops on hook.

Pc – popcorn st: 4dc into next st, remove hook from loop and insert into first dc just worked and into loop just left, yo and draw through all loops on hook.

Pf – puff st: (yo, insert hook into st and draw through a loose loop) 4 times, yo and draw through first 8 loops on hook, yo and draw through rem 2 loops.

Panel 1 (worked over 20 sts)

1st row (RS) 1dc into each of next 8 sts, pc into next st, 1dc into each of next 2 sts, pc into next st, 1dc into each of next 8 sts.

2nd row 1sc into each of next 5 sts, pf into next st, 1sc into each of next 8 sts, pf into next st, 1sc into each of next 5 sts.

3rd row 1dc into each of next 3 sts, * skip next st, inserting hook from front to back work 1dtr around stem – called 1dtr front – of dc 2 sts to left and 2 rows below, 1dc into each of next 3 sts, skip next st, 1dtr front around dc 2 rows below and now 2 sts to right * *, 1dc into next dc, pc into each of next 2 sts,

1dc into next st, rep from * to * * once more, 1dc into each of next 3 sts.

4th row 1sc into each of next 4 sts, pf into next st, 1sc into next st, pf into next st, 1sc into each of next 6sc, pf into next st, 1sc into next st, pf into next st, 1sc into each of next 4 sts.

5th row 1dc into next st, *skip next st, 1dtr around dtr to left 2 rows below, 1dc into each of next 7 sts, skip next st, 1dtr around dtr to right 2 rows below * *, rep from * to * * once more, 1dc into next st.

6th row 1sc into each of next 4 sts, pf into next st, 1sc into next st, pf into next st, 1sc into each of next 6 sts, pf into next st, 1sc into next st, pf into next st, 1sc into each of next 4 sts.

7th row 1dc into each of next 3 sts, *skip next st, 1dtr front around dtr to right 2 rows below, 1dc into each of next 3 sts, skip next st, 1dtr front around dtr to left 2 rows below *, 1dc into next st, pc into each of next 2 sts, 1dc into next st, rep from * to * * once more, 1dc into each of next 3 sts.

8th row 1sc into each of next 5 sts, pf into next st, 1sc into each of next 8 sts, pf into next st, 1sc into each of next 5sts.

9th row 1dc into each of next 5 sts, *skip next st, leaving last loop of each st on hook work 1dtr front around

━━ SPECIAL TECHNIQUE ━━

working puff stitch

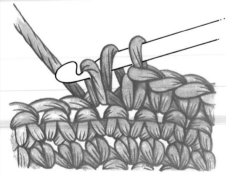

1 Puff stitch can be worked with either the right or the wrong side facing. Work to the position of the puff stitch. Wind the yarn over the hook, insert the hook into the next stitch and draw through a loose loop — three loops on the hook.

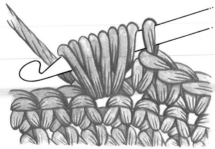

2 * Wind the yarn over the hook, insert the hook into the same stitch and draw through a loose loop — five loops on the hook. Rep from * twice more — nine loops on the hook — making sure that all loops are sufficiently loose.

3 Wind the yarn over the hook and draw through the first eight loops on the hook. (This would be very difficult if the loops had been worked tightly.) Wind the yarn over the hook and draw through the remaining two loops onto the hook to complete the puff stitch.

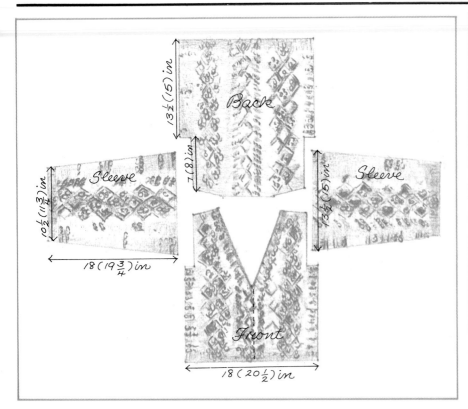

dtr to right 2 rows below and 1dtr front around dtr to left 2 rows below, yo and draw through rem 3 loops on hook * *, 1dc into each of next 2 sts, (pc into next st, 1dc into each of next 2 sts) twice, rep from * to ** once more, 1dc into each of next 5 sts.

10th row 1sc into each of next 5 sts, pf into next st, 1sc into each of next 8 sts, pf in next st, 1sc in each of next 5 sts.

11th row 1dc into each of next 3 sts, * skip next st, 1dtr around dtr to left 2 rows below. 1dc into each of next 3 sts, skip next st, 1dtr around dtr to right 2 rows below * *, 1dc into next st, pc into each of next 2 sts, 1dc into next st, rep from * to * * once more, 1dc into each of next 3 sts.

4th–11th rows form pat of Panel 1. Rep them as required.

Panel 2 (worked over 3 sts)

1st row (RS) 1dc into next st, pc into next st, 1dc into next st.

2nd row Pf into next st, 1dc into next st, pf into next st.

First and 2nd rows form pat of Panel 2. Rep them as required.

Panel 3 (worked over 9 sts)

1st row 1dc into next st, pc into next st, 1dc into each of next 5 sts, pc into next st, 1dc into next st.

2nd row 1sc into each of next 2 sts, cb into next st, 1sc into each of next 3 sts, cb into next st, 1sc into each of next 2 sts.

3rd row 1dc into each of next 3 sts, pc into next st, 1dc into next st, pc into next st, 1dc into each of next 3 sts.

4th row 1sc into each of next 4 sts, cb into next st, 1sc into each of next 4 sts.

5th row 1dc into each of next 4 sts, pc into next st, 1dc into each of next 4 sts.

6th row As 4th row.

7th row As 3rd row.

8th row As 2nd row.

First – 8th rows form pat of Panel 3. Rep them as required.

Pullover

Back

Using larger hook, make 66 [74]ch.

Base row (WS) Sl st into 3rd ch from hook, ch 2, br into next ch, (sl st into next ch 2, br into next ch) 1 [3] times, 1sc into each of next 55ch, (ch 2, br into next ch, sl st into next ch) 2 [4] times, 1 sc into last ch. Turn. 65 [73] sts.

1st row (RS) ch 3, skip first st, (1dc into next sl st, 1sc into next br) 2 [4] times, work first rows of panels as follows: Panel 1, Panel 2, Panel 3, Panel 2, Panel 1, (1sc into next br, 1dc into next sl st) 2 [4] times, 1dc into top of turning ch. Turn.

2nd row (Ch 2, br into next dc, sl st into next sc) 2 [4] times, work 2nd rows of panels as follows: Panel 1, Panel 2, Panel 3, Panel 2, Panel 1, (sl st into next sc, ch 2, br into next dc) 2 [4] times, 1sc into top of turning ch. Turn.

3rd row ch 3, skip first st, (1sc into next br, 1dc into next sl st) 2 [4] times, work next rows of panels as set, (1dc into next sl st, 1 sc into next br) 2 [4] times, 1dc into first of first 2ch. Turn.

4th row Ch 1, skip first st, (sl st into next sc, ch 2, 1br into next dc) 2 [4] times, work next rows of panels as set, (ch 2, br into next dc, sl st into next sc) 2 [4] times, 1sc into top of turning ch. Turn.

Cont working border of br and panels as set, rep panel pats as previously instructed, until 34 [38] rows in all have been worked from the foundation ch.

Shape armholes

Next row Sl st across first 6 [8] sts, ch 1, skip sl st at base of first ch, 1sc into each of next 0 [2]sts, work panels as set, 1sc into each of next 1 [3] sts, turn. 55 [59] sts.

Next row Ch 3, skip first st, 1dc into each of next 0 [2] sts, work panels as set, 1dc into each of next 1 [3] sts. Turn.

Cont to work panels and edge sts as set until 18 [20] rows have been worked from beg of armhole.

Shape shoulders

Next row Sl st across first 7 sts, 1sc into each of next 7 sts, 1dc into each of next 27 [31] sts, 1sc into each of next 7 sts. Fasten off.

Front

Work as for back until 26 [34] rows have been worked.

Shape neck

Next row Pat across 28 [32] sts, 1sc into each of next 4sc, turn. 32 [36] sts.

Next row Ch 3, skip first st, 1dc into each of next 3 sts, pat to end. Turn.

** Next row Pat across 28 [32] sts, 1sc into next st, work next 2sc tog, 1sc into last st. Turn. 31 [35] sts.

Next row Ch 3, skip first st, 1dc into each of next 2 sts, pat to end. Turn.

2nd size only: shape armhole

Next row Sl st across first 8 sts, ch 1, skip sl st at base of first ch, pat to last 3 sts, work next 2sc tog, 1sc into last st. Turn.

1st size only

Next row Pat across 28 sts, work next 2sc tog, 1sc into last st. Turn. 30sts.

Both sizes

Next row Ch 3, skip first st, 1dc into next st, pat to end. Turn.

Next row Pat across 24 [21] sts, pf into next st, 1sc into next st, pf into next st, work next 2sc tog, 1sc into last st. Turn. 29 [26] sts.

Next row Ch 3, skip first st, 1dc into each of next 2 sts, pc into next st, pat to end. Turn.

1st size only: shape armhole

Next row Sl st across first 6 sts, ch 1, skip sl st at base of first ch, pat across 18 sts, pf into next st, 1sc into next st, pf into next st, work next 2sc tog, 1sc into last st. Turn. 23 sts.

2nd size only

Next row Pat across 20 sts, pf into next st, 1sc into next st, pf into next st, work next 2sc tog, 1sc into last st. Turn. 25 sts.

Both sizes

Next row Ch 3, skip first st, 1dc into each of next 2 sts, pc into next st, pat to end. Turn.

Next row Pat across 17 [19] sts, pf into next st, 1sc into next st, pf into next st, work next 2sc tog, 1sc into last st. Turn. 22 [24] sts.

Next row Ch 3, skip first st, 1dc into each of next 2 sts, pc into next st, pat to end. Turn.

Keeping panel and neck edge pats correct, cont to dec one st at neck edge on next and every following alternate row until 16 [18] sts rem.

Next row Ch 3, skip first st, 1dc into each of next 2 sts, pc into next st, 1dc into each of next 2 sts, pat to end. Turn.

2nd size only: shape shoulder

Next row Sl st across first 7 sts, 1sc into each of next 7 sts, 1dc into each of next 4dc. Fasten off.

1st size only

Next row Pat across 9 sts, 1sc into next st, pf into next st, 1sc into next st, pf into next st, work next 2sc tog, 1sc into last st. Turn. 15 sts.

Next row Ch 3, skip first st, 1dc into each of next 2 sts, pc into next st, 1dc into next st, pat to end. Turn.

Shape shoulder

Next row Sl st across first 7 sts, 1sc into each of next 7 sts, 1dc into next st. Fasten off. ******

Both sizes

Return to first row of neck shaping, skip next st next st and rejoin yarn to next st, ch 1, skip first st, pat to end. 32 [36] sts. Complete to match other side of neck, reversing all shaping.

Sleeves (both alike)

Using larger hook make 39 [43] ch.

Base row (WS) Sl st into 3rd ch from hook, ch 2, br into next ch, (sl st into next ch, ch 2, br into next ch) 1 [2] times, 1sc into each of next 28ch, (ch 2, br into next ch, sl st into next ch) 2 [3] times, 1sc into last ch. Turn. 38 [42] sts.

1st row Ch 3, skip first st, (1dc into next sl st, 1sc into next br) 2 [3] times, 1dc into next st, work first rows of panels as follows: Panel 2, Panel 1, Panel 2, 1dc into next st, (1sc into next br, 1dc into next sl st) 2 [3] times, 1dc into top of turning ch. Turn.

2nd row (Ch 2, br into next dc, sl st into next sc) 2 [3] times, 1sc into next st, work 2nd rows of panels as follows: Panel 2, Panel 1, Panel 2, 1sc into next st, (sl st into next sc, ch 2, br into next dc) 2 [3] times, 1sc into last st. Turn.

3rd row Ch 3, skip first st, (1sc into next br, 1dc into next sl st) 2 [3] times, 1dc into next st, work next row of panels as set, 1dc into next st, (1dc into next sl st, 1sc into next br) 2 [3] times, 1dc into top of turning ch. Turn.

Shape sleeve

4th row Ch 1, 1sc into first st at base of first ch, (sl st into next sc, ch 2, br into next dc) 2 [3] times, 1sc into next st, work next row of panels as set, 1sc into next dc) 2 [3] times, 1sc into next st, work next row of panels as set, 1sc. Cont to rep panels as previously instructed, while *at the same time* inc one st at each end of every following 4th row until there are 48 [54] sts. Work even until 46 [50] rows have been worked. Fasten off.

To finish

Do not press. Pin out all pieces to size. Spray lightly with water and leave to dry naturally.

Waistbands (both alike)

With RS facing and using knitting needles, pick up and K 65 [73] sts from foundation ch.

1st ribbing row K1, (P1, K1) to end.

2nd ribbing row P1, (K1, P1) to end.

Rep first and 2nd ribbing rows 6 more times.

Bind off loosely in ribbing.

Cuffs (alike)

With RS facing and using knitting needles, pick up and K 37 [41] sts from foundation ch.

Rep first and 2nd ribbing rows 7 more times. Bind off loosely in ribbing. Using leftover yarn split in half, join shoulder and side seams. Join sleeve seam, leaving open approx 2 [2¾] in at top edge. Set in sleeve, joining open edges to underarm edges.

Neck border

With RS facing and using larger hook, join yarn to left shoulder seam.

Next row Ch 1, working 1sc into each st and into each sc row end and 2sc into each dc row end, work in sc across back neck and down right front, work 1sc into skipped st at front neck, marking this st with a contrasting thread, work in sc up left front, sl st to first ch.

Next row Ch 1, work in sc to right

shoulder seam, skip next st, work in sc to 2 sts before marked st, work next 2sc tog, 1sc into marked st, work next 2sc tog, work in sc to last st, skip last st, sl st to first ch.
Rep last row once more. Fasten off.

Cardigan

Back and sleeves
Work as for Pullover.

Left front
Using larger hook, make 33 [37] ch.
Base row (WS) Sl st into 3rd ch from hook, ch 2, br into next ch, (sl st into next ch, ch 2, br into next ch) 1 [3] times, 1sc into each ch to end. Turn. 32 [36] sts.
1st row Ch 3, skip first st, 1dc into each of next 3 sts, work first rows of panels as follows: Panel 2, Panel 1, (1sc into next br, 1dc into next sl st) 2 [4] times. 1dc into top of turning ch. Turn.
2nd row (Ch 2, br into next st, sl st into next st) 2 [4] times, work 2nd rows of panels as follows: Panel 1, Panel 2, 1sc into each of last 4 sts. Turn.
3rd row Ch 3, skip first st, 1dc into each of next 3 sts, work next row of panels as set, (1dc into next sl st, 1sc into next br) 2 [4] times, 1dc into top of turning ch. Turn.

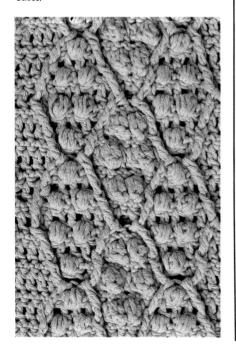

4th row Ch 1, skip first st, (sl st into next st, ch 2, br into next st) 2 [4] times, work next row of panels as set, 1sc into each of last 4 sts. Turn.
Cont working borders and panels as set, rep panel pats as previously instructed, until 28 [36] rows have been worked. Work from * * to * * as for Pullover front.

Right front
Using larger hook, make 33 [37] ch.
Base row (WS) 1sc into 3rd ch from hook, 1sc into each of next 26ch, (ch 2, br into next ch, sl st into next ch) 2 [4] times, 1sc into last ch. Turn. 32 [36] sts.
1st row Ch 3, skip first st, (1dc into next sl st, 1sc into next br) 2 [4] times, work first rows of panels as follows: Panel 1, Panel 2, 1dc into each of last 4 sts. Turn.
2nd row Ch 1, skip first st, 1sc into each of next 3 sts, work 2nd rows of panels as follows: Panel 2, Panel 1, (sl st into next sc, ch 2, br into next dc) 2 [4] times. 1sc into top of turning ch. Turn.
Complete as for left front, reversing all shaping.

To finish
Work back waistband and cuffs as for Pullover.
Front waistbands (both alike)
With RS facing and using knitting needles, pick up and K 31 [35] sts from foundation ch. Rep first and 2nd ribbing rows 7 times.
Bind off loosely in ribbing.
Join shoulder, side and sleeve seams and set in sleeves as for Pullover.

Front band
Woman's version Mark positions of 4 buttonholes on right front. With RS facing and using larger hook, join yarn to first row end on lower RH edge.
Next row Working 1sc into each st, into each ribbing row end and into each sc row end and 2sc into each dc row end, work in sc up right front, across back neck and down left front. Turn.
Next row Work in sc. Turn.
Next row (Work in sc to marker, ch 2, skip next 2sc) 4 times, work in sc to end. Turn.
Next row Work in sc to first 2ch sp, (2sc into next 2ch sp, work in sc to next 2ch sp) 4 times, work in sc to end. Turn.
Man's version Mark positions of 4 buttonholes on left front, and complete front band as for woman's version, reversing positions of buttonholes.

Buttons (make 4)
Wind off several inches of yarn to stuff button.
Using smaller hook, ch 5, join with a sl st to form a ring.
1st round Ch 3, leaving last loop of each st on hook work 2dc into ring, yo and draw through all 3 loops on hook, (leaving last loop of each st on hook, work 3dc into ring, yo and draw through all 4 loops on hook) 3 times, sl st into 3rd of first 3ch.
2nd round Ch 1, (work next 2sc tog) twice, inserting spare yarn as button closes, sl st to first ch. Fasten off firmly. Sew on buttons to front band to correspond with buttonholes.

Adapting the pullover and cardigan

Combine puff and popcorn stitches with other crochet bobbles to create a highly textured fabric.

Intricately patterned garments such as the basic pullover and cardigan are very difficult to adapt radically; it is much safer, if you wish to vary their appearance, to introduce contrasting colors when working the bobbles. Remember to introduce the new color when completing the last stitch in the old color.

Using puffs and popcorns
Puffs and popcorns can be incorporated into plain crochet fabrics; puffs are usually worked in a single crochet fabric and popcorns in double crochet.
These bobble stitches, however, may alter the gauge, so change hook size accordingly. Estimate carefully the amount of yarn you will need. Use up a ball of yarn patterning across the width of the back. Divide the area of the garment by the area of the sample; the result is the number of balls needed.

Pattern Library: Puff and popcorn patterns

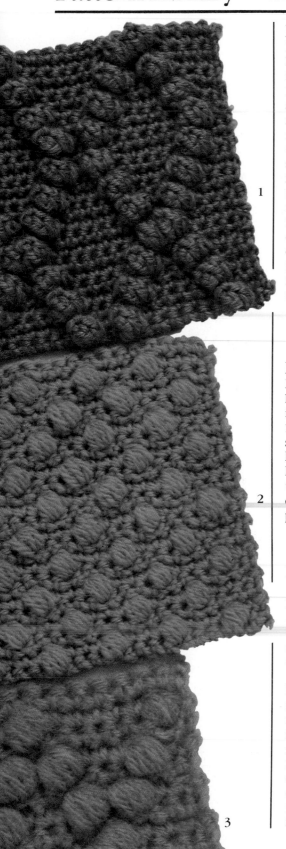

Popcorn lattice (1)

Make a multiple of 10ch plus 3 extra.
Base row 1sc into 2nd ch from hook, 2sc into each ch to end. Turn.
1st row (RS) Ch 1 to count as first sc, skip first st, 1sc into next st, *4dc into next st, remove hook from loop and insert it into first dc just worked and into loop just left, yo and draw through all loops on hook – popcorn st or pc formed –, 1sc into each of next 6 sts, pc into next st, 1sc into each of next 2sts, rep from * to end. Turn.
2nd and every alternate row. Ch 1 to count as first sc, skip first st, 1sc into each st to end. Turn.
3rd row Ch 1 to count as first sc, skip first st, 1sc into each of next 2 sts, * (pc into next st, 1sc into each of next 4 sts) twice, rep from * ending last rep with 3sc. Turn.
5th row Ch 1 to count as first sc, skip first st, 1sc into each of next 3 sts, *pc into next st, 1sc into each of next 2sts, pc into next st, 1sc into each of next 6 sts, rep from * ending last rep with 4sc. Turn.
7th row Ch 1 to count as first sc, skip first st, 1sc into each of next 4 sts, *pc into each of next 2 sts, 1sc into each of next 8 sts, rep from * ending last rep with 5sc. Turn.
9th row As 5th row.
11th row As 3rd row.
13th row As first row.
14th row As 2nd row.
Rep first-14th rows throughout.

Puff stitch (2)

Make a multiple of 4ch plus 2 extra.
Base row 1sc into 2nd ch from hook, 1sc into each ch to end. Turn.
1st row (WS) Ch 1 to count as first sc, skip first st, 1sc into next st, *(yo, insert hook into next st and draw through a loose loop) 4 times, yo and draw through first 8 loops on hook, yo and draw through rem 2 loops on hook – puff st or pf formed –, 1sc into each of next 3 sts, rep from * ending last rep with 2sc. Turn.
2nd row Ch 1 to count as first sc, skip first st, 1sc into each st to end. Turn.
3rd row Ch 1 to count as first sc, skip first st, *1sc into each of next 3 sts, pf into next st, rep from * to last 4 sts, 1sc into each of last 4 sts. Turn.
4th row As 2nd row.
Rep first-4th rows throughout.

Puff stitch crosses (3)

Make a multiple of 6ch plus 4 extra.
Base row 1sc into 2nd ch from hook, 1sc into each ch to end. Turn.
1st row (RS) Ch 1 to count as first sc, skip first st, *(yo, insert hook into next st and draw through a loose loop) 5 times, yo and draw through first 10 loops on hook, yo and draw through rem 2 loops on hook – puff st or pf formed –, 1sc into each of next 5sts, rep from * to last 2 sts, pf into next st, 1sc into last st. Turn.
2nd and every alternate row Ch 1 to count as first sc, skip first st, 1sc into each st to end. Turn.
3rd row Ch 1 to count as first sc, skip first st, 1sc into next st, *pf into next st, 1sc into each of next 3 sts, pf into next st, 1sc into next st, rep from * to last st, 1sc into last st. Turn.
5th row Ch 1 to count as first sc, skip first st, *1sc into each of next 2 sts, pf into next st, 1sc into next st, pf into next st, 1sc into next st, rep from * to last 2 sts, 1sc into each of last 2 sts. Turn.
7th row Ch 1 to count as first sc, skip first st, 1sc into each of next 3 sts, *pf into next st, 1sc into each of next 5 sts, rep from * ending last rep with 4sc. Turn.
9th row As 5th row.
11th row As 3rd row.
12 row As 2nd row.
Rep first-12th rows throughout.

Floral patterns

Of all natural forms, flowers have most often served as inspiration for needlework. Blossoms and petals worked on crochet add a new dimension to garments – such as this beach robe – and accessories.

The basic floral beach robe

Sizes
C-5-7[C-10-12:misses'10-12:14-16]
Length 19½[21¼:28½:30]in
Sleeve seam 12½[15:17½:18]in

Note: *Instructions for larger sizes are in brackets [ ]; where there is only one set of figures it applies to all sizes.*

Materials
11[15:18:22]oz of a tightly-spun fingering yarn
Size B crochet hook

Gauge
22hdc and 20 rows to 4in worked on size B hook

To save time, take time to check gauge.

Back and fronts (worked in one piece to armholes)
Make 143 [164:185:206] ch *loosely.*
Base row (RS) 1hdc into 3rd ch from hook, 1hdc into each ch to end. Turn.
142 [163:184:205] sts.
1st row Ch 2, 1hdc into sp between hdc to end, working last hdc in top of 2ch. Turn.
Rep last row twice more.
4th row Ch 2, 1hdc into sp between hdc

3 times, * 6dc around stem of next hdc on previous row, turn, 6dc around stem of next hdc on previous row, join with a sl st to first dc, turn – flower worked –, 1hdc into sp between hdc 6 times, rep from * to last 5 sts, work 1 flower, 1hdc into sp between hdc to end. Turn.
5th row Ch 2, 1hdc into each sp between hdc and each sl st to end. Turn.
6th-9th rows As first row.
10th row Ch 2, 1hdc into sp between hdc 7 times, * work flower, 1hdc into sp between hdc 6 times, rep from * to last 8 hdc, work flower, 1hdc into sp between hdc to end. Turn.
11th row As 5th row.
12th row As 2nd row.
These 12 rows form the pat. Cont in pat until work measures 9[10¼:13½:14]in, ending with a WS row.

Shape fronts
Note: Keep pat correct throughout.
Dec row Sl st into top of first hdc, 2ch, pat to within last 2 sts. Turn. 2 sts dec.
Keeping continuity of pat correct, dec 1 st at each end of every following alternate [alternate:3rd:3rd] row until 16 [16:16:17] decs have been worked at both ends of the row.
At the same time when work measures

13½ [13¼:19½:19½] in, divide work for back and fronts thus:
Leave center 82 [97:114:127] sts for back and cont on end sts only for fronts.

Right and left fronts
Keeping armhole edge straight, cont to dec at front edge as set until 14 [17:19:22] sts rem.
Work even until work measures 19½ [21¼:28½:30] in. Fasten off.

Back
With WS facing, skip next 14 [17:21:24] sts and rejoin yarn to next hdc, ch 2, pat into next 53 [61:71:77] hdc, turn. 54 [62:72:73] sts.
Keeping pat correct, cont on these sts until armholes measure same as front armholes. Fasten off.

Sleeves (both alike)
Make 74 [86:100:114] ch *loosely.*
Base row 1hdc into 3rd ch from hook, 1hdc into each ch to end. Turn. 71 [85:99:103] sts.
1st row Ch 2, 1hdc into sp between hdc to end. Turn.
Rep last row twice more.
4th row Ch 2, 1hdc into sp between hdc

SPECIAL TECHNIQUE
working raised flowers

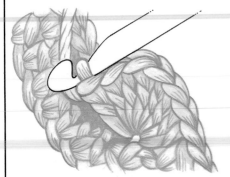

1 On the flower row, begin with two chains followed by (one half double into the space between the next two half doubles) three times. To work the first half of the flower, work six doubles around the stem of the next half double on the previous row, inserting the hook from front to back.

2 To work the second half of the flower, turn, and work six doubles around the stem of the next half double on the previous row. Insert the hook from front to back as before. You will find this easier if you hold the work upside down as shown. Join with a slip stitch to the first double.

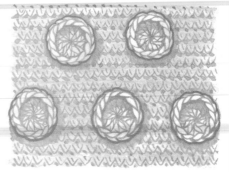

3 Then work (one half double in the space between the next two half doubles) six times. Continue spacing flowers in this way to the last four stitches and end with a half double worked as before. On the next flower row, begin with seven half doubles worked between half doubles to move the position of the flowers.

3 times, * work flower, 1hdc into sp between hdc 6 times, rep from * to last 4 hdc, work flower, 1hdc into sp between hdc to end. Turn.

5th-9th rows As 5th-9th rows on back and fronts.

10th row Ch 2, 1hdc into sp between hdc 7 times, * work flower, 1hdc into sp between hdc 6 times, rep from * to end. Turn.

11th and 12th rows As 11th and 12th rows on back and fronts.

These 12 rows form the pat. Cont in pat until sleeve measures 12½[15:17½:18] in. Mark last row with a contrasting thread. Cont in pat until sleeve measures 13¾[16½:19½:20½] in. Fasten off.

To finish
Do not press.
Join shoulder and sleeve seams.
Set in sleeves.

Front band
With RS facing, join yarn to left shoulder seam.

1st round Work one around of evenly into edge of work, working down left front, along lower edge, up right front and across back neck, so that the number of sts is divisible by 4, join with a sl st to first st.

2nd round Ch 1, 1sc into first sc, * skip next sc, 5dc into next sc, skip next sc, 1sc into next sc rep from * to last 3 sts, skip next sc, 5dc into next sc, join with a sl st to first ch.
Fasten off.

Sleeve band
With RS facing, join yarn to lower edge at sleeve seam.

1st round Work one round of sc evenly into edge of work so that number of sts is divisible by 4, join with a sl st to first st.

2nd round Work as for front band. Fasten off.

Make a twisted cord of the length required and thread it evenly through the sts at the waist.

Back and Fronts

9½(11:13:14)in

9(7½:9:10½)in

13¾(13¾:19½:19½)in

25½(29:33:36½)in

9(10½:13½:14)in

Sleeve

13¾(16½:19½:20½)in

12½(15:17½:20½)in

Adapting the basic floral beach robe

Use floral patterns to bring interesting textures to your crochet.

The simple flowers on the beach robes on page 69 are worked as part of the main pattern by working doubles around the stem of half doubles.

A simple, but effective variation would be to work the doubles in a color contrasting with that of the background, changing color either at random or in a regular pattern.

Other variations
Those with more experience might like to work the flowers in a different type of yarn. A slightly bouclé yarn could be interesting, a glitter yarn would make the garment into an evening wrap.

The stitches that form the flowers could be varied to form petals: for example, instead of working six doubles around the stem, you could work (one half double and two doubles) twice or (one double and two triples) twice. You should, of course, check your gauge carefully before working the pattern in this or any other variation.

Individual flowers
Instead of working an all-over pattern, you could simply work a plain half double fabric, then sew individual crochet flowers onto it, arranging them as you like. Leaves and stems could also be added, using crochet or embroidery.

Pattern Library: Floral patterns

Daisy (1)

Use 2 colors, A and B. Using A, wind yarn twice around index finger to form a ring, remove ring from finger.
1st round Ch 1, 8sc into ring, sl st to first ch. Fasten off. Pull end of yarn to close center of ring.
2nd round * Using B make 5ch, with WS facing, sl st to first sc on first round, ch 1, 1sc into each of next 4ch, 3sc into last ch, working into other edge of ch, 1sc into each of next 4ch, sl st to same sc on first round, fasten off, rep from * into each sc of first round.

Tulip (3)

Make 10ch.
1sc into 2nd ch from hook, 1sc into each of next 7ch, 3sc into last ch. Working into other edge of foundation ch work 1sc into each of next 8ch, 3sc into turning ch. Working into *back* loop only of each sc work 1sc into each of next 8sc. Turn.
Ch 1, skip first sc, working into *front* loop only of each sc, work 1sc into each of next 8sc, 3sc into next sc, 1sc into each of next 8sc. Turn. Ch 1, skip first sc, working into *back* loop only of each sc, work 1sc into each of next 7sc, sl st into next sc. Fasten off.

Dahlia (4)

Make 5ch, join with a sl st to form a ring.
1st round Ch 1, 12sc into ring, sl st to first ch.
2nd round Working into *back* loop only of each sc, ch 12, sl st to first sc, * sl st into next sc, ch 12, sl st into same sc, rep from * to end.

3rd round Work as for 2nd round, but work into the *front* loop only of each sc and work 8ch only between sl st. Fasten off.

Forget-me-not pattern (2)

Make a multiple of 3ch plus 5 extra.
Base row (RS) (2dc, ch 2, 1sc) into 5th ch from hook, * skip next 2ch, (2dc, ch 2, 1sc) into next ch, rep from * to last 3ch, skip 2ch, 1sc into last ch. Turn.
1st row Ch 3 to count as first dc, * (2dc, ch 2, 1sc) into next 2ch sp, rep from * to end, 1sc into 4th of first 4ch. Turn.
2nd row As first, but ending with 1sc into 3rd of first 3ch. Turn.
Rep 2nd row throughout for pat.

Periwinkle (5)

Make 6ch, join with a sl st to form a ring.
1st round Ch 3, 20dc into ring, sl st to 3rd of first 3ch.
2nd round Ch 1, 1sc into sl st of previous round, (ch 1, 1dc into next dc, 2dc into next dc, 1dc into next dc, ch 1, 1sc into next dc) 5 times, to first ch. Fasten off.

Rose (6)

Make 4ch, join with a sl st to form a ring.
1st round Ch 5, (1dc, ch 2) 7 times into ring, sl st to 3rd of first 5ch.
2nd round Ch 1, (1sc, 1dc, 1tr, 1dc, 1sc) into each 2ch sp to end, sl st to first ch. Turn.
3rd round With WS of work facing, (ch 3, 1sc under both vertical threads at base of next sc) 8 times. Turn.
4th round Ch 1, (1sc, 2dc, 1tr, 2dc, 1sc) into each 3ch sp to end, sl st to first ch. Turn.
5th round With WS of work facing, (ch 4, sl st under both horizontal threads between 2 petals on last round) 8 times. Turn.
6th round Ch 1, (1sc, 2dc, 3tr, 2dc, 1sc) into each 4ch sp to end, sl st to first ch. Fasten off.

Wallflower pattern (7)

Make a multiple of 8ch plus 5 extra.
Base row 1dc into 4th ch from hook, * ch 2, skip next 3ch, 1sc (ch 4, 1sc) 3 times into next ch, ch 2, skip next 3ch, 1dc into next ch, rep from * to last ch, 1dc into last ch. Turn.
1st row (RS) Ch 4, 1tr into first dc, (ch 2, 1sc, ch 4, 1sc) into next dc, ch 3, skip next 4ch loop, 1dc into next 4ch loop, ch 3, * 1sc, (ch 4, 1sc) 3 times into next dc, ch 3, skip next 4ch loop, 1dc into next 4ch loop, ch 3, rep from * ending with (1sc, ch 4, 1sc, ch 3) into last dc, 1dc into top of turning ch. Turn.
2nd row Ch 2, 1sc into next 3ch loop, * ch 3, 1sc into next dc, ch 3, skip next 4ch loop, 1sc into next 4ch loop, rep from *, ending with ch 3, 1sc into next dc, ch 3, 1sc into last tr, 1sc into top of turning ch. Turn.
3rd row Ch 2, skip first sc, 1sc into next sc, * 1sc into each of next 3ch, 1sc into next sc, rep from *, ending with 1sc into top of turning ch. Turn.
4th row Ch 2, skip first sc, 1sc into each sc to end, 1sc in top of turning ch. Turn.
5th row Ch 3, skip first sc, 1dc into next sc, * ch 2, skip next 3sc, 1sc, (ch 4, 1sc) 3 times into next sc, ch 2, skip next 3sc, 1dc into next sc, rep from * to end, 1dc into turning ch. Turn.
First-5th rows form the pat. Rep them throughout.

Elongated stitches

Dazzling patterns of zigzags, triangles and bricks can be added to a single crochet fabric by working longer stitches in a contrasting yarn. Two shades of gray are used for this good-looking vest.

The basic elongated-stitch vest

Sizes

Men's sizes 38-40 [40-42]
Length (from back neck) 19½in
Note: *Instructions for the larger size are in brackets* []; where there is only one set of figures it applies to both sizes.

Materials

8 [9] oz of a knitting worsted in main color A
4 [6] oz in contrasting color B
Sizes C and F crochet hooks
Pair of size 4 knitting needles

Note: *Strand yarn not in use loosely up side of work. Change colors by using new color to complete last st worked in old color.*

Gauge
15sc and 22 rows to 4in worked on size F hook. Knitting ribbing gauge 27 sts and 30 rows to 4in worked on size 4 needles.

To save time, take time to check gauge.

Left front (both sizes worked alike)
Using larger hook and A, make 3ch.
Base row 1sc into 3rd ch from hook. Turn.
1st row Ch 2, 1sc into 2nd ch from hook, 1sc into next sc, 1sc into turning ch. Turn.
2nd row Ch 2, 1sc into 2nd ch from hook, (1sc into each of next 2sc, 2sc into last sc). Turn.
3rd row Ch 2, 1sc into 2nd ch from hook, 1sc into each sc to last sc, 2sc into last sc. Turn.
Rep last row 3 more times. 13sc. Change to B.
7th row Ch 2, 1sc into 2nd ch from hook, (1sc into each of next 2sc, 1sc into next st one row below, 1sc into next st 2 rows below, 1sc into next st 3 rows below, 1sc into next st 4 rows below, 1sc

into next st 5 rows below, 1sc into next st 4 rows below, 1sc into next st 3 rows below, 1sc into next st 2 rows below, 1sc into next st one row below, 1sc into next st of previous row, 2sc into last st. Turn.
Rep 3rd row 5 times. 25sc.
Change to A.
13th row Ch 2, 1sc into 2nd ch from hook, 1sc into each of next 3sc, *1sc into next st one row below, 1sc into next st 2 rows below, 1sc into next st 3 rows below, 1sc into next st 4 rows below, 1sc into next st 5 rows below, 1sc into next st 4 rows below, 1sc into next st 3 rows below, 1sc into next st 2 rows below, 1sc into next st one row below, 1sc into next st of previous row, rep from * once more, 1sc into next sc, 2sc into last st. Turn.
Rep 3rd row 3 times. 33sc.
17th and 18th rows Ch 1, skip first sc, 1sc into each st to end. Turn.
Change to B.
19th row Ch 1, skip first sc, 1sc into next sc, *1sc into st one row below, 1sc into next st 2 rows below, 1sc into next st 3 rows below, 1sc into next st 4 rows below, 1sc into next st 5 rows below, 1sc into next st 4 rows below, 1sc into next st 3 rows below, 1sc into next st 2 rows

below, 1sc into next st one row below, 1sc into next st of previous row, rep from * twice more, 1sc into turning ch. Turn.
20th-24th rows As 17th row.
Change to A.
25th row Ch 1, skip first sc, 1sc into next st 5 rows below, *1sc into next st 4 rows below, 1sc into next st 3 rows below, 1sc into next st 2 rows below, 1sc into next st one row below, 1sc into next st of previous row, 1sc into next st one row below, 1sc into next st 2 rows below, 1sc into next st 3 rows below, 1sc into next st 4 rows below, 1sc into next st 5 rows below, rep from * twice more, 1sc into turning ch. Turn.
26th-30th rows As 17th row.
Keeping color sequence correct, work 19-30th rows twice more, then work 19th to 25th rows once more.
Shape front
Keeping pat correct, beg front shaping:
62nd row Ch 1, skip first sc, 1sc into each st to end. Turn.
63rd row Ch 1, skip first sc, 1sc into each sc to end, dec 1 st at inner edge by omitting 1sc into turning ch. Turn.
64th-66th rows As 62nd row.
67th row As 63rd row.

SPECIAL TECHNIQUE
Working a pointed lower edge

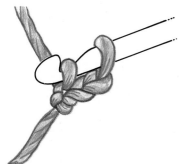

1 The pointed lower edges on the fronts of the basic vest are worked by increasing from a small number of chains, while at the same time keeping the elongated-stitch pattern correct. Begin with three chains and work one single crochet into the third chain from the hook. Turn.

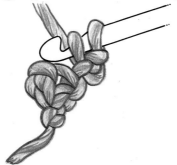

2 On the next row begin with two chains and increase by working one single crochet into the second chain from the hook. Work one single crochet into the next single crochet and finish the row with one single crochet into the turning chain. Turn.

3 The third row begins as before with two chains. Work one single crochet into the second chain from the hook, one single crochet into each of the next two single crochets and two single crochet into the last single crochet. Turn. Continue increasing in this way for the required width.

68th row As 62nd row.

Shape armhole
Cont to dec 1st at inner edge on every 4th row, *at the same time* beg armhole shaping:

69th row Sl st into each of first 3sc, 1sc into each st to end. Turn.

70th row Ch 1, skip first sc, 1sc into each of next 25sc. Turn.

71st row As 63rd row.

72nd row Ch 1, skip first sc, 1sc into each of next 22sc, turn.

73rd row As 62nd row.

74th row Ch 1, skip first sc, 1sc into each of next 21sc, turn.

75th row As 63rd row.

76th row Ch 1, skip first sc, 1sc into each of next 19sc, turn.

77th row As 62nd row.

78th row Ch 1, skip first sc, 1sc into each of next 18sc, turn.

79th row As 63rd row.

Keeping armhole edge straight, cont in pat, dec 1st at inner edge on every following 4th row, until 10sc rem and work measures 9½in from beg of armhole.

Next row Sl st into each of first 3sc, 1sc into each st to end. Turn.

Next row Ch 1, skip first sc, 1sc into each of next 5sc. Turn.

Next row Sl st into each of first 3sc, 1sc into each st to end. Turn. Fasten off.

Right front (both sizes worked alike)
Work as for left front, reversing all shaping.

Front border
Mark positions of 4 buttonholes on left front.

1st row With RS facing and using smaller hook, join A to lower side edge of right front, and work 1sc into each row end or st to top of shoulder, make 40ch for back neck border, cont down left front and lower edge, working 1sc into each row end and st as before. Turn.

2nd row Ch 1, skip first sc, *1sc into each sc to sc at point, 3sc into next sc, 1sc into each sc to corner, 2sc into next sc, (1sc into each sc to buttonhole marker, ch 3, skip next 3sc) 4 times, 1sc into each sc to beg of front shaping, 2sc into next sc, 1sc into each sc to 40ch at

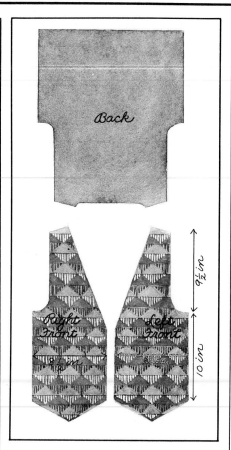

back neck *, 1sc into each of next 40ch, rep from * to *, omitting buttonholes and reversing order of working.

3rd row Ch 1, skip first sc, 1sc into each sc to end, inc at points and corners as on last row and omitting 1sc into turning ch. Turn.

4th row As 3rd row, but do not turn.

5th row Ch 1, skip first sc, *working from left to right*, 1sc into each sc to end (see page 18). Fasten off.

Buttons (make 4 alike)
Using smaller hook and A, leave an end of 20in and work ch 3, 9dc into 3rd ch from hook, sl st to top of 3ch, 1sc into each dc.
Break yarn and thread into yarn needle. Wind 20in length of yarn into tight little ball and insert into button. Thread the yarn in the needle through the button and draw up tightly to form a round button.
Sew buttons to right front to match buttonholes.

Back
Using knitting needles and A, cast on 122 [134] sts.
Work in K1, P1 ribbing until work measures same as side fronts to armholes including band at lower edge.

Shape armholes
Keeping pat correct, bind off 7 [13] sts at beg of next 2 rows.
Dec 1 st at both ends of every following row until 80 sts rem.
Work even until work measures 10in from beg of armhole shaping.

Shape shoulders
Bind off 3 sts at beg of next 4 rows.
Next row Bind off 3 sts, pat 44 sts, turn, bind off 24 sts, pat to end.
Cont on rem sts, bind off 3 sts at beg of every row until no more sts rem.
Fasten off. Work other shoulder to match.

To finish
Press or block as appropriate, pressing crochet only.
Seam shoulders and back neck.
Join side seams.

Armhole borders (both alike)
1st round Using smaller hook and A, beg at underarm seam and work in sc around armhole edge. Join with a sl st to first st. Turn.

2nd round Ch 1, skip first sc, 1sc into each sc to end, join with a sl st to first ch. Turn.

3rd and 4th rounds As 2nd round, but do not turn at end of 4th round.

5th round Work one round of sc from left to right as for front border.
Fasten off.

Adapting the elongated-stitch vest

Use our patterns to crease beautiful zigzag fabrics

Color variations

It is possible to vary the basic vest quite considerably by using different color combinations.

We have used a soft combination of grays for this vest, but bright, contrasting colors would be equally attractive. Try red and yellow or black and white.

Substituting patterns

Using another elongated-stitch pattern to work the fronts of the basic vest is more difficult, and you should make certain that the pattern can be fitted into the basic shaping. For this reason, it is best to use a variation that has exactly the same number of stitches and rows in the repeat as the basic pattern.

Finally, make sure to check very carefully to see where the points fall on the sample – for example, whether they fall in between or on top of each other – and make sure that you understand the pattern before you begin to crochet.

Pattern Library: Elongated-stitch patterns

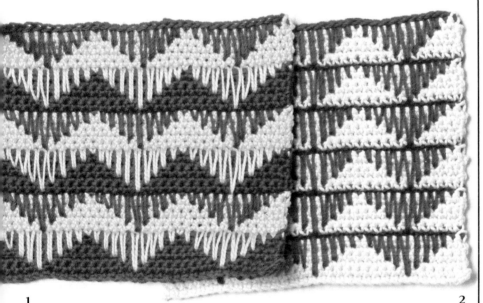

1

2

Slanted diamonds (3)

Use 2 colors, A and B.

Using A, make a multiple of 8ch plus 4 extra.

Base row 1sc into 2nd ch from hook, 1sc into each ch to end. Turn.

1st row Ch 1, skip first sc, 1sc into each sc to end. Turn.

2nd-7th rows Work in sc.

8th row (RS) Using B, ch 1, skip first sc, 1sc into next sc, *1sc into next sc 7 rows below, 1sc into next sc 6 rows below, 1sc into next sc 5 rows below, 1sc into next sc 4 rows below, 1sc into next sc 3 rows below, 1sc into next sc 2 rows below, 1sc into next sc 1 row below, 1sc into next sc of previous row, rep from * to turning ch, 1sc into turning ch. Turn.

9th-15th rows Using B, work in sc.

16th row As 8th row, using A.

Rep first-16th rows throughout.

Zigzag (1)

This pattern could be used to make the vest on page 74.

Use 2 colors, A and B.

Using A, make a multiple of 10ch plus 4 extra.

Base row 1sc into 2nd ch from hook, 1sc into each ch to end. Turn.

1st row Ch 1, skip first sc, 1sc into each sc to end. Turn.

2nd-5th rows Work in sc.

6th row (RS) Using B, ch 1, skip first sc, 1sc into next sc, *1sc into next sc one row below, 1sc into next sc 2 rows below, 1sc into next sc 3 rows below, 1sc into next sc 4 rows below, 1sc into next sc 5 rows below, 1sc into next sc 4 rows below, 1sc into next sc 3 rows below, 1sc into next sc 2 rows below, 1sc into next sc one row below, 1sc into next sc of previous row, rep from * to turning ch, 1sc into turning ch. Turn.

7th-11th rows Using B, work in sc.

12th row As 6th row, using A.

Rep. first-12th rows throughout.

Triangles (2)

This pattern could be used to make the vest on page 74.

Work as for Zigzag, but work base row, first-5th and 7th-11th rows in A, and 6th and 12th rows in B.

3

4

6

Three-color points (7)

Use 3 colors, A, B and C.

Using A, make a multiple of 6ch plus 4 extra.

Base row 1sc into 2nd ch from hook, 1sc into each ch to end. Turn.

1st row Ch 1, skip first sc, 1sc into each sc to end. Turn.

2nd and 3rd rows Work in sc.

4th row (RS) Using B, ch 1, skip first sc, 1sc into next sc, *1sc into next sc one row below, 1sc into next sc 2 rows below, 1sc into next sc 3 rows below, 1sc into next sc 2 rows below, 1sc into next sc one row below, 1sc into next sc of previous row, rep from * to end, 1sc into turning ch. Turn.

5th-7th rows Using B, work in sc.

8th row Using C, work as 4th row.

9th-11th rows Using C, work in sc.

12th row Using A, work as 4th row.

Rep first-12th rows throughout, ending with a 4th, 8th or 12th row.

Arrows (4)

Use 2 colors, A and B.

Using A, make a multiple of 8ch plus 4 extra.

Base row 1sc into 2nd ch from hook, 1sc into each ch to end. Turn.

1st row Ch 1, skip first sc, 1sc into each sc to end. Turn.

2nd-7th rows Work in sc.

8th row (RS) Using B, ch 1, skip first sc, 1sc into next sc, *1sc into next sc 7 rows below, 1sc into next sc 6 rows below, 1sc into next sc 5 rows below, 1sc into next sc 4 rows below, 1sc into next sc 3 rows below, 1sc into next sc 2 rows below, 1sc into next sc one row below, 1sc into next sc of previous row, rep

from * to turning ch, 1sc into ch.

9th-15th rows Using B, work in sc.

16th row Using A, ch 1, skip first sc, 1sc into next sc, *1sc into next sc, 1sc into next sc one row below, 1sc into next sc 2 rows below, 1sc into next sc 3 rows below, 1sc into next sc 4 rows below, 1sc into next sc 5 rows below, 1sc into next sc 6 rows below, 1sc into next sc 7 rows below, rep from * to turning ch, 1sc into turning ch. Turn.

Rep first-16th rows throughout.

Parti-color arrows (6)

Work as for Arrows, but work base row, first-8th and 9th-15th rows in A, and 8th and 16th rows in B.

into next sc 4 rows below, rep from * to turning ch, 1sc into turning ch. Turn.

5th-7th rows Using B, work in sc.

8th row Using A, ch 1, skip first sc, 1sc into each of next 4sc, *1sc into next sc 4 rows below, 1sc into each of next 7sc of previous row, rep from * to last 7 sts, 1sc into next sc 4 rows below, 1sc into each of next 5 sts of previous row. Turn.

Rep first-8th rows throughout, ending with a 4th or 8th row.

Bricks (5)

Use 2 colors, A and B.

Using A, make a multiple of 8ch plus 4 extra.

Base row Using A, 1sc into 2nd ch from hook, 1sc into each ch to end. Turn.

1st row Using B, ch 1, skip first sc, 1sc into each sc to end.

2nd and 3rd rows Work in sc.

4th row (RS) Using A, ch 1, skip first sc, 1sc into next sc 4 rows below, *1sc into each of next 7sc of previous row, 1sc

5

Patchwork

Beautiful fabrics can be formed by sewing together crochet motifs.
Although geometric motifs such as squares and hexagons can be
used, diamonds are especially suitable for patchwork; sew them
together to make a colorful harlequin-style sweater.

The basic harlequin sweater

Size

Misses' sizes 12-16
Length 23in
Sleeve seam 19½in

Materials

11oz of a sport yarn in main color A
4oz in contrasting colour B
6oz in C
4oz in D and E
Size C crochet hook
Pair of size 2 knitting needles
Size 2 circular knitting needle, 16in long

Gauge

22sts and 17 rows to 4in in motif pattern worked on size C hook

To save time, take time to check gauge.

Note: *The sweater is made up of diamond-shaped and triangular motifs with a ribbed crochet yoke and knitted waistband and cuffs. The motifs are worked separately and sewn together.*

Diamond motif

Make 2 motifs in A, 2 in B and 4 each in C, D and E.
* *Using size C hook, make 3ch.
1st row (WS) 1sc into 2nd ch from hook, 1sc into next ch. 2 sts. Turn.
2nd row Ch 3, 1dc into first (edge) st, 2dc into next st. Turn. 4 sts.

3rd row Ch 1, 1sc into first (edge) st, 1sc into each st, 2sc into top of turning ch. Turn. 6 sts.
4th row Ch 3, 1dc into first (edge) st, 1 dc into each st to last st, 2dc into last st. Turn. 8sts.
Rep 3rd and 4th rows, inc one st at each end of row until there are 40 sts in all.
Next row Ch 1, 1sc into each st to end, 1sc into turning ch. Turn. * *
Next row (dec) Ch 3 to count as first dc, skip first st; keeping last loop of each st on hook, work 1dc into each of next 2sts, yo and through all loops on hook – called dec 1 – 1dc into each st to last 3 sts, dec 1, 1dc into top of turning ch. Turn. 38sts.
Next row (dec) Ch 1, skip first 2 sts, 1sc into each st to last 2 sts, skip one st, 1sc into last st. Turn. 36sts.
Rep last 2 rows until 4 sts rem.
Next row Ch 3, skip first st, dec 1, turn. 2 sts.
Next row Ch, 1sc into each st. Fasten off.

Triangular motif

Make 5 motifs in A, 4 in B, 9 in C and 6 each in D and E.
Work as for diamond motif from * * to * *. Fasten off.

Split diamond motifs for underarm (Make 2)

Using C, work as for diamond motif

from * * to * *. Cont dec as for diamond motif until 30 sts rem, thus ending with a RS row.
Divide for armhole
Next row Ch 1, skip first 2 sts, 1sc into each of next 17 sts, turn.
Next row Ch 3, skip first st, 1dc into each st to last 3 sts, dec 1, 1dc into last st. Turn. Cont dec one st on every row at outer edge until one st rem. Fasten off. Return to skipped dc and complete to match first half.
Work one more motif in D.

Half triangle (right)

Using A, make 21ch.
Base row (WS) 1sc into 2nd ch from hook, 1sc into each st to end. 20sts.
1st row (dec) Ch 3, skip one st, 1dc into each st to last 3 sts, dec 1, 1dc into turning ch. Turn. 19 sts.
2nd row (dec) Ch 1, skip first 2 sts, 1sc into each st to end. Turn. 18 sts.
Rep first and 2nd rows until one st rem. Fasten off. Using B, make another half triangle in the same way.

Half triangle (left)

Using A, make 21ch. Work base row as for half triangle (right).
1st row (dec) Ch 3, skip first st, dec 1, 1dc into each st to end. 19 sts.
2nd row (dec) Ch 1, 1sc into each st to last 2 sts, skip one st, 1 sc into last st. 18

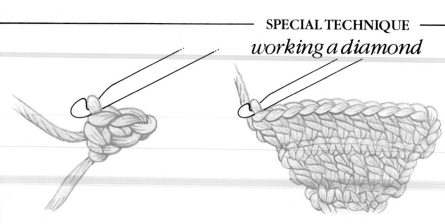

SPECIAL TECHNIQUE
working a diamond

1 *Begin the diamond with three chains. Work one single crochet into the second chain from the hook and one single crochet into the last chain to form two stitches.*

2 *On the next and every following row, increase one stitch at each end of the alternating double and single crochet rows until the diamond is the required width.*

3 *Work one row without shaping. Decrease one stitch at each end of the next and every following row until two stitches remain. Work one row and fasten off.*

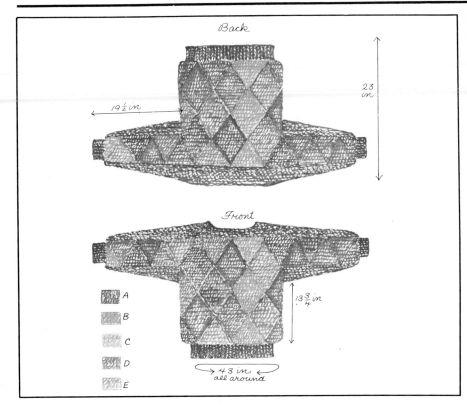

Back

$19\frac{1}{2}$ in

23 in

Front

A

B

C

D

E

$13\frac{3}{4}$ in

43 in all around

sts. Complete as for half triangle (right), reversing shaping.
Using B, make another half triangle.

To finish

Sleeves
Join 5 triangular motifs and 1 half triangle to form front and back of each sleeve as shown in the diagram

Underarm sections
Left front and right back Using A and with RS of work facing, start at apex of triangle at underarm and work 100sc along lower edge of sleeve.
Work into back loop only of each st throughout.
1st row Ch 1, 1sc into each st to end. Turn.

Shape sleeve seam
2nd row Ch 1, 1sc into each of next 90 sts, turn.
3rd and every alternate row Sl st over first 10 sts, 1sc into each st to end. Turn.
4th row Ch 1, 1sc into each of next 70 sts, turn.
6th row Ch 1, 1sc into each of next 50 sts, turn.
8th row Ch 1, 1sc into each of next 30

sts, turn.
10th row Ch 1, 1sc into each of next 10 sts, turn. Fasten off.

Right front and left back
Using A and with RS facing, start at base of half triangle and work 100sc along lower edge of sleeve. Work into back loop only of each st throughout.
1st row Ch 1, 1sc into each st to end. Turn.

Shape sleeve seam
2nd and every alternate row Sl st over first 10 sts, 1sc into each st to end.
3rd row Ch 1, 1sc into into each of next 80 sts, turn.
5th row Ch 1, 1sc into each of next 60 sts, turn.
Cont shaping in this way on every alternate row and complete as for left front and right back sections.

Back
Join motifs as in diagram, attaching corresponding sleeve sections. Join straight edge of each underarm section to opening in split diamonds.

Back yoke
Using A and with RS facing, start at right cuff * *, work 320sc evenly along top to

left cuff. Work into back loop only of each st throughout.
Next row Ch 1, 1sc into each st to end. Work 5 more rows in same way.

Shape top
Next 2 rows Sl st over 12 sts, 1sc into each st to last 12 sts, turn. * *
Next 7 rows Sl st over 16 sts, 1sc into each st to last 16 sts, turn. Fasten off.
Mark rem 48 sts at center for back neck with contrasting thread.

Front
Join motifs as in diagram, then join underarm sections as for back.

Front yoke
Using A and with RS facing, beg at left cuff and work as for back yoke from * * to * *.
Next 2 rows Sl st over 16 sts, 1sc into each st to last 16 sts, turn.

Shape front neck
Next row (WS) Sl st over 16 sts, 1sc into each of next 98 sts, turn.
Cont working on these sts for right side of neck shaping.
Next row Sl st over 6 sts, 1sc into each of next 76 sts, turn.
Next row Sl st over 16 sts, 1sc into each of next 54 sts, turn.
Next row Sl st over 6 sts, 1sc into each of next 32 sts, turn.
Next row Sl st over 16 sts, 1sc into each of next 16 sts. Fasten off.
With WS of work facing, skip center 12 sts, rejoin yarn to next st, 1sc into each st to last 16 sts, turn.
Complete as for right side of neck, reversing shaping.

Neck border
Join shoulder and top arm seam. Using A and with RS facing, work 1 row sc around neck opening. Fasten off.

Cuffs
Using A and with RS facing and using knitting needles, pick up and K 50 sts along lower edge of each sleeve and work 2in in K1, P1 ribbing. Bind off loosely in ribbing.

Waistband
Join sleeve seams. With RS facing, using A and circular needle. Pick up and K 204 sts along lower edge and work $2\frac{1}{4}$in K1, P1 ribbing. Bind off loosely in ribbing.

Adapting the basic patchwork sweater

Work a variation of the basic sweater or design your own colorful patchwork crochet fabric with the diamond motifs.

Crochet lends itself particularly well to patchwork, since many favorite afghan motifs – such as the traditional granny square – can be joined together to make colorful fabrics. On these two pages and on pages 121-122 you'll find other motifs that can be used to make beautiful patchwork crochet.

Diamonds
The diamond is a shape that is especially well-suited to patchwork. Some alternatives to the plain diamonds in the basic sweater are given in the Pattern Library. A random design needs very little planning, but if you want to construct a regular patchwork, you should draw a plan of how you want the diamonds to fit together. Note that striped shapes will form strikingly different patterns, depending on how they are joined. Any of these samples can be used for the basic sweater.

1

Pattern Library: Patchwork patterns

(edge) st, 2dc into next st, changing to B while working last st. Turn. 4 sts.
3rd row Using B, Ch 1, 1sc into first (edge) st, 1sc into each st, 2sc into top of turning ch. Turn. 6 sts.
4th row Using B, Ch 3, 1dc into first st, 1dc into each of next 2 sts, 2dc into last st, changing to A while working last st. Turn. 8 sts.
Cont to work stripes as set, working from diamond motif pattern on page 80 until there are 40 sts, changing to C at end of row.
Next row Using C, ch 1, 1sc into each st to end, changing to B at end of row. Beg with B cont working in stripe pat working from diamond motif on page 80.

Narrow striped pattern (1)
Use two main colors, A and B, plus one extra color C, for center row. Work 2 rows each in A and B. Using A, make 3ch.
1st row 1sc into 2nd ch from hook, 1sc into next ch. Turn. 2 sts.
2nd row Using A, Ch 3, 1dc into first

Triple-color diamond (2)
Use 3 colors, A, B and C. Work diamond motif pattern as shown on page 80, working 14 rows in A, 13 rows in B and 14 more rows in C.

Half-triangle diamond (3)
Use three colors, A, B and C, with C a sharply contrasting color.
Using A, work diamond motif pattern as shown on page 80 until there are 40 sts in all, changing to C at end of last row.
Next row Using C, ch 1, 1sc into each st to end. Turn, changing to B at end of this row.
Using B, complete diamond motif as shown on page 80.

2

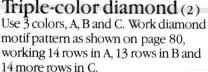

3

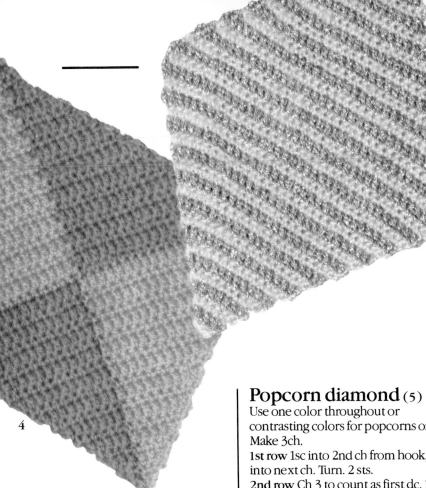

4

7

5

6

Mohair and gold diamond (7)

Use mohair (A) and glitter yarn (B) throughout. Using A, make 3ch.
1st row Using A, 1sc into 2nd ch from hook, 1sc into next ch, changing to B while working last sc. Turn. 2 sts.
2nd row Using B, ch 3, 1dc into first (edge) st, 2dc into next st, changing to A while working last st. Turn. 4 sts. Cont in pat as set working every dc row in B, working from diamond motif pattern shown on page 80.

Popcorn diamond (5)

Use one color throughout or contrasting colors for popcorns only. Make 3ch.
1st row 1sc into 2nd ch from hook, 1sc into next ch. Turn. 2 sts.
2nd row Ch 3 to count as first dc, 1dc into first (edge) st, 2dc into last st. Turn. 4 sts.
3rd row Ch 1, 1sc into first (edge) st, 1sc into each st, 2sc into last st. Turn. 6 sts.
4th row Ch 3, 1dc into first (edge) st, 1dc into next st, 1 popcorn into each of next 2 sts; 1dc into next st, 2dc into turning ch. Turn.
5th row Ch 1, 1sc into first (edge) st, 1sc into each st and into top of each popcorn, to last st, 2sc into last st. Turn. 10 sts.
Cont working diamond motif (page 80), working 2 popcorns on alternate rows until 6 sts rem.

Center stripes (6)

Use main color A for triangle at each end of diamond, with contrasting colors B and C for stripes at center. Work diamond motif pattern in A until there are 22 sts in all. 10 rows have been worked. Change to B. Cont in pat working (1 row B, 1 row C) 9 times. Work one row in B. Change to A. Complete diamond as given on page 80.

Harlequin diamond (4)

Use 2 colors coded as A and B. Use separate balls of yarn for each color and twist colors at center tó make a neat joining, changing colors while working last st in each color and making sure that colors are always changed on WS. Using A, make 3ch.
1st row Using A, 1sc into 2nd ch from hook, using B, 1sc into next ch. Turn. 2 sts.
2nd row Using B, ch 3, 1dc into first (edge) st, using A, 2dc into next st. Turn. 4 sts.
Cont in diamond pattern (page 80) as set until there are 40 sts in all. Break off A and B.
Next row (reverse colors) Using B (over A), ch 1 to count as first sc, 1sc into each of next 19 sts, changing to A while working last sc, using A, 1sc into each st to end. Turn.
Cont working in A and B as set and complete diamond motif as given on page 80.

Rice and bullion stitches

Although rice and bullion stitches need some practice, they are fascinating to work and form rich, dense fabrics. You can also use them for contrasting details, as on this baseball jacket.

The basic baseball jacket

Sizes
C-7 [C-8:C-10:C-12]
Length 16 [18:18:20] in
Sleeve seam 12 [13½:15:16½] in
Note: *Instructions for larger sizes are in brackets* [ ]*; where there is only one set of figures it applies to all sizes.*

Materials
11 [11:13:13] oz of a knitting worsted in main color A
4 [4:6:6] oz in contrasting color B
Size G crochet hook
Pair of size 3 knitting needles
Open-ended zipper, 14 [16:16:18] in long

Gauge
17 sts and 12 rows to 4in in pat worked on size G hook

To save time, take time to check gauge.

Pocket linings (make 2)
Using A, make 22 [24:24:26] ch.
Base row 1dc into 4th ch from hook, 1dc into each ch to end. Turn. 20 [22:22:24] sts.
1st row (WS) Ch 1 to count as first sc, skip first st, 1sc into each dc to end, ending with 1sc into top of first 3ch. Turn
2nd row Ch 3, skip first st, 1dc into each sc to end, ending with 1dc into first ch. Turn.
First and 2nd rows form pat.
Pat 5[5:7:7] more rows, ending with a first row. Fasten off.

Left front
* * Using A, make 33 [35:37:39] ch.
Work base row and pat rows as for pocket linings. 31 [33:35:37] sts. Pat 5 [5:7:7] more rows, ending with a first row. * *
Divide for pockets
Next row Pat next 11 [11:13:13] sts, with RS facing pat across 20 [22:22:24]

sts of pocket lining, turn. 31 [33:35:37] sts.
Pat 8 [8:10:10] more rows, ending with a 2nd row. Fasten off.
With RS facing, rejoin A to next sc at base of pocket opening.
Shape pocket
Dec one st at pocket edge on next and every following row until 11 [13:11:13] sts rem, ending with a 2nd row.
Next row Pat to end, skip first 11 [13:11:13] sts of pocket linings, 1sc into next st of pocket lining, pat to end. Turn. 31 [33:35:37] sts.
Cont in pat until front measures 12½ [14½:14½:15¾] in, ending with a first row.
Shape neck
Next row Pat to within last 7 [8:8:9] sts, work next 2 sts tog, turn. 25 [26:28:29] sts.
Dec one st at neck edge on next 5 rows. 20 [21:23:24] sts. Fasten off.

Right front
Work as for left front from * * to * *
Divide for pockets
Next row Pat 18 [20:20:22] sts, work next 2sts tog, turn. 19 [21:21:23] sts.
Shape pocket
Dec one st on pocket edge on next and every following row until 11 [13:11:13] sts rem. Fasten off.
Next row Rejoin A to first st of pocket lining, pat to end, with RS facing work 1dc into next st at base of pocket opening, pat to end. Turn. 31 [33:35:37] sts.
Pat 8 [8:10:10] more rows.
Next row Pat 20 [22:22:24] sts, pat across first side of pocket. Turn. 31 [33:35:37] sts. Turn.
Cont in pat until work measures 12½ [14½:14½:15¾] in, ending with a first row.
Shape neck
Next row Sl st across first 6 [7:7:8] sts, work next 2 sts tog, pat to end. Turn. 25 [26:28:29] sts.
Complete as given for left front.

Back
Using A, make 63 [67:71:75] ch.
Work base row and pat rows as for pocket linings. 61 [65:69:71] sts. Pat 1 [3:3:5] more rows, ending with a first row.
Beg rice st jacquard
1st row (RS) Using A pat next 19 [21:23:25] sts, using B yo 8 times, insert hook into next st, yo and draw through all 9 loops on hook, ch 1 – rice st formed –, rice st into each of next 22 sts, using A pat to end. Turn.
2nd and every alternate row Pat to end, working 1sc in B into each rice st of previous row.
3rd row Using A pat next 19 [21:23:25] sts, (using B rice st into each of next sts, using A pat next 17 sts) twice, using A pat to end. Turn.
5th and 7th rows As 3rd row.
9th row Using A pat next 19 [21:23:25] sts, (using B rice st into each of next 3 sts, using A pat next 7 sts) twice, using A pat to end. Turn.
11th row Using A pat next 24 [26:28:30] sts, (using B rice st into each of next 3 sts, using A pat next 7 sts) twice, using A pat to end. Turn.
13th, 15th, 17th and 19th rows As 11th row.
21st row Using A pat next 24 [26:28:30] sts, using B rice st into each of next 3 sts, using A pat next 7 sts, using B rice st into each of next 8 sts, using A pat to end. Turn.
23rd row Using A pat next 24 [26:28:30] sts, (using B rice st into each of next 3 sts, using A pat next 12 sts) twice, using A pat to end. Turn.
25th row Using A pat next 24 [26:26:28:30] sts, (using B rice st into

each of next 3 sts, using A pat next 10 sts) twice, using A pat to end. Turn.
27th row Using A pat next 24 [26:28:30] sts, (using B rice st into each of next 3 sts, using A pat next 8 sts) twice, using A pat to end. Turn.
29th row Using A pat next 24 [26:28:30] sts, (using B rice st into each of next 3 sts, using A pat next 6 sts) twice, using A pat to end. Turn.
31st row Using A pat next 24 [26:28:30] sts, (using B rice st into each of next 3 sts, using A pat next 4 sts) twice, using A pat to end. Turn.
33rd row Using A pat next 24 [26:28:30] sts, using B rice st into each of next 8 sts, using A pat to end. Turn.
34th row As 2nd row.
Cont in A only, working in pat until work measures same as fronts to shoulders, ending with a first row. Fasten off.

Sleeves (alike)
Using A, make 46 [50:54:58] ch. Work base row and pat rows as for pocket linings. 44 [48:52:56] sts. Cont in pat until sleeve measures 7 [8½:10¼:11½]in, ending with a first row.
Next row Using B, ch 3, skip first st, rice st into each st to turning ch, 1dc into turning ch. Turn.

Next row Using B, ch 1 to count as first sc, skip first st, 1sc into each st to end, ending with 1sc into top of turning ch. Turn.
Next 2 rows Pat 2 rows in A.
Rep last 4 rows once more.
Pat 2 more rows in A. Fasten off.

To finish
Front waistbands (alike)
With RS facing and using knitting needles and B, pick up and K 41 [43:45:47] sts from lower edge.
1st ribbing row (WS) K1, (P1, K1) to end.
2nd row P1, (K1, P1) to end.
Rep ribbing rows for 3½in, ending with a first row. Bind off loosely in ribbing.
Back waistband
With RS facing, using knitting needles and B, pick up and K 81 [85:89:91] sts from lower edge.
Rep ribbing rows as for front waistbands for 3½in, ending with a first row. Bind off loosely in ribbing.
Cuffs (alike)
With RS facing and using knitting needles and B, pick up and K 44 [48:52:56] sts from lower edge.
Dec row P3[5:2:4], P2 tog, (P2 [2:3:3], P2 tog), to last 3 [5:3:5] sts, P to end. 34 [38:42:46] sts. Work 3½in of K1, P1

ribbing. Bind off loosely in ribbing.

Pocket borders (alike)
With RS facing and using crochet hook, join B to first row end on pocket edge.
Next row Ch 3, work a row of rice st into edge, working one st into sc row ends and 2 sts into dc row ends and ending with 1dc. Turn.
Next row Ch 1 to count as first sc, skip first st, 1sc into each rice st to end, 1sc into top of 3ch.
Fasten off. Join shoulder seams. Mark depth of armholes 5½ [6:6½:7]in from shoulders on back and fronts. Set in sleeves between markers, matching center of sleeve with shoulder seam. Join side and sleeve seams. Turn waistband and cuffs to WS and slip stitch in place. Sew pocket linings to WS of fronts and ends of pocket borders to RS fronts.

Left front edging
With RS facing and using crochet hook, join A to first row end on neck edge.
Next row Work in sc along front edge, working one sc into each sc row end and 2sc into each dc row end, to beg of waistband, using B work in sc through double thickness of waistband to lower edge. Turn.

SPECIAL TECHNIQUE
stitch-by-stitch seaming

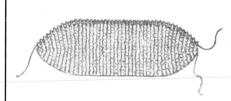

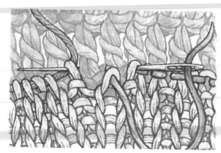

1 The collar on the basic jacket is attached to the neck edge by a particularly neat method of seaming. Knit the collar, shaping the short rows as instructed in the pattern. Do not bind off, but break the yarn and leave the stitches on a spare needle or length of yarn.

2 Stretching the collar to fit if necessary, pin the wrong side of the last row of the collar to the right side of the neck edge. Align the short ends of the collar with the last row of the front edgings, overlapping the collar with the neck by about ¼in.

3 Using yarn to match the collar, backstitch the collar to the neck edge. Insert the needle through the loops of the last row and remove the needle or yarn from the loops as you sew. Fold the collar to the wrong side; slip stitch it in place around the neck.

Work 2 more rows of sc in B.
Fasten off.

Right front edging
With RS facing and using crochet hook, join B to lower edge of waistband.
Next row Work in sc to top of waistband, working through double thickness, using A work in sc along front edge as for left front edging. Turn. Work 2 more rows of sc in B.
Fasten off.

Collar
Using knitting needles and B, cast on 81 [87:87:93] sts.
Shape collar
Beg with a 2nd row, work 2 ribbing rows as for front waistband throughout and *at the same time:*
1st row Rib to last st, turn.
2nd row Sl 1, rib to last st, turn.
3rd and 4th rows Sl 1, rib to last 2 sts, turn.
5th and 6th rows Sl 1, rib to last 4 sts, turn.
7th and 8th rows Sl 1, rib to last 6 sts, turn.
9th and 10th rows Sl 1, rib to last 9 sts, turn.
11th and 12th rows Sl 1, rib to last 12 sts, turn.

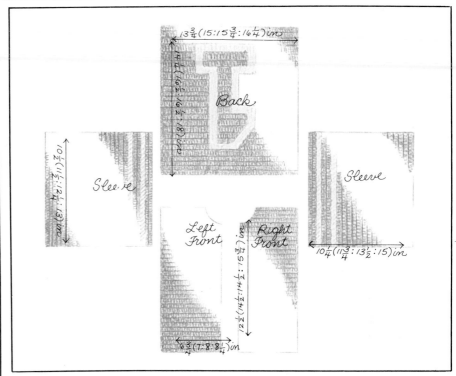

13th row Sl 1, rib to end.
14th row Rib to end across all sts.
15th-25th rows As 12th, 11th, 10th, 9th, 8th, 7th, 6th, 5th, 4th, 3rd and 2nd rows.
Work 2nd row, 13th and 14th rows once more. Break yarn and leave sts on a spare length of yarn.
Place WS of last row of collar on RS of neck and sew in place, working neat backstitch through open loops of last row. See Special Technique, opposite. Double collar to WS to slip stitch in place. Sew in the zipper.

Adapting the basic baseball jacket

Vary the jacket's look by using softer, pastel shades or working a different number or letter.

The basic baseball jacket has contrasting rice-stitch sleeve bands and a number on the back.

It would be quite possible to work more rice stitch bands on the sleeves or to work a different number or letter.

Charting a number
Draw the outline of the back of the jacket on graph paper so that one square equals one stitch. Draw a line between the center stitch on the lower and top edges to indicate the center back.

Draw each stitch of the outline of the number on the graph, at the same time centering the number on the center back line. Remember that, since the number will be worked in alternate rows of rice stitch (on double pattern rows) and single crochet, the chart will be taller than the crocheted number.

Pattern Library: Rice and bullion patterns   1

Simple rice stitch (1)
Make a multiple of 2ch plus 5 extra.
Base row Yo 8 times, insert hook into 5th ch from hook, yo and draw through all loops on hook – rice st formed –, * ch 1, skip next ch, rice st into next ch, rep from * to end. Turn.
Pattern row Ch 3, skip first st, * rice st into next 1ch sp, ch 1, rep from * to turning ch, rice st into top of turning ch. Turn.
Rep pat row throughout.

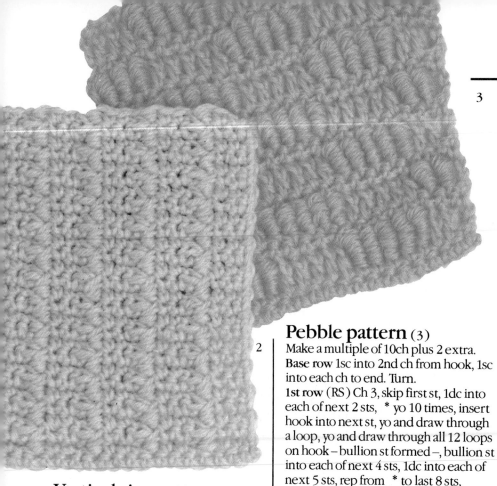

3

Picket fence (5)
Make any number of ch plus 3 extra.
Base row Yo 5 times, insert hook into 4th ch from hook, yo and draw through a loop, yo and draw through all 7 loops on hook – bullion st formed –, * bullion st into next st, rep from * to end. Turn.
1st row (WS) ch 1 to count as first sc, skip first st, 1sc into each st to end. Turn.
2nd row Ch 3, skip first st, bullion st into each st to end. Turn.
First and 2nd rows form pat. Rep them throughout.

2

Pebble pattern (3)
Make a multiple of 10ch plus 2 extra.
Base row 1sc into 2nd ch from hook, 1sc into each ch to end. Turn.
1st row (RS) Ch 3, skip first st, 1dc into each of next 2 sts, * yo 10 times, insert hook into next st, yo and draw through a loop, yo and draw through all 12 loops on hook – bullion st formed –, bullion st into each of next 4 sts, 1dc into each of next 5 sts, rep from * to last 8 sts, bullion st into each of next 5 sts, 1dc into last 3 sts. Turn.
2nd row Ch 1 to count as first sc, skip first st, 1sc into each st to end. Turn.
3rd row Ch 3, skip first st, bullion st into each of next 2 sts, * 1dc into each of next 5 sts, bullion st into each of next 5 sts, rep from * to last 8 sts, 1dc into each of next 5 sts, bullion st into each of next 2 sts, 1dc into last st. Turn.
4th row As 2nd row.
Rep first–4th rows throughout.

5

Vertical rice pattern (2)
Make a multiple of 4ch plus 5 extra.
Base row 1sc into 2nd ch from hook, 1sc into each ch to end. Turn.
1st row Ch 1 to count as first sc, skip first st, * 1sc into each of next 2 sts, yo 3 times, insert hook into next st, yo and draw through all loops on hook – rice st formed –, ch 1, skip next st, rep from * to last 3 sts, 1sc into each of last 3 sts.
2nd row Ch 1 to count as first sc, skip first st, 1sc into each of next 2 sts, * rice st into next 1ch sp, ch 1, skip next st, 1sc into each of next 2 sts, rep from * to last st, 1sc into last st. Turn.
Rep 2nd row throughout.

4

Rice with doubles (4)
Make an odd number of ch plus 4 extra.
Base row (RS) Yo 5 times, insert hook into 5th ch from hook, yo and draw through all loops on hook – rice st formed, * ch 1, skip next ch, rice st into next ch, rep from * to end. Turn.
1st row Ch 3, skip first st, * 1dc into next 1ch sp, 1dc into next rice st, rep from * to turning ch, 1dc into sp formed by turning ch, skip next turning ch, 1dc into next turning ch. Turn.
2nd row Ch 4, skip first 2 sts, * rice st into next st, ch 1, skip next st, rep from * to last st, rice st into last st. Turn.
Rep first and 2nd throughout.

Horizontal patterns

Horizontal patterns are highly versatile, being suitable for anything from fashionable garments, such as this casual cardigan, to the simplest baby clothes. Choose beautiful yarns and colors to display the strong crosswise lines of these useful patterns.

The basic striped cardigan

Size
Misses' sizes 34-38
Length including waistband 21¼in
Sleeve seam 19¼in

Materials
6oz of a knitting worsted in main color
A
6oz in contrasting color B
4oz in contrasting color C
2oz in each of contrasting colors D and
E
Sizes G and H crochet hooks
5 buttons
Note: *The cardigan is worked in two
sections, each beginning at the cuff,
which are then joined at the center
back.*

Gauge
15sc and 14 rows to 4in worked on size
G hook

To save time, take time to check gauge.

Left side
Cuff Using smaller hook and A, make
21ch.
Base row 1sc into 2nd ch from hook, 1sc
into each ch to end. Turn. 20 sts.
Next row Ch 1, skip first st, 1sc into *back*
loop only of each st to end. Turn.
Rep last row 34 more times.
Change to larger hook, and use loop on
hook to beg to work into one edge of
cuff:
Next row (RS) Ch 3, skip first row end,
1dc into each row end to end. Turn. 36
sts.
Next row Ch 1, skip first st, 1sc into next
st, (2sc into next st, 1sc into each of next
7 sts) 4 times, 2sc into next st, 1sc into
last st. Turn. 41 sts.

Pattern band A
Change to B.
1st row (RS) Work in sc, inc one st at
each end of the row. 43 sts.
2nd row (RS) Work in dc.
Change to A.
3rd row Work in sc, inc one st at each
end of the row. 45 sts.
4th row Work in sc.
Change to B.
5th row Ch 1, skip first st, *inserting
hook from front to back work 1dc
around stem of next st on last dc row –
1dc front below worked – 1sc into each
of next 2sc, rep from * to last 2 sts, 1dc
front below, 1sc into last st. Turn.
6th row Work in dc.
Rep 3rd-6th rows once more, inc one st

at each end of 7th row, and working
each dc front below on 9th row into
corresponding dc on 4th row. 47 sts.
Next row Change to D and work in sc
working into back loops only and inc
one st at each end of row. 49 sts.
Next row Change to A and work in sc.

Pattern band B
Change to C.
1st row (RS) Ch 4, skip first st, *1dc into
next st, 1hdc into next st, 1sc into each
of next 3 sts, 1hdc into next st, 1dc into
next st, 1tr into next st, rep from * to
end. Turn.
Change to D.
2nd row Ch 1, 1sc into first tr, *ch 3,
leaving last loop of each st on hook
work 1dc into each of next 7 sts, yo and
draw through all 8 loops on hook – half
whirl formed –, ch 3, 1sc into next tr, rep
from * to end, working last sc into top of
turning ch. Turn.
3rd row Ch 1, 1sc into first sc, *(6dc, 1tr)
into sp at top of half whirl, 1sc into next
sc, rep from * to end. Turn. Change to C.
4th row As for first row.
Next row Change to A and work in sc.
Next row Change to D and work in sc.
Next row Change to E and work in sc
working into front loops only.

SPECIAL TECHNIQUE

whirl pattern

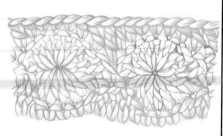

1 *Pattern band B on the basic cardigan
is a two-color whirl pattern. Using the
first color, work the first, graduated-stitch
(see page 41) row as given in the pattern.
Change to the second color. After working
the edge stitch, work seven doubles
together into the next seven stitches to
form the first half whirl.*

2 *Continue in this way to the end of the
row. Complete the whirl on the third
row by working six doubles and one triple
into the space formed at the top of each
group of seven doubles. Work one single
crochet into each single crochet between
half whirls to anchor the whirl.*

3 *Return to the first color and for the
last pattern row follow the
instructions given for the first pattern
row. This straightens the top edge to allow
you to work the next row of the basic
cardigan instructions.*

Cont in dc, working in stripe sequence as follows: 1 row in E, 2 rows in B, 3 rows in C, 2 rows in D, 2 rows in E, 3 rows in B, 3 rows in C.
At the same time shape sleeve thus:
Next row Work in dc.
Next 2 rows Work in dc, inc one st at each end of row.
Working in stripe sequence as above, rep last 3 rows 5 times in all. 69 sts.
Next row Work in dc. Do not turn.

Shape bodice
Using C, at the end of last row of stripe sequence, work 27 ch. Turn and remove hook from loop. Using spare length of C, work 26ch and fasten off. Return to loop just left.
Next row (WS) 1sc into 2nd ch from hook, 1sc into each of next 25ch, 1sc into each of 69 sts on top of sleeve, 1sc into each of 26ch just worked. Turn. 121 sts.
Next row Change to B and work in dc.
Next 3 rows Work in sc, working one row each in E, D and A.
Change to C and work the 4 rows of pat band B, omitting all incs.
Next 4 rows Work in sc, working one row each in A, D, E and B.
Cont with B and work the 10 rows of pat band A, working one more sc at end of 5th row and omitting all incs.
Next row Change to E and work in sc.
Next row Change to C and work in dc.**

Back bodice extension
Next row With RS facing and using C, ch 1, skip first st, 1sc into each of next 49 sts, turn. 50 sts.
Shape back neck
Next row Sl st over first 3 sts, ch 1, skip first st, 1sc into each st to end. Turn. 48 sts.
Next row Ch 1, skip first st, 1sc into each st to last 3 sts, work 2sc tog, 1sc into last st. Turn.
Next row Ch 3, work 2dc tog, 1dc into each st to end. Turn. 46 sts.
Change to B and work 2 rows in dc.
Change to C and work 1 row in dc and 1 row in sc. Fasten off.

Right side
Work as for left side to **.
Fasten off.

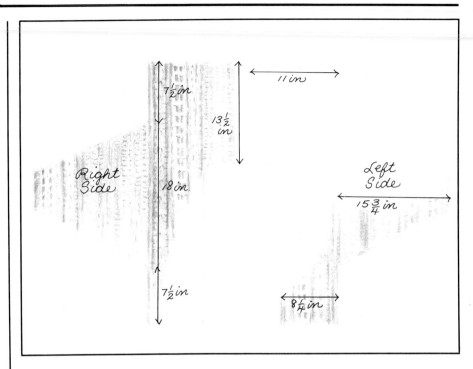

Back bodice extension
Next row With RS facing and using C, rejoin yarn to 72nd st of row, ch 1, skip first st, 1sc into each st to end. 50 sts.
Complete to match left back neck, reversing all shaping.
Fasten off, but do not cut yarn.

To finish
With RS tog, join center back seam with crochet sl st. Fasten off.
Press center back seam lightly.
Join underarm and side seams, carefully matching stripes at underarm.

Striped border
1st row With RS facing, join C to first st on lower edge, ch 1, skip first st, 1sc into each st up right front, 1sc into each row end on back neck (at the same time place colored markers at beg of RH back bodice extension, center back seam and beg of LH back bodice extension), and 1sc into each st down left front. Turn.
Next 7 rows Work in sc, working 2sc tog at each of the markers on the back neck and working in stripe sequence as follows: 2 rows in B, 1 row in E, 1 row in D, 1 row in A, 1 row in B and 1 row in A. Fasten off.

Waistband
Using smaller hook and A, make 21ch. Work in single crochet ribbing as for cuff until work measures 27in, or your waist measurement, when slightly stretched. Fasten off.
Using smaller hook and A, work 1 row of sc into row ends on lower edge to finish edge and ease in fullness.
Sew waistband to lower edge of bodice from RS, easing in fullness. Do not press seam.

Buttonhole band
Mark positions of 5 buttonholes on lower right front.
1st row Using smaller hook and with RS facing, join A to first st on lower edge, ch 1, skip first st, 1sc into each st up right front, 1sc into each sc across back neck, working 2sc tog at markers, and 1sc into each st down left front. Turn.
2nd row Ch 1, skip first st, *work in sc to position of buttonhole, ch 2, skip next 2 sts, 1sc into next st, rep from * 4 times more, 1sc into each st to end. Turn.
3rd row Work in sc.
4th row Work in crab st (see page 18). Fasten off.
Sew buttons to left front to correspond with buttonholes.

Adapting the basic striped cardigan

Use the Pattern Library to make several versions of the basic, simply-shaped cardigan.

Simple substitutions
The basic cardigan is worked from cuff to cuff in horizontal bands of pattern and simple stripes to produce a vertically-striped garment.
Any of the samples in the Pattern Library could be substituted – the easiest method being to work the cardigan in any or all of the simple, striped patterns.

Enlarging the cardigan
The cardigan will fit Misses' sizes 34 to 38, but it can easily be made larger by working more rows on the sleeves and on the back bodice extension.
Work enough waistband to fit, when slightly stretched, around your waist; sew it to the lower edge, easing any fullness to fit.

Pattern Library: Horizontal patterns

1

Fancy clusters (1)
Make a multiple of 9ch plus 2 extra.
Base row (RS) 1sc into 2nd ch from hook, *1sc into each of next 3ch, (ch 7, 1sc into next ch) 3 times, 1sc into each of next 3ch, rep from * to end. Turn.
1st row Ch 7, *(leaving last loop of each st on hook work 4dc into next 7ch loop, yo and draw through all 5 loops on hook – cluster formed –, ch 2) twice, cluster into next 7ch loop, ch 6, rep from * to end, omitting 6ch at end of last rep and working ch 2, 1dtr into last sc. Turn.
2nd row Ch 1, skip first dtr, *(2sc into next 2ch loop) 3 times, 6sc into next 6ch loop, rep from * to end, omitting 6sc at end of last rep and working 2sc into sp formed by turning ch. Turn.
3rd row Ch 3, skip first st, 1dc into each st to end. Turn.
4th row Ch 1, skip first st, *1sc into each of next 3 sts, (ch 7, 1sc into next st) 3 times, 1sc into each of next 3 sts, rep from * to end. Turn.
Rep first–4th rows throughout, ending with a 2nd row.

Note: *This pattern can be worked in one color or in two colors as shown.*

Simple clusters (3)
Make a multiple of 2ch plus 2 extra.
Base row (RS) 1sc into 2nd ch from hook, 1sc into each ch to end. Turn.
1st row Ch 3, leaving last loop of each dc on hook work 2dc into first st, yo and draw through all 3 loops on hook – cluster worked –, *skip next st, (1dc, 1 cluster) into next st, rep from * to last 2 sts, skip next st, 1dc into last st. Turn.
2nd row Ch 1, skip first st, *1sc into top of next cluster, 1sc into next dc, rep from * to end, ending with 1sc into top of turning ch.
Rep first and 2nd rows throughout.

3

Narrow stripes (2)
Use 2 colors, A and B, and work alternate rows of hdc and sc, changing color after every row or every alternate row.

2

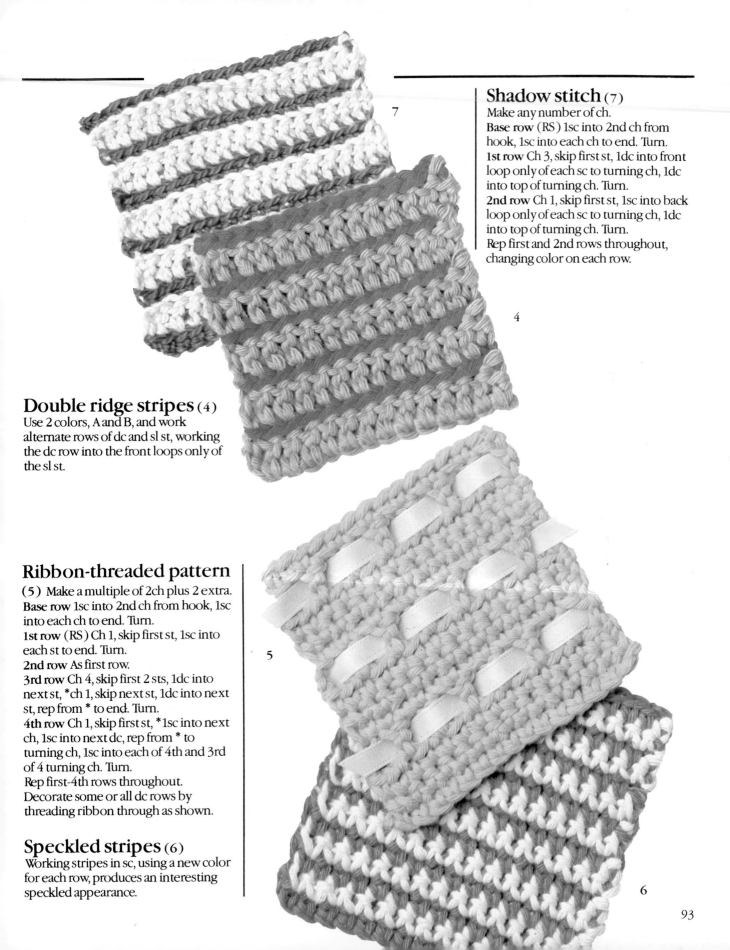

7

Shadow stitch (7)

Make any number of ch.
Base row (RS) 1sc into 2nd ch from hook, 1sc into each ch to end. Turn.
1st row Ch 3, skip first st, 1dc into front loop only of each sc to turning ch, 1dc into top of turning ch. Turn.
2nd row Ch 1, skip first st, 1sc into back loop only of each sc to turning ch, 1dc into top of turning ch. Turn.
Rep first and 2nd rows throughout, changing color on each row.

4

Double ridge stripes (4)

Use 2 colors, A and B, and work alternate rows of dc and sl st, working the dc row into the front loops only of the sl st.

Ribbon-threaded pattern

(5) Make a multiple of 2ch plus 2 extra.
Base row 1sc into 2nd ch from hook, 1sc into each ch to end. Turn.
1st row (RS) Ch 1, skip first st, 1sc into each st to end. Turn.
2nd row As first row.
3rd row Ch 4, skip first 2 sts, 1dc into next st, *ch 1, skip next st, 1dc into next st, rep from * to end. Turn.
4th row Ch 1, skip first st, *1sc into next ch, 1sc into next dc, rep from * to turning ch, 1sc into each of 4th and 3rd of 4 turning ch. Turn.
Rep first-4th rows throughout.
Decorate some or all dc rows by threading ribbon through as shown.

5

Speckled stripes (6)

Working stripes in sc, using a new color for each row, produces an interesting speckled appearance.

6

Lacets

Lacets are V-shaped stitches, which can either be used by themselves to create a variety of openwork patterns or be combined with blocks and spaces to form lacy filet fabrics. Here they are used for a cool summer T-shirt.

The basic lacet T-shirt

Sizes

Men's sizes 38 [40:42]
Length 25 [25½:26] in
Sleeve seam 8¼in
Note: *Instructions for larger sizes are in brackets [ ]; where there is only one set of figures it applies to all sizes.*

Materials

13 [15:16] oz of a sport yarn
Size B crochet hook
Pair of size 2 knitting needles
3 small buttons

Gauge

7 pat reps and 20 rows to 4in worked on size B hook

To save time, take time to check gauge.

Back

Using knitting needles, cast on 145 [149:157] sts. Work in K1, P1 ribbing until work measures 2½in. Bind off loosely in ribbing until one loop rem. Transfer loop to crochet hook.
1st row (RS) Ch 5, *skip next bound-off st, 1sc into next bound-off st, ch 2, skip next bound-off st, 1dc into next bound off st, ch 2, rep from * to end, omitting last 2ch and working 1dc into last bound-off st. 36 [37:39] pat reps.
2nd row Ch 1, 1sc into first dc, *ch 3, 1sc into next dc, rep from * to end, working last sc into 3rd turning ch. Turn.
3rd row Ch 5, *1sc into next 3ch sp, ch 2, 1dc into next sc, ch 2, rep from * to end, omitting last 2ch and working 1dc into last sc. Turn.
2nd and 3rd rows form the pat.
Cont in pat until work measures 16½in, ending with a 2nd pat row.

Yoke

Next row Ch 3, skip first st, *2dc into next 3ch sp, 1dc into next sc, rep from * to end. Turn.
109 [112:118] sts.

Shape armholes

Next row Sl st over first 9dc, ch 3, 1dc into each of next 92 [95:101] dc, turn leaving 8dc unworked. 93 [96:102] sts. * *
Work even in dc until work measures 25 [25½:26] in. Fasten off.

Front

Work as for back to * *.

Divide for front opening

Next row Ch 3, skip first st, 1dc into each of next 42 [44:47] sts, turn. 43 [45:48] sts.
Cont in dc on these sts only until work measures 22 [22½:23] in, ending at neck edge.

Shape neck

Next row Sl st over first 8dc, ch 3, work in dc to end. Turn.
Dec 1dc at neck edge on every row until 31 [32:33] dc rem.
Work even until work measures same as back.
Fasten off.
Return to beg of front opening, skip next 7 [6:6] dc and rejoin yarn to next st. Complete other side to match.

Sleeves (both alike)

Using knitting needles, cast on 93 [101:109] sts. Work in K1, P1 ribbing until work measures 1½in. Bind off in ribbing until one loop rem. Transfer loop to crochet hook. Work first-3rd rows as for back, then 2nd row once more. 23 [25:27] pat reps.

Shape sleeve

Next row Ch 4, 1dc into sc at base of

SPECIAL TECHNIQUE

finishing a front opening

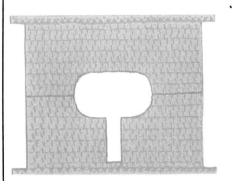

1 The front opening usually begins just above the start of the armhole shaping. Work each side separately, reversing shaping on the second side. Press or block the front and back as instructed in the pattern. Join shoulder seams.

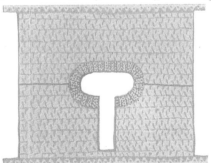

2 With right side facing, pick up stitches evenly around the neck and work in ribbing as required. Bind off loosely in ribbing.

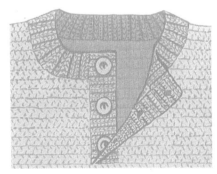

3 Pick up stitches on each side of the neck, including the row ends of the neckband. Remember to work buttonholes in the ribbing. Lap the buttonhole band over the button band and sew both neatly to the beginning of the front opening.

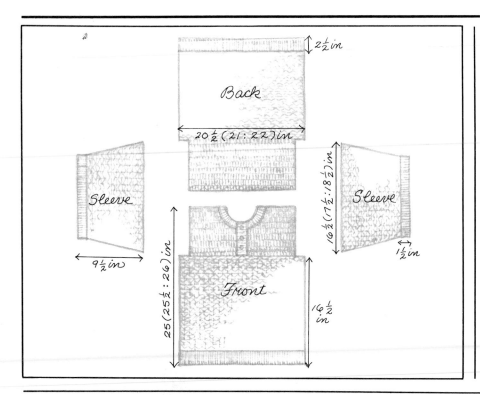

Back

20½ (21:22) in

2½ in

Sleeve

9½ in

Sleeve

16½ (17½:18½) in

1½ in

25 (25½:26) in

Front

16½ in

4ch, pat to last sc, (1dc, ch 1, 1dc) into last sc. Turn.

Next row Ch 1, 1sc into first dc, ch 1, 1sc into next dc, pat to last 2 sts, 1sc into last dc, ch 1, 1sc into 3rd of 4 turning ch. Turn.

Next row Ch 5, 1sc into next 1ch sp, ch 2, 1dc into next sc, pat to end, ending with ch 2, 1sc into next 1ch sp, ch 2, 1dc into last sc. Turn.

Pat 7 rows without shaping.

Rep last 10 rows twice more.

29 [31:33] pat reps. Work even in pat until sleeve measures 9½in. Fasten off.

Neckband

Join shoulder seams. With RS facing and using knitting needles, pick up and K 110 [116:122] sts around neck edge. Work in K1, P1 ribbing for 10 rows. Bind off in ribbing.

Button band

With RS facing and using knitting

Pattern Library: Lacet patterns

1

Crossed lacets (1)

This could be used for the T-shirt on page 94.

Make a multiple of 8ch plus 2 extra.

Base row 1sc into 2nd ch from hook, *ch 4, skip next 3ch, 1sc into next ch, rep from * to end. Turn.

1st row (RS) Ch 3, skip first st, *3dc into next 4ch sp, 1dc into next sc, ch 2, 1sc into next 4ch sp, ch 2, 1dc into next sc, rep from * to end. Turn.

2nd row Ch 5, *1sc into first of next 5dc, ch 4, 1sc into last of same 5dc, ch 4, rep from * omitting 4ch at end of last rep and working last sc into top of turning ch. Turn.

3rd row Ch 5, *1sc into first 4ch sp, ch 2, 1dc into next sc, 3dc into next 4ch sp, 1dc into next sc, ch 2, rep from * omitting 2ch at end of last rep and working last dc into 3rd of 5 turning ch. Turn.

4th row Ch 1, 1sc into first dc, *ch 4, 1sc into last of next 5dc, ch 4, 1sc into first of next 5dc, rep from * to end working last sc into 3rd turning ch. Turn.

Rep first-4th rows throughout.

Vertical lacets (2)

Make a multiple of 8ch plus 7.

Base row (RS) 1dc into 4th ch from hook, 1dc into each of next 3ch, *ch 2, skip next ch, 1sc into next ch, ch 2, skip next ch, 1dc into each of next 5ch, rep from * to end. Turn.

1st row Ch 3, skip first dc, 1dc into each of next 4dc, *ch 3, skip next (2ch, 1sc, 2ch), 1dc into each of next 5dc, rep from * to end. Turn.

2nd row Ch 3, skip first dc, 1dc into each of next 4dc, *ch 2, 1sc into next 3ch sp, ch 2, 1dc into each of next 5dc, rep from * to end, working last dc into top of turning ch. Turn.

Rep first and 2nd rows throughout.

2

needles, pick up and K 50 [54:48] sts down right side of neck. Work in K1, P1 ribbing for 10 rows. Bind off in ribbing.

Buttonhole band

Pick up and K sts down left side of neck as for button band. Work 5 rows in K1, P1 ribbing ending at top of neck.
Buttonhole row Rib 6, *bind off 3 sts, rib 12 [13:14] *, rep from * to * once, bind off 3 sts, rib to end.
Next row Rib to first buttonhole, *cast on 3 sts, rib 12 [13:14], rep from * once, cast on 3 sts, rib to end. Work 13 more rows in ribbing. Bind off.

To finish

Join side seams. Join sleeve seams, leaving top 7 rows open. Set in sleeves, sewing 7 rows at sleeve top to sts of armhole shaping. Overlap buttonhole band over button band and sew ends to dc at base of neck opening. Sew on buttons.

Adapting the basic lacet T-shirt

Some of the lacet patterns in this section could be used for the T-shirt. Others could be used for edgings.

The patterns suitable for the T-shirt are so designated under their names. Make a sample first, using your chosen yarn and hook, then calculate the number of pattern repeats that will produce a fabric of the desired width.

Lacet edgings

These patterns can also be adapted for use as edgings on household linens. You should experiment before you begin the edging to ensure that your chosen pattern can be used, but the following method can be applied to most simple lacet patterns. Work chains the length of the edging plus about 20 extra.

Work the base row of your chosen lacet patterns into the chains.
When the edging is the required length, turn, and work the first pattern row. Fasten off. If you want a deeper edging, work more pattern rows before fastening off.
Do not worry about the few chains left unworked after the base row. After fastening off, cut the beginning slip knot and undo the chains.

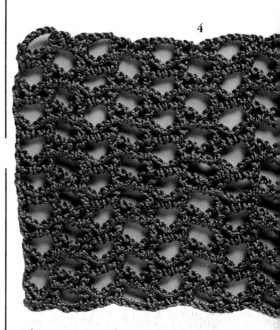

4

Cluster lacet (3)

This could be used for the T-shirt on page 94.
Make a multiple of 6ch plus 3 extra.
Base row 1dc into 4th ch from hook, *ch 2, skip next ch, 1sc into next ch, ch 2, skip next ch, 1dc into each of next 3ch, rep from *, ending last rep with 1dc into each of last 2ch. Turn.
1st row (RS) Ch 3, skip first dc, 1dc into next dc, *ch 3, 1dc into first of next 3dc, leaving last loop of each st on hook work 5dc into next dc, yo and draw through all 6 loops on hook – cluster formed –, 1dc into next dc, rep from * omitting cluster in last rep and working last dc into top of turning ch. Turn.
2nd row Ch 3, skip first dc, 1dc into next dc, *ch 2, 1sc into next 3ch sp, ch 2, 1dc into next dc, 1dc into top of cluster, 1dc into next dc, rep from * ending last rep with 1dc into last dc, 1dc into top of turning ch.
Rep first and 2nd rows throughout.

Alternating lacets (4)

Make a multiple of 8ch plus 9.
Base row (RS) 1sc into 7th ch from hook, ch 2, skip next ch, 1dc into next ch, *ch 3, skip next 3ch, 1dc into next ch, ch 2, skip next ch, 1sc into next ch, ch 2, skip next ch, 1dc into next ch, rep from * to end. Turn.
1st row Ch 6, skip first dc, *1dc into next dc, ch 2, 1sc into next sp, ch 2, 1dc into next dc, ch 3, 1dc into next dc, rep from * to end. Turn.
2nd row Ch 5, 1sc into first sp, ch 2, *1dc into next dc, ch 3, 1dc into next dc, ch 2, 1sc into next sp, ch 2, rep from * to end, ending skip first 3 turning ch, 1dc into next ch. Turn.
Rep first and 2nd rows throughout.

3

Openwork patterns

A variety of attractive lacy fabrics can be made from different combinations of loops, clusters and shells. Use them to make beautiful shawls, like the one shown here, and evening clothes.

The basic lace shawl

Size
Shawl measures about 70in in diameter.

Materials
22oz of a sport yarn
Size H crochet hook

Gauge
7 3dc clusters to 4in in pattern worked on size H hook

To save time, take time to check gauge.

Note: *Never use a knot to join in a new ball of yarn; instead, splice the ends together. (See Special Technique.)*

Shawl
Make 4ch, join into a ring with a sl st.
1st round Ch 3 to count as first dc, work 11dc into ring, sl st into 3rd of first 3ch. 12dc.
2nd round Ch 5 to count as first dc and 2ch sp, *1dc into next dc, 2ch, rep from * all around, sl st to 3rd of first 5ch.

3rd round 1sc into same place as sl st, *2sc into next 2ch sp, 1sc into next dc, rep from * ending with 2sc into last sp, sl st into first sc. Turn.
4th round Ch 2, leaving last loop of each st on hook, work 2dc into first st, yo and draw through all loops on hook – called 2dc Cl –, *ch 2, skip 1sc, leaving last loop of each st on hook, work 3dc into next sc, yo and draw through all loops on hook – called 3dc Cl –, rep from * to end, ending with ch 2, sl st into top of first Cl. Turn.
5th round Work 4sc into each sp to end, sl st into first sc.
6th round Ch 5, *skip 1sc, 1dc into next sc, ch 2, rep from * to end, sl st into 3rd of first 5ch.
7th round Ch 5, *3dc Cl into next dc, ch 2, 1dc into next dc, ch 2, rep from * ending with 3dc Cl into next dc, ch 2, sl st into 3rd of first 5ch.
8th round Ch 1 to count as first sc, 1sc into first sp, *1sc into next 3dc Cl, 2sc into next sp, rep from * to end, sl st

into first ch.
9th round As 4th round.
10th round *3sc into next sp, 4sc into next sp, rep from * ending with 4sc into last sp, sl st into first sc.
11th round 1sc into same place as sl st, *ch 1, skip 1sc, 1sc into next sc, rep from * ending with ch 1, sl st into first sc.
12th round Sl st into first 1ch sp, ch 3, 1dc into same sp, *2dc into each 1ch sp, rep from * to end of round, sl st into 3rd of first 3ch.
13th round Ch 2, work 2dc Cl into same place as sl st, ch 1, skip 1dc, *3dc Cl into next dc, ch 1, skip 2dc, rep from * to end, sl st into first 2dc Cl.
14th round *1sc into next sp. ch 5, rep from * ending with ch 2, 1dc into first sc at beg of round.
15th-19th rounds 1sc into loop just made, *ch 5, 1sc into next loop, rep from * ending with ch 2, 1dc into first sc.
20th round 1sc into loop just made,

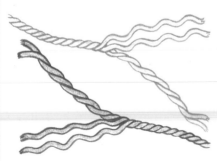
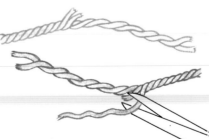

*ch 3, 1sc into next loop, rep from * ending with ch 3, sl st into first sc.
21st round 1sc into same place as sl st, *3sc into next loop, 1sc into next sc, rep from * ending with 3sc into last loop, sl st into first sc. Turn.
22nd round As 4th round.
23rd round 2sc into each of first 2 sps, 3sc into each following sp, sl st into first sc.
24th round As 6th round.
25th round As 7th round.
26th round *2sc into each of next 5 sps, 3sc into next sp, rep from *ending with 1sc into each of last 2 sps, sl st into first sc. Turn.
27th round Ch 2, 2dc Cl into first st, *ch 2, skip 1sc, 3dc Cl into next sc,

ch 2, skip 2sc, 3dc Cl into next sc, rep from * omitting 3dc Cl at end of last rep, sl st into first 2dc Cl. Turn.

28th round 3sc into each sp to end, sl st into first sc.
29th round As 11th round.
30th round As 12th round.
31st round Ch 2, 2dc Cl into same place as sl st, *ch 1, skip 2dc, 3dc Cl into next dc, rep from * ending with ch 1, sl st into top of first 2dc Cl.
32nd round As 14th round.
33rd-39th rounds As 15th round.
40th round As 20th round.
41st round As 21st round, inc 4sc evenly in round.
42nd round Ch 2, 2dc Cl into same place as sl st, *ch 2, skip 1sc, 3dc Cl into next sc, (ch 2, skip 2sc, 3dc Cl into next sc) twice, rep from * omitting a Cl at end of last rep, sl st into top of first 2dc

Adapting the basic shawl

Openwork patterns combine chain lace and groups, clusters and shells in various ways. Any of the ones shown could be used to make a pretty shawl.

Using openwork patterns

Openwork patterns can be worked in either rounds or rows, and so are suitable for making not only shawls, but also bags, scarves, summer tops and evening wraps. Worked in crochet cot-

ton, they have a crisp look; for evening wear, choose one of the many pretty glitter yarns available.

The patterns can also be worked in strips and used as decoration – either as a lace insertion or as edging – on household items, baby clothes and adults' garments.

Pattern Library: Openwork patterns

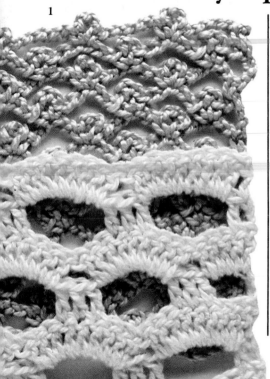

1

Picot chain lace (1)

Make a multiple of 4 plus 1ch with 5 extra turning ch.
Base row (1sc, ch 3, 1sc) into 10th ch from hook, ch 5, skip 3ch, (1sc, ch 3, 1sc) into next ch, rep from * to last 4ch, ch 5, skip 3ch, 1sc into last ch. Turn.
Pattern row Ch 5, *(1sc, ch 3, 1sc) into 3rd ch of next 5ch loop, ch 5, rep from * to end, 1sc into 3rd of last 5ch loop. Turn.
Rep pat row throughout.

Diamond eyelets (2)

Make a multiple of 8ch plus 3 extra turning ch.
Base row 1dc into 4th ch from hook, 1dc into next ch, *ch 5, skip 5ch, 1dc into each of next 3ch, rep from *, ending with 1dc into each of last 2ch. Turn.

1st row Ch 3 to count as first dc, *9dc into next 5ch sp, rep from * to end, 1dc into top of turning ch. Turn.
2nd row Ch 5 to count as first dc and 2ch sp, *skip first 3dc of next 9dc group, 1dc into each of next 3dc at center of group, ch 5, skip next 3dc of same group, rep from *, ending with 3dc at center of last 9dc group, ch 2, 1dc into top of turning ch. Turn.
3rd row Ch 3, 4dc into first 2ch sp, *9dc into next 5ch sp, rep from * to end, working 4dc into last 2ch sp before turning ch, 1dc into 3rd of 5 turning ch. Turn.
4th row Ch 3, skip 1dc, 1dc into next dc, ch 5, 1dc into each of 3 center dc of next 9dc group, rep from * to end, ending with skip 3dc of last 9dc group and first 3dc of last 5dc group, 1dc into next dc, 1dc into turning ch. Turn.
Rep first-4th rows throughout.

Cl. Turn.

43rd round 2sc into first sp, 3sc into each following sp all around, sl st into first sc.

44th round As 6th round, working ch 1 instead of ch 2 between dc.

45th round As 7th round, working ch 1 instead of ch 2 between dc.

46th round 3sc into each of first 3 sps, 2sc into each following sp all around, sl st into first sc. Turn.

47th round As 27th round.

48th round *2sc into next sp, 3sc into next sp, rep from *, working 2sc into last sp.

49th round As 11th round.

50th round As 12th round.

51st round As 31st round, working ch 2

instead of ch 1 between each 3dc Cl.

52nd round As 14th round.

53rd-61st rounds As 15th round.

62nd round As 20th round.

63rd round 1sc into same place as sl st, *2sc into next sp, 1sc into next sc, 3sc into next sp, 1sc into next sc, rep from * ending with 3sc into last sp, sl st into first sc.

64th round As 4th round.

65th round As 28th round.

66th round As 44th round.

67th round As 45th round.

68th round 3sc into first sp, 2sc into each following sp, sl st into first sc. Turn.

69th round As 4th round, but skipping 2sc instead of ch 1 between 3dc Cls.

70th round 2sc into first sp, ch 3 into

each following sp all around, sl st into first sc.

71st round As 11th round.

72nd round As 12th round.

73rd round As 30th round, working ch 2 instead of ch 1 between each 3dc Cl.

74th round As 14th round.

75th-78th rounds As 15th round.

79th round 1sc into loop just made, *ch 5, 1sc into next sc, rep from * to end, ending with ch 5, sl st into first sc.

80th round 1sc into same place as sl st, *ch 6, 1sc into next sc, rep from * to end, ending with ch 6, sl st into first sc.

81st round As 79th round, working ch 7 instead of ch 6 for each loop.

Fasten off.

Double block and picot (3)

Make a multiple of 10 plus 7ch with 2 extra turning ch.

Base row 1dc into 4th ch from hook, 1dc into each of next 4ch, *ch 3, skip 2ch, (1sc, ch 3, 1sc) into next ch – called picot sc –, ch 3, skip 2ch, 1dc into each of next 5ch, rep from * to end, 1dc into last ch. Turn.

1st row Ch 3 to count as first dc, 1dc into each of next 5dc, ch 5, 1dc into each of next 5dc, rep from * to end, 1dc into top of turning ch. Turn.

2nd row Ch 6 to count to first dc and 3ch sp, picot sc into center of first 5dc block, ch 3, 5dc into next 5ch sp, ch 3,

picot sc into center of next 5dc block, ch 3, rep from * to end, 1dc into top of turning ch. Turn.

3rd row Ch 8 to count as first dc and 5ch sp, *skip next picot, 1dc into each of next 5dc, ch 5, rep from * to end, 1dc into 3rd of 6 turning ch. Turn.

4th row Ch 3 to count as first dc, 5dc into first 5ch sp, *ch 3, 1 picot sc into center dc of next 5dc block, ch 3, 5dc into next 5ch sp, rep from * to end, 1dc into 3rd of 8 turning ch. Turn.

5th row As 2nd row.

2nd-5th rows form pat; rep them throughout.

3

4

Crown lace (4)

Make a multiple of 10 plus 7ch.

Base row 1dc into 4th ch from hook, 1dc into each of next 3ch, *ch 3, skip 2ch, 1sc into next ch, ch 3, skip 2ch, 1dc into each of next 5ch, rep from * to end. Turn.

1st row Ch 3, skip first dc, 1dc into each of next 4dc, *ch 4, 1dc into each of next 5dc, rep from * ending with 1dc into each of last 4dc, 1dc into top of turning ch. Turn.

2nd row Ch 6, 1sc into center dc of next 5dc group, * Ch 3, 5dc into next 4ch

sp, ch 3, 1sc into center dc of next 5dc group, rep from * ending with ch 3, 1dc into top of turning ch. Turn.

3rd row Ch 6, skip first sc, *1dc into each of next 5dc, ch 5, rep from * ending with ch 4, 1dc into 3rd of turning ch. Turn.

4th row Ch 3, 4dc into first ch sp, *ch 3, 1sc into center dc of 5dc group, ch 3, 5dc into next 5ch sp, rep from * ending with 4dc into last sp, 1dc into turning ch. Turn.

Rep first-4th rows throughout.

Shells

Shells are probably the best known of crochet stitches, and their popularity is well justified. Use these lacy fabrics, formed from groups of double crochet, to make traditional baby clothes, such as this christening gown and shawl, as well as lightweight sweaters and lacy edgings.

The basic christening gown and shawl

Sizes
Dress Size Newborn – 6 month
Length 30in
Sleeve seam 1½in
Shawl 43in square

Materials
Dress 10oz of a baby yarn
Approx 2yd of ¼in-wide, double-faced satin ribbon
5 small buttons
Shawl 16oz of a baby yarn
Approx 6yd of ¼in-wide, double-faced satin ribbon
Size E crochet hook

Gauge
16sts and 10 rows to 4in in double crochet worked on size E hook

To save time, take time to check gauge.

Gown
Skirt and bodice
Make 184ch.
Base row 2dc into 4th ch from hook, *skip next 2ch, 1sc into next ch, skip next 2ch, 5dc into next ch, rep from * to last 6ch, skip next 2ch, 1sc into next ch, skip next 2ch, 3dc into last ch. Turn.
Beg pattern
1st row (RS) Ch 1, 1sc into first dc, ch 2, leaving last loop of each st on hook work 3dc into next sc, yo and draw through all 4 loops on hook – called cluster –, *ch 2, 1sc into 3rd of next 5dc, ch 2, cluster into next sc, rep from * to turning ch, ch 2, 1sc into top of turning ch. Turn.
2nd row Ch 3, 2dc into first sc, 1sc into next cluster, *5dc into next sc, 1sc into next cluster, rep from * to last sc, 3dc into last sc. Turn.

First and 2nd rows form the pat.
Cont in pat until work measures 24in, ending with a WS row.

Bodice
Next row Ch 3, 1dc into first dc, *(skip next dc, 1dc into next dc) 24 times, skip next dc, 2dc into next dc, rep from * twice more. Turn. 80 sts.
Next row Ch 3, skip first dc, 1dc into each of next 29 sts, 1sc into next st, skip next 2 sts, 5dc into next st, skip next 2 sts, 1sc into next st, 1dc into each of next 6 sts, 1sc into next st, skip next 2 sts, 5dc into next st, skip next 2 sts, 1sc into next st, 1dc into each of last 30 sts. Turn.

SPECIAL TECHNIQUE
beginning the bodice

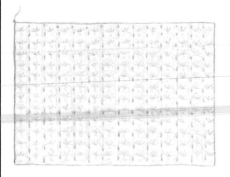

1 *The skirt and bodice of the dress are worked in one piece to the armholes, the skirt edges being sewn together to form the center back seam. Work the skirt for the length required, ending with a second pattern row.*

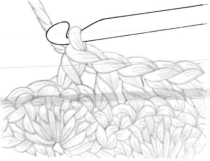

2 *Turn and work three chains and one double into the first double. *Skip the next double and work one double into the next double. Repeat from * 24 times. Skip the next double, then work two doubles into the next double.*

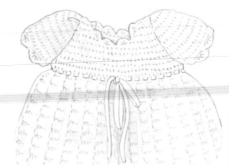

3 *Continue in this way to the end of the row so that there are 80 stitches. When the garment is completed, thread narrow satin ribbon between stitches on the first row of the bodice and tie in a bow at the center front. Use buttons in a color matching the ribbon.*

Rep last row twice more.

Divide for backs and front
Next row Ch 3, skip first st, 1dc into each of next 17 sts, turn. 18 sts.
Left back
Cont on these sts only for bodice left back.

Shape armhole
Next row Ch 3, skip first st, work next 2dc tog, 1dc into each st to end. Turn. 17 sts.
Next row Ch 3, skip first st, 1dc into each st to last 3 sts, work next 2dc tog, 1dc into last st. Turn. 16 sts.

Work even for 3 more rows in dc.
Shape neck
Next row Sl st across first 7 sts, ch 3, skip st at base of 3ch, 1dc into each st to end. Turn. 10 sts.
Next row Ch 3, skip first st, 1dc into each st to last 3 sts, work next 2dc tog,

1dc into last st. 9 sts. Fasten off.

Front

With RS facing, return to sts skipped at beg of left back, skip next 4 sts and using hook, rejoin yarn to next st.

Next row Ch 3, skip first st at base of joining, 1dc into each of next 7 sts, 1sc into next sc, 5dc into 3rd of next 5dc, 1sc into next sc, 1dc into each of next 6dc, 1sc into next sc, 5dc into 3rd of next 5dc, 1sc into next dc, 1dc into each of next 8 sts, turn.

Shape armholes

Next row Ch 3, skip first st, work next 2dc tog, pat to last 3 sts, work next 2dc tog, 1dc into last st.

Rep last row once more.

Work even for 2 rows in pat.

Shape right front neck

Next row Ch 3, skip first st, 1dc into each of next 5 sts, 1dc into next sc, 1dc into next dc, skip next dc, 1dc into next dc, turn. 9 sts.

Next row Ch 3, skip first st, 1dc into each st to end. Turn.

Rep last row once more.

Fasten off.

Left front neck

With WS facing, return to sts skipped at beg of front neck, and rejoin yarn to 3rd dc of next shell.

Next row Ch 3, skip first st at base of joining, skip next dc, 1dc into next dc, 1dc into next sc, 1dc into each of next 6 sts. 9 sts.

Complete to match first side of neck, reversing all shaping.

Right back

With RS facing, return to sts skipped at beg of front, skip next 4 sts and rejoin yarn to next st.

Next row Ch 3, skip first st at base of joining, 1dc into each st to end. Turn. 18 sts.

Complete to match left back, reversing all shaping.

Sleeves

Make 28ch.

Base row (RS) 1dc into 4th ch from hook, 1dc into each ch to end. Turn. 26 sts.

Next row Ch 3, skip first st, *2dc into next st, 1dc into next st, 2dc into next st,

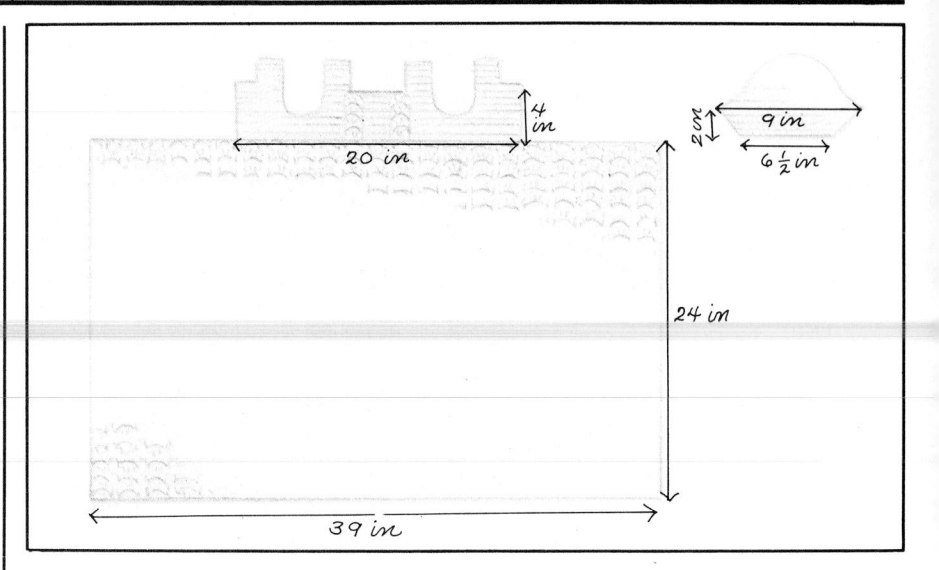

1dc into each of next 2 sts, rep from * to end. Turn. 36 sts.

Next 2 rows Ch 3, skip first st, 1dc into each st to end. Turn.

Shape top

Next row Sl st across first 3 sts, ch 3, 1dc into each st to last 2 sts, turn. 32 sts.

Next row Ch 3, skip first st, work next 2dc tog, 1dc into each st to last 3 sts, work next 2dc tog, 1dc into last st. Turn. 30 sts.

Rep last row until 22 sts rem.

Work even in dc for 2 more rows.

Fasten off.

To finish

Press or block, according to yarn used.

Join shoulder seams.

Join skirt seam including first row of bodice to form center back.

Join sleeve seams. Set in sleeves, easing in the fullness.

Neck and bodice edging

With RS facing join yarn to top of center back seam at beg of left back bodice.

Next row Ch 1, 1sc into same place as joining, (5dc into top of st at next row end, 1sc into top of st at next row end) 4 times, 5dc into top of st at corner of left back bodice, 1sc into top of 4th st on neck edge, 5dc into top of st at neck row end, 1sc into shoulder seam, skip next row end, 5dc into next row end, 1sc into next row end, 5dc into center dc of next shell, 1sc into top of next sc, 5dc between 3rd and 4th of next 6dc, 1sc

into top of next sc, 5dc into center dc of next shell, 1sc into next row end, 5dc into next row end, skip next row end, 1sc into shoulder seam, 5dc into top of st at next row end, 1sc into 3rd st on neck edge, 5dc into top of st at corner of right back bodice, (1sc into top of st at next row end, 5dc into top of st at next row end) 4 times, 1sc into top of center-back seam. Fasten off.

Sleeve edgings (both alike)

With RS facing join yarn to first st on lower edge.

Next row Ch 1, 1sc into next st, *skip next 2 sts, 5dc into next st, skip next 2 sts, 1sc into next st, rep from * to end. Fasten off.

Skirt edging

With RS facing join yarn to center back seam.

Next row Ch 3, 2dc into same place as joining, *skip next 2 sts, 1sc into next st, skip next 2 sts, 5dc into next st, rep from * to last 6 sts, skip next 2 sts, 1sc into next st, skip next 2 sts, 2dc into last st, sl st to top of first 3ch. Fasten off.

Thread ribbon through first row of bodice, adjust gathers to fit and tie ribbon in a bow at center front.

Sew buttons to bottom of center dc of 5 shells on right back edge of bodice.

Use holes formed when working corresponding shells on left back edge of bodice as buttonholes.

Shawl

Center square
Make 160ch. Work base row as for Gown skirt.
Cont in pat as for skirt until work measures approx 35in and 94 rows in all have been worked. Do not turn at end of last row, but cont working into row ends.

Edging
1st round Ch 3, **1dc into first row end, *(2dc into next row end, 1dc into next row end) twice, 3dc into next row end, 1dc into next row end, rep from * to last 3 row ends, 2dc into next row end, 1dc into next row end, 2dc into last row end, 3dc into st at corner, 1dc into each of next 156 sts, 3dc into st at corner**, rep from ** to ** once more, ending last rep with 2dc into base of 3ch, sl st to top of 3ch. 636 sts.
2nd and 3rd rounds Ch 3, skip first st, (1dc into each st to center dc of 3 corner dc, 3dc into corner dc) 4 times, 1dc into

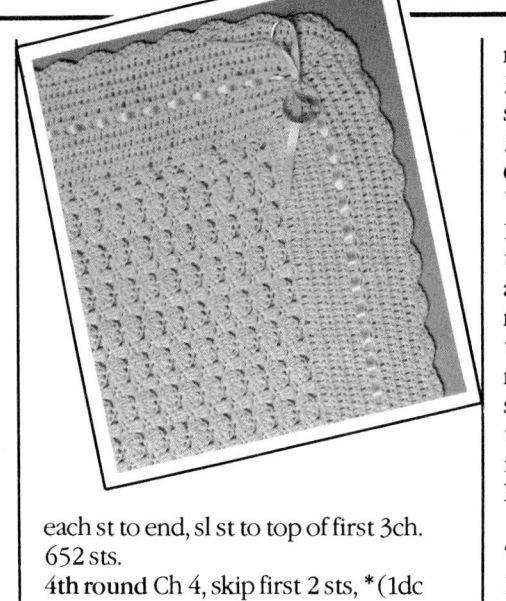

each st to end, sl st to top of first 3ch. 652 sts.
4th round Ch 4, skip first 2 sts, *(1dc into next st, ch 1, skip next st) to within 3 sts of next corner st, 1dc into each of next 3 sts, 3dc into corner st, 1dc into each of next 3 sts, rep from * 3 times more, sl st to top of first 3ch.
5th round Ch 3, skip first st, *(1dc into

next 1ch sp, 1dc into next dc) to within 3 sts of next corner st, 3dc into corner st, 1dc into each of next 3 sts, rep from * 3 times more, sl st to top of first 3ch.
6th-9th rounds As 2nd and 3rd rounds. 700 sts. Fasten off.
10th round With RS facing, rejoin yarn to a corner st, ch 3, 4dc into same place as joining, *(skip next 2 sts, 1sc into next st, skip next 2 sts, 5dc into next st) to within 6 sts of next corner st, skip next 2 sts, 1sc into next st, skip next 3 sts, 5dc into next corner st, rep from * 3 times more, omitting 5dc at end of last rep, sl st to top of first 3ch.
Fasten off.

To finish
Press or block, according to yarn used.
Cut ribbon into four equal lengths.
Thread a length of ribbon through the holes on the 4th round of the edging on each side of the shawl.
Tie the ends of ribbon in a neat bow at each corner.

Adapting the basic shell pattern

Shell patterns are ideal for delicate, traditional baby clothes such as christening gowns.

Christening gowns are traditionally made in white or cream, but there is no reason why you should not introduce pastel-colored yarn as a contrast.
For example, the double crochet rows on the dress and shawl could be striped. Similarly, a color could be introduced when working the shell edging. If you do decide to use another color, buy ribbon and buttons to match.

Designing with shells
Unless you are experienced, increasing and decreasing can be difficult when working shell patterns, so avoid shaping wherever possible. Instead, make simple garments from squares and rectangles; some possibilities include summer tops, scarves, T-shaped pullovers and cardigans.

Pattern Library: Shell patterns

Little shells (1)
Make an odd multiple of 3ch plus 1 extra.
Base row (RS) 1dc into 4th ch from hook, *skip next 2ch, (1dc, ch 3, 1dc) into next ch, rep from * to last 3ch, skip next 2ch, 1dc into last ch. Turn.
1st row Ch 3, 1dc into first dc, *(1dc, ch 3, 1dc) into next 3ch sp, (3dc, ch 1, 3dc) into next 3ch sp, rep from * to last 3ch sp, (1dc, ch 3, 1dc) into last 3ch sp, 1dc into top of turning ch. Turn.

2nd row Ch 3, 1dc into first dc, (1dc, ch 3, 1dc) into each ch sp to end, 1dc into top of turning ch. Turn.
First and 2nd rows form the pat. Rep them throughout.

1

2

Vertical shells (2)

Make a multiple of 12ch plus 2 extra.
Base row 1sc into 8th ch from hook, *ch 5, skip next 3ch, 1sc into next ch, rep from * to last 2ch, ch 2, skip next ch, 1dc into next ch. Turn.
1st row (RS) Ch 1, 1sc into first dc, *7dc into next 5ch sp, 1sc into next 5ch sp, ch 5, 1sc into next 5ch sp, rep from * to last 5ch sp, 7dc into last 5ch sp, 1sc into 3rd turning ch. Turn.
2nd row Ch 5, *skip next dc, 1sc into next dc, ch 5, skip next 3dc, 1sc into next dc, ch 5, 1sc into next 5ch sp, ch 5, rep from * to last shell, skip next dc, 1sc into next dc, ch 5, skip next 3dc, 1sc into next dc, ch2, 1dc into last sc. Turn.
First and 2nd rows form the pat. Rep them throughout.

Shells with picot (3)

Make a multiple of 8ch plus 3 extra.
Base row (RS) 1dc into 4th ch from hook, *1dc into next ch, ch 3, skip next ch, 1sc into next ch, ch 3, sl st into first of 3ch just worked – picot formed –, ch 3, skip next ch, 1dc into each of next 4ch, rep from * ending last rep with 3dc. Turn.
1st row Ch 1, 1sc into first dc, *1sc into each of next 2dc, ch 5, 1sc into each of next 3dc, rep from * ending last rep with 1sc into top of turning ch. Turn.
2nd row Ch 1, 1sc into first sc, *ch 3, 5dc into next 5ch loop, ch 3, skip next 2sc, 1sc into next sc, picot, ch 3, rep from * to last 5ch loop, 5dc into last 5ch loop, ch 3, 1sc into last sc. Turn.
3rd row Ch 5, *1sc into each of next 5dc, ch 5, rep from * ending last rep with ch 2, 1dc into last sc. Turn.
4th row Ch 3, 2dc into first dc, *ch 3, skip next 2sc, 1sc into next sc, picot, ch 3, 5dc into next 5ch loop, rep from * ending last rep with 3dc into 3rd turning ch. Turn.
First-4th rows form the pat. Rep them throughout.

Openwork shells (4)

Make a multiple of 6ch plus 4 extra.
Base row 1sc into 2nd ch from hook, *ch 3, skip next 2ch, 1sc into next ch, rep from * to last 2ch, ch 1, 1sc into last ch. Turn.

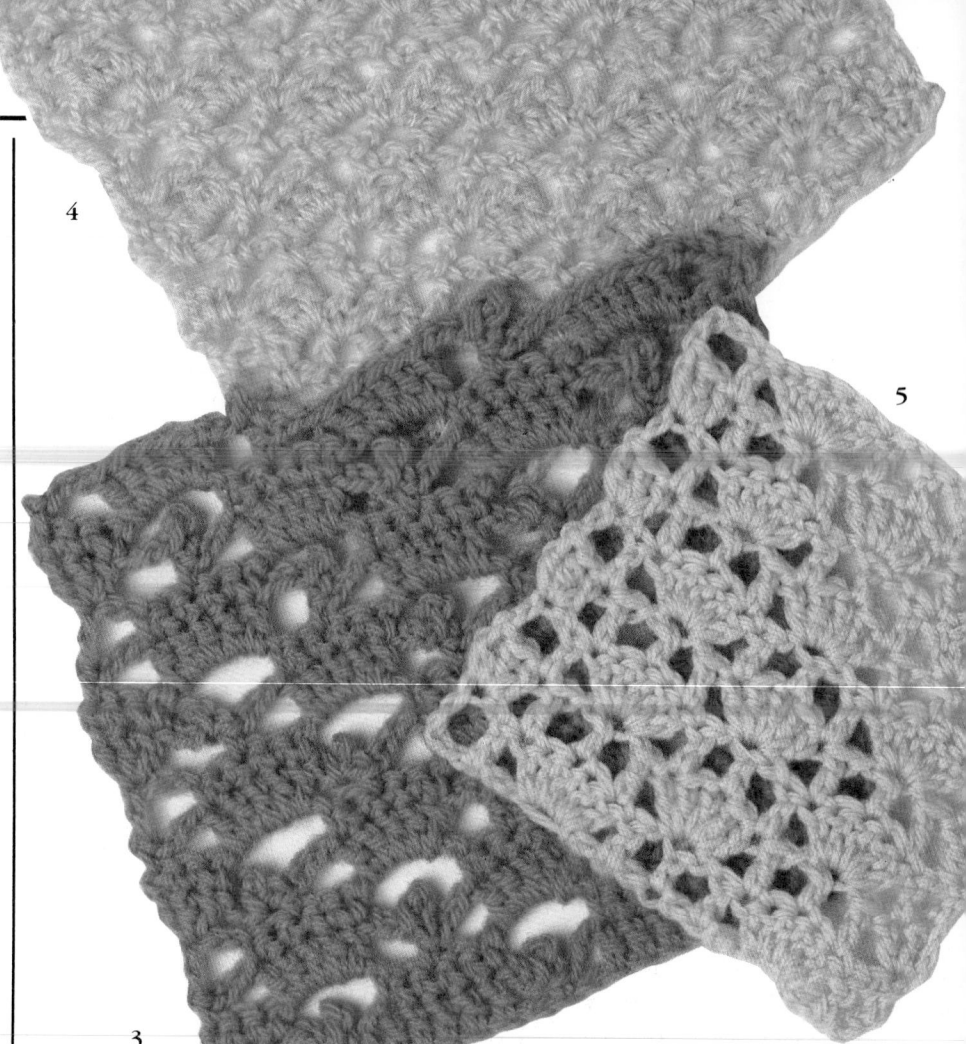

4

5

3

1st row (RS) Ch 1, 1sc into first 1ch sp, *ch 2, 3dc into next 3ch sp, ch 2, 1sc into next 2ch sp, rep from * to turning ch, ch 2, 1dc into top of turning ch. Turn.
2nd row Ch 4, *1sc into next 2ch sp, ch 3, rep from * to last 2ch sp, 1sc into last 2ch sp, ch 1, 1dc into top of turning ch. Turn.
3rd row Ch 2, 1dc into first sc, *ch 2, 1sc into next 3ch sp, ch 2, 3dc into next 3ch sp, rep from * to turning ch, ch 1, 1dc into sp formed by turning ch. Turn.
4th row Ch 1, 1sc into first 1ch sp, *ch 3, 1sc into next 2ch sp, rep from * to turning ch, ch 1, 1sc into top of turning ch. Turn.
First-4th rows form the pat. Rep them throughout.

Shells and doubles (5)

Make a multiple of 10ch plus 5 extra.
Base row 1dc into 7th ch from hook, *skip next 2ch, 5dc into next ch, skip next 2ch, 1dc into next ch, (ch 1, skip next ch, 1dc into next ch) twice, rep from * omitting ch 1 and 1dc from end of last rep. Turn.
1st row Ch 3, 2dc into first dc, *1dc into first dc of shell, ch 1, 1dc into 3rd dc of shell, ch 1, 1dc into 5th dc of shell, skip next dc, 5dc into next dc, rep from * ending last rep with 3dc into top of turning ch. Turn.
2nd row Ch 4, skip first 2dc, 1dc into next dc, *skip next dc, 5dc into next dc, 1dc into first dc of shell, ch 1, 1dc into 3rd dc of shell, ch 1, 1dc into 5th dc of shell, rep from * ending last rep with skip next dc, 1dc into next dc, ch 1, 1dc into top of turning ch. Turn.
First and 2nd rows form the pat. Rep them throughout. The work is reversible.

106

Filet motifs

Filet crochet is derived from two basic stitches – double crochet and chain stitch. Motifs are created against a trellis of chain stitch and spaced doubles by building up blocks of doubles. Fine cotton is well-suited to this work and has been used for the summer top shown here.

The basic filet sun top

Sizes
Misses' sizes 12-14 [14-16]
Length 14in excluding straps
Note: *Instructions for larger sizes are in brackets [ ]; where there is one set of figures it applies to all sizes.*

Materials
About 1200yd of a size 20 crochet cotton
Size 9 steel crochet hook
5 buttons

Gauge
20 sps and 20 rows to 4in worked on size 9 steel hook

To save time, take time to check gauge.

Top (both sizes)
Make 207ch.
1st row 1dc into 4th ch from hook, 1dc into each of next 2ch, (ch 2, skip 2ch, 1dc into next ch) twice, (2 sps made), 1dc into each of next 3ch (block made), now work 60 sps, 1 block, 2 sps, 1 block. Turn.
2nd row Ch 3, skip first dc, 1dc into each of next 3dc (block made over block at beg of row), (Ch 2, 1dc into next dc) twice, (2 sps made over 2 sps), 1dc into

each of next 3dc (block made over block), now work 47 sps, (2dc into next sp, 1dc into next dc) twice, (2 blocks made over 2 sps), now work 11 sps, 1 block, 2 sps, 1dc into each of next 2dc, 1dc into next ch (block made over block at end of row). Turn.
3rd row 1 sl st into each of first 4dc (1 block dec) ch 3, (2dc into next sp, 1dc into next dc) twice, ch 2, skip 2dc, 1dc into next dc (sp made over block), now work 10 sps, 1 block, 2 sps, 1 block, 23 sps, 2 blocks, 22 sps, 2 blocks. Turn.
4th row Ch 5, 1dc into 4th ch from hook, 1dc into next ch, 1dc into next dc, (block inc at beg of row) 2 sps, 1 block, 20 sps, 1 block, 2 sps, 1 block, 22 sps, 1 block, 2 sps, 1 block, 10 sps, 1 block, 1 sp, ch 2, skip 2dc, insert hook into next ch and draw yarn through, yo and draw through one loop on hook (a foundation ch made), complete as a dc, *yo, insert hook into foundation ch and draw yarn through, yo and draw through one loop on hook (another foundation ch made) complete as a dc, rep from * twice more (a block inc at end of row), ch 3. Turn.
1st size only
5th–88th rows Work from chart, noting that 88th row is marked by arrow.

Turn chart and work from 88th row marked by arrow back to first row. Fasten off.
2nd size only
5th–94th rows Work from chart, noting that 94th row is marked by an asterisk. Turn chart and work from 94th row marked by * back to first row. Fasten off.

Buttonhole band (both sizes)
1st row Join yarn to 3rd dc made on last row, 1sc into same place as joining, (2sc into next sp, 1sc into next dc) twice, 1sc into each of next 3dc, (2sc into next sp, 1sc into next dc) 60 times, 1sc into each of next 3dc (2sc into next sp, 1sc into next dc) twice, ch 1. Turn.
2nd row 1sc into each of first 58sc, (ch 5, skip 5sc, 1sc into each of next 28sc) 4 times, ch 5, skip 5ch, 1sc into each of next 4sc, ch 1. Turn.
3rd row (1sc into each sc, 5sc into next 5ch sp) 5 times, 1sc into each sc, ch 5. Turn.
4th row Skip first 3sc, 1dc into next sc, (ch 2, skip 2sc, 1dc into next sc) 65 times. Fasten off.

Button band (both sizes)
1st row Join yarn to 3rd dc made on first row, 1sc into same place as joining, (2sc

— SPECIAL TECHNIQUE —
making a crochet cord

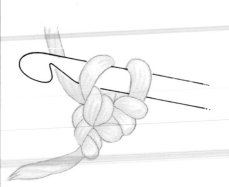
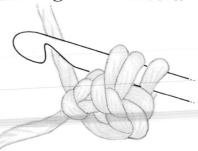

1 Start with 2 chains. Hold them between finger and thumb of left hand and work 1 single crochet into 2nd chain from hook. Turn the work so that foundation chain is at top. Insert hook into back loop and work 1 single crochet into foundation loop of 2nd chain made at beginning.

2 Turn chain so that bottom is now at top next to hook and insert hook into the 2 loops at side of chain.

3 Take yarn over and through 2 loops on hook. Yarn over hook and through remaining 2 loops to make a twisted stitch. By turning stitches in this way you achieve a twisted cord.

into next sp, 1sc into base of next dc) twice, 1sc into base of each of next 3dc, (2sc into next sp, 1sc into base of next dc) 60 times, 1sc into base of each of next 3dc, (2sc into next sp, 1sc into base of next dc) twice, ch 1. Turn.
2nd row 1sc into each sc, ch 1. Turn.
3rd row 1sc into each sc, ch 5. Turn.
4th row As 4th row of buttonhole band.

Shoulder straps (make 2)
Make 9ch.
1st row 2 blocks. Turn.
2nd row Ch 5, inc 1 block, 2 sps, inc 1 block. Turn.
3rd row Ch 3, 1 block, 2 sps, 1 block. Turn.
4th row Dec 1 block, ch 3, 2 blocks. Turn.
Rep 2nd to 4th rows until work measures 14½in, or desired length. Fasten off.

To finish
Sew shoulder straps in place, making sure they are positioned comfortably. Sew buttons to correspond with buttonholes.

Cord (make 2)
Beg with 2ch; holding this between finger and thumb of left hand, work 1sc into 2nd ch from hook, turn, inserting hook into back of loop, work 1sc into foundation loop of 2nd ch made, *turn, insert hook into 2 loops at side, yo and draw through 2 loops on hook, yo and draw through rem 2 loops, rep from * until work measures 47in, or desired length. Fasten off. Slot cords through at waistline and top.
Dampen and pin out to measurements. Leave to dry.

Adapting the filet sun top

Substitute another filet pattern by working from one of the following charts, placing the motifs on a plain filet net background.

Filet crochet, traditionally worked in fine cottons, is really a simple form of lace, originally inspired by filet guipure lace. It had its heyday at the end of the 19th century, when filet crochet could be seen decorating almost any piece of household linen, baby clothes and underwear.

The motifs are worked on a basic net background with spaces filled in with blocks of crochet to create the different motifs. The motifs can either be small and scattered all over the fabric, or quite large and used either individually or in groups to create denser patterns over the basic net.

The basic patterns
The basic net is made by working individual doubles with either one or two chains between, depending on the size of mesh required. The blocks are formed by working one or two doubles into these spaces. The size of the net must be determined before creating a filet design; if you are working from a printed pattern, this will be specified at the beginning of the instructions.

Using a filet chart
Since many filet designs are fairly intricate, the pattern is set out in the form of a chart, since row-by-row instructions for the motifs would be far too complicated and lengthy. Each blank square on the chart represents a space (*not* a stitch), and each block is indicated by a symbol – for example – a ●, as here, or an X – so that you can see how many blocks to work in one row to form the pattern.
Right side rows are usually worked by reading the chart from right to left, and wrong side rows from left to right. When making a filet chart for your own design, remember that although spaces and blocks are represented by squares on the graph paper, these do not represent the actual size of the space or block. It is therefore important to make a gauge swatch in the yarn and pattern of your choice so that you can judge the size of the completed motif, and adjust it if necessary.

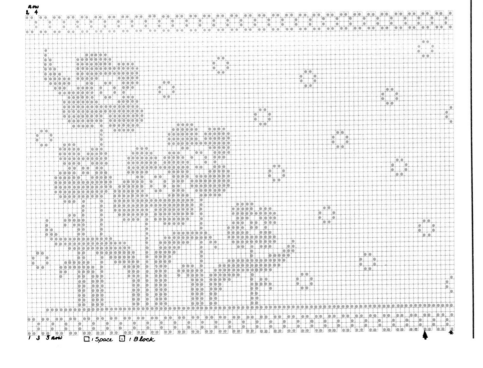

Pattern Library: Filet patterns

Cupid's bow (1)
Worked over a basic net of 1dc and 1ch with 1dc worked into each 1ch sp to form blocks.

1st motif row Ch 4, 1dc into next dc, (Ch 1, 1dc into next dc) 29 times, 1dc into 1ch sp, 1dc into next dc, (ch 1, 1dc into next dc) to end of row, working last dc into 3rd of 4 turning ch. Following chart, work rem 32 rows of motif.

Heart
Worked over a basic net of 1dc and 1ch with 1dc worked into each 1ch sp to form blocks.

1st motif row Ch 4, 1dc into next dc, (ch 1, 1dc into next dc) 4 times, 1dc into next 1ch sp, 1dc into next dc, (ch 1, 1dc into next dc) to end of row working last dc into 3rd of 4 turning ch.
Following chart work rem 9 rows of motif.

1

2

Swans (2)
Worked over a basic net of 1dc and 1ch with 1dc worked into each 1ch sp to form blocks.

1st motif row Ch 4, 1dc into next dc, (ch 1, 1dc into next dc) 4 times, (1dc into 1ch sp, 1dc into next dc) 17 times, (ch 1, 1dc into next dc) to end of row working last dc into 3rd of 4 turning ch.
Following chart, work rem 28 rows of motif.

Small swan
Worked over a basic net of 1dc and 1ch with 1dc worked into each 1ch sp to form blocks.

1st motif row Ch 4, 1dc into next dc, (ch 1, 1dc into next dc) 3 times, 1dc into 1ch sp, (1dc into next dc) 9 times, (ch 1, 1dc into next dc) to end of row, working last dc into 3rd of 4 turning ch.
Following chart work rem 12 rows of motif.

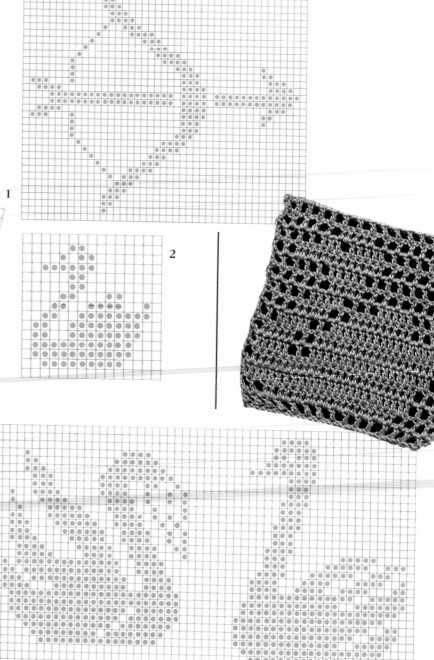

Large butterfly (3)

Worked over a basic net of 1dc and 2ch with 2dc worked into each 2ch sp to form blocks.

1st motif row Ch 5, 1dc into next dc, (ch 2, 1dc into next dc) 14 times, (2dc into next 2ch sp, 1dc into next dc) 4 times, (ch 2, 1dc into next dc) to end of row, working last dc into 3rd of first 5 turning ch.

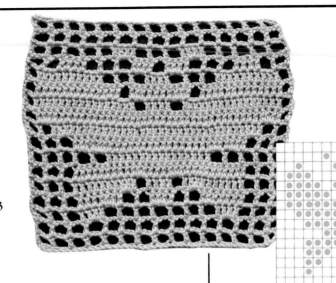

3

Small butterfly

Worked over a basic net of 1dc and 2ch with 2dc worked into each 2ch sp to form blocks.

1st motif row Ch 5 to count as first dc and 2ch sp, 1dc into next dc, (ch 2, 1dc into next dc) 3 times, 2dc into next 2ch sp, 1dc into next dc, (ch 2, 1dc into next dc) 7 times, 2dc into 2ch sp, 1dc into next dc, (ch 2, 1dc into next dc) 3 times, working last dc into 3rd of first 5 turning ch.

Following chart work rem 12 rows of motif.

Birds (4)

Worked over a basic net of 1dc and 1ch with 1dc worked into each 1ch sp to form blocks.

1st motif row Ch 4, 1dc into next dc, ch 1, 1dc into next dc, 1dc into 1ch sp, 1dc into next dc, (ch 1, 1dc into next dc) to end of row, working last dc into 3rd of 4 turning ch.

Following chart, work rem 38 rows of motif.

Flying bird

Worked over a basic net of 1dc and 1ch with 1dc worked into each 1ch sp to form blocks.

1st motif row Ch 4, 1dc into next dc, (ch 1, 1dc into next dc) 13 times, 1dc into next 1ch sp, 1dc into next dc, (ch 1, 1dc into next dc) 14 times, working last dc into 3rd of 4 turning ch.

Following chart, work rem 10 rows of motif.

4

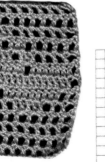

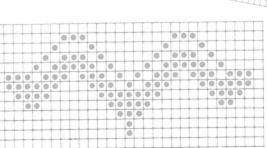

111

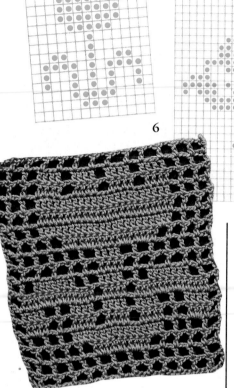

6

Treble clef and musical notes (5)

Worked over a basic net of 1dc and 1ch with 1dc worked into each 1ch sp to form blocks.

1st motif row Ch 4, 1dc into next dc, (ch 1, 1dc into next dc) 37 times, (1dc into 1ch sp, 1dc into next dc) 7 times, (ch 1, 1dc into next dc) to end of row, working last dc into 3rd of 4 turning ch.
Following chart, work rem 35 rows of motif.

Musical note

Worked over a basic net of 1dc and 1ch with 1dc worked into each 1ch sp to form blocks.

1st motif row Ch 4, 1dc into next dc, (ch 1, 1dc into next dc) 5 times, (1dc into 1ch sp, 1dc into next dc) 4 times, (ch 1, 1dc into dc) to end of row, working last dc into 3rd of 4 turning ch.
Following chart, work rem 11 rows of motif.

Tulip (6)

Worked over a basic net of 1dc and 2ch with 2dc worked into each 2ch sp to form blocks.

1st motif row Ch 5, 1dc into next dc, (ch 2, 1dc into next dc) 11 times, (2dc into 2ch sp, 1dc into next dc) 4 times, (ch 2, 1dc into next dc) 3 times, (2dc into 2ch sp, 1dc into next dc) twice, (ch 2, 1dc into next dc) to end of row, working last dc into 3rd of 5 turning ch.
Following chart, work rem 29 rows of motif.

Small tulip

Worked over a basic net of 1dc and 2ch with 2dc worked into each 2ch sp to form blocks.

1st motif row Ch 5, 1dc into next dc, (ch 2, 1dc into next dc) 4 times, (2dc into next 2ch sp, 1dc into next dc) 3 times, (ch 2, 1dc into next dc) to end of row, working last dc into 3rd of 5 turning ch.
Following chart, work rem 13 rows of motif.

5

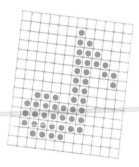

Irish crochet

Elaborate Irish crochet fabrics, formed from a rich combination of flowers, leaves, shamrocks and picot mesh, all worked in fine cotton, are among the most beautiful of crochet laces. Use the technique to make this charming blouse for a little girl and a pretty bolero.

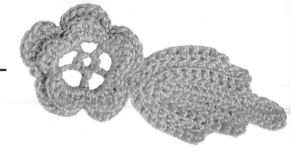

The basic Irish crochet patterns

Child's blouse
Sizes
C-4 [C-5:C-6]
Length 13¾[15:16] in
Sleeve seam 3½in
Note *Instructions for larger sizes are given in brackets [ ]; where there is only one set of figures it applies to all sizes.*

Materials
485[485:610] yd of a size 5 crochet cotton
Size B crochet hook
1 small button

Gauge
8 loops and 17 rows to 4in in mesh pat worked on size B hook

To save time, take time to check gauge.

Back
Make 79 [82:85] ch.
Base row 1sc into 7th ch from hook, * Ch 4, skip next 2ch, 1sc into next ch, rep from * to end. Turn. 25[26:27] 4ch loops.
Pattern row Ch 6, * 1sc into next 4ch loop, Ch 4, rep from * to last loop, 1sc into last loop. Turn.
Rep pat row until work measures 8¼[9:10] in.

Shape armholes
Next row Sl st across first 4ch loop and to center of next loop, 1sc into center of same loop, work 22 [23:24] loops. Turn.
Rep last row once more, working 20 [21:22] loops. Turn. * *
Next row Sl st across first 4ch loop and to center of next loop, 1sc into center of same loop, work 19 [20:21] loops. Turn.
Work even until work measures 13[14:15¼] in.

Shape shoulders
Next row Sl st across first 2 4ch loops and to center of next loop, 1sc into same loop, work 14 [15:16] loops. Turn.
Rep last row once more, working 10 [11:12] loops. Turn.
Next row Sl st across first 4ch loop and to center of next loop, 1sc into center of same loop, work 8[9:10] loops. Turn.
Next row Sl st to center of first 4ch loop, 1sc into same loop, work 7 [8:9] loops. Fasten off.

Front
Work as for back to * *

Divide for neck
Next row Sl st across first 4ch loop and to center of next loop, 1sc into center of same loop, work 9 [10:10] loops, turn.
Work even on these loops only until work measures 12 [12½:13¾] in ending at neck edge.

Shape neck
Next row Sl st across next 2 4ch loops, 1sc into next sc, ch 6, 1sc into first 4ch loop, pat to end. Turn. 7 [8:8] loops.
Pat 1 row without shaping.
Next row Sl st to center of first 4ch loop, 1sc into same loop, pat to end. Turn. 6 [7:7] loops.
Pat 1 row without shaping.
Rep last shaping row once more.
5 [6:6] loops.

Shape shoulder
Next row Sl st across first 2 4ch loops and to center of next loop, 1sc into same loop, pat to end. Turn. 2 [3:3] loops.
Next row Ch 6, 1sc into first loop, ch 4, 1sc into next loop.
Fasten off.
Rejoin yarn to next 4ch loop at beg of neck division and work 2nd side of neck to correspond with first, reversing all shaping.

SPECIAL TECHNIQUE
working raised motifs

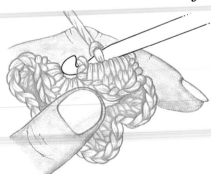
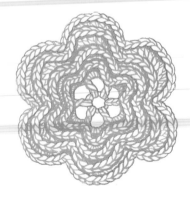

1 The outer petals of the flowers on the blouse and bolero on page 113 are worked behind the previous rounds to give a three-dimensional appearance. Work the first two rounds as instructed in the pattern to form a small flower.

2 Holding the work as shown and inserting the hook from back to front, work one single crochet around the stem of the next double on the first round. Work five chains. Continue in this way, ending with a slip stitch to the first single crochet. On the next round work in the chain loops to form the petals.

3 To form a many-layered motif like the rose on the bolero, repeat step 2, working the single crochet around the corresponding single crochet on the next-to-last round. The petals are made larger by working more chains and then more graduated stitches (see page 41) on the following round.

Sleeves (both alike)
Make 52 [55:58] ch.
Base row As for back. 16 [17:18] loops.
Cont in pat as for back until work measures 3½in.

Shape top
Next row Sl st across first 4ch loop and to center of next loop, 1sc into same loop, pat across 13 [14:15] loops. Turn.
Next row Sl st to center of first 4ch loop, 1sc into same loop, pat across 12 [13:14] loops. Turn. Pat 2 rows without shaping.
Next row Sl st to center of first 4ch loop, 1sc into same loop, pat across 11 [12:13] loops. Turn.
Next row Sl st to center of first 4ch loop, 1sc into same loop, pat across 10 [11:12] loops. Turn.
Rep last 4 rows, work one loop less on each dec row until 8 [9:10] loops rem. Rep last 2 rows only until 4 [5:6] loops rem.
Fasten off.

To finish
Join shoulder seams. Set in sleeves. Join side and sleeve seams, using an invisible seam.

Lower edging
With RS facing, join yarn to a side seam, ch 1, * 2sc into first loop, ch 3, sl st to first of 3ch – picot formed –, 3sc into next loop, picot, rep from * all around lower edge, ending with sl st to first ch. Fasten off.

Neck edging
With RS facing, join yarn to a shoulder seam and work as for lower edging.

Sleeve edgings
With RS facing, join yarn to sleeve seam and work as for lower edging.

Rosebud
Make 6ch, join with a sl st to form a ring.
1st round Ch 6, (1dc, ch 3) 5 times into ring, sl st into 3rd of 6 ch.
2nd round (1sc, 1hdc, 3dc, 1hdc, 1sc) into each 3ch loop.
3rd round Working behind last round, 1sc round first dc on first round, * ch 5, 1sc around next dc on first round, rep from * ending with sl st into first sc.
4th round (1sc, 1hdc, 5dc, 1hdc, 1sc) into each 5ch loop, sl st to first sc. Fasten off. Work 3 more rosebuds in same way.

Leaf
Make 16ch.
Base row 1sc into 3rd ch from hook, 1sc into each ch to last ch, 3sc into last ch, 1sc into each ch along opposite side of foundation ch, 1sc into turning ch.
On following rows work into *back* loop only of each st:
1st row 1sc into each of next 11sc. Turn.
2nd row Ch 1, skip first st, 1sc into each of next 10sc, (1sc, ch 1, 1sc) into center sc, 1sc into each sc to within 4sc of tip of leaf, turn.
3rd row Ch 1, skip first sc, 1sc into each sc to 1ch at base of leaf, (1sc, ch 1, 1sc) into 1ch sp, 1sc into each sc to within 3sc of previous row.
4th and 5th rows As 3rd.
6th row As 3rd, working 3sc into 1ch sp at base of leaf.
Fasten off. Work 5 more leaves in the same way.

To finish
Sew motifs around neck as shown in the photograph. Sew button to left-hand edge of neck opening. Work 6ch. Fasten off. Sew ch to neck opposite button to form loop.

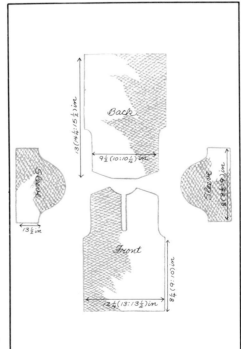

Traditional Irish bolero
Note: *Before beginning, see Know-How, page 154. Because of the method of working, it is not possible to give exact yarn quantity, size and gauge.*

Materials
A size 5 crochet cotton as required (bolero shown was made from about 970yd)
Size B crochet hook
Paper dressmaking pattern for simple bolero
Medium-weight interfacing – amount as specified for main fabric on pattern

Rose
Make 8ch, join with a sl st to form a ring.
1st round Ch 6, (1dc, ch 3) 7 times into ring, sl st to 3rd of 6ch.
2nd round (1sc, 1hdc, 3dc, 1hdc, 1sc) into each 3ch loop.
3rd round Working behind last round, 1sc around first dc on first round, (ch 5, 1sc around next dc) 7 times, ch 5, sl st to first sc.
4th round (1sc, 1hdc, 5dc, 1hdc, 1sc) into each 5ch loop.
5th round Working behind last round, 1sc around first sc of 3rd round, (ch 7, 1sc around next sc) 7 times, ch 7, sl st to first sc.
6th round (1sc, 1hdc, 7dc, 1hdc, 1sc) into each 7ch loop.
7th round Working behind last round, 1sc around first sc of 5th round, (ch 9, 1sc around next sc) 7 times, ch 9, sl st to first sc.
8th round (1sc, 1hdc, 9dc, 1hdc, 1sc) into each 9ch loop, sl st to first sc. Fasten off. Make one more rose in the same way.

Rosebud
Work as for child's blouse. Make 21.

Leaf
Work as for child's blouse. Make 22.

To finish
Cut out back and fronts of bolero from interfacing, omitting seam allowances around neck, armholes and front and lower edges. Join side seams.

Baste motifs in place on interfacing as shown.

Join yarn to first motif and work picot mesh as follows:

Base row * Ch 2, 1 picot (ch 3, sl st into first of 3ch), ch 3, 1 picot, ch 2, sl st into next motif or same motif, rep from * to end. Turn.

Pattern row Ch 2 or sl st along a motif as necessary, * 1 picot, ch 3, rep from * to end.

Cont filling in between motifs, working straight rows of picot mesh across back. When all motifs are joined and interfacing covered with picot mesh, remove all basting. Join shoulder seams.

Edging
Working over a cord of 3 strands of thread, * (3sc, 1 picot) into each ch loop all around neck, front and lower edges and around armholes.

Adapting the basic Irish patterns

Use the rich motifs and meshes of Irish crochet to work either modern or traditional lace.

Adapting the blouse
The child's blouse is adapted simply by substituting motifs from among those given here for those given in the basic pattern. You could sew smaller motifs around the neckline as shown on page 113, or arrange larger motifs over the bodice. Use matching sewing thread to sew the motifs invisibly to the mesh. If you do not want to substitute motifs, vary the blouse by working the motifs in the pattern in contrasting colors.

Adapting the bolero
The basic bolero could be worked using any of the motifs or meshes given here, though a picot mesh is traditional. The bolero shown has motifs around the front and edges only, but using motifs all over the bolero would create a beautifully ornate fabric.

Pattern Library: Irish crochet patterns

Fancy clover (1)
Make 7ch, join with a sl st to form a ring.
1st round Ch 1, 15sc into ring, sl st to first sc.
2nd round *Ch 4, skip next sc, (1dc, ch 2, 1dc) into next sc, ch 4, skip next sc, sl st into each of next 2sc, rep from *, ending with sl st into last sc.
3rd round * (3sc, ch4, 3sc) into next 4ch loop, (2sc, ch 4, 2sc) into next 2ch loop, (3sc, ch 4, 3sc) into next 4ch loop, sl st between 2sl st of 2nd round, rep from * to end.
Stem Ch 16, 1sc into 2nd ch from hook, 1sc into each ch to end, sl st to base of clover. Fasten off.

Bluebell (2)
Make 10ch. From now on, work over a cord.
Base row 1sc into 2nd ch from hook, 1sc into each of next 7ch, 5sc into into last ch, 1sc into each of next 8ch along opposite side of foundation, 3sc over cord only, 1sc into each of next 7sc, 3sc over cord only. Turn. From now on work into back loop only of each st.
1st row Ch 1, skip first sc, 1sc into each of next 10sc, 3sc into end sc, 1 sc into each of next 8sc, 3sc over cord only. Turn.
2nd row Ch 1, skip first sc, 1sc into each of next 13sc, work 20sc over cord for stem. Fasten off.

Honeycomb mesh (3)
Make a multiple 4ch plus 10.
Base row 1dc into 10th ch from hook, * ch 4, skip next 3ch, 1dc into next ch, rep from * to end. Turn.
Pattern row Ch 8, 1dc into first 4ch loop, *ch 4, 1dc into next 4ch loop, rep from * to end. Turn.
Rep pat row for desired length.

Triple leaf (4)
Make 15ch. From now on work each st over a cord.
1st row 1sc into 2nd ch from hook, 1sc into each of next 12ch, 5sc into last ch, 1sc into each ch along opposite side of foundation ch, work 3sc over cord only, working into back loop of each st, work 1sc into each of next 11sc. Turn.
From now on work into back loop only of each st.
2nd row Ch 1, skip first sc, 1sc into each of next 11sc, 3sc into center of 3sc of previous row, 1sc into each of next 12sc. Turn.
3rd row Ch 1, skip first st, 1sc into each of next 12sc, 3sc into center sc of 3sc of previous row, 1sc into each of next 10sc. Turn.
4th row Ch 1, skip first st, 1sc into each of next 10sc, 3sc into center sc of 3sc of previous row, 1sc into each of next 11sc. Turn.
5th row Ch 1, skip first st, 1sc into each of next 11sc, 3sc into center sc of 3sc of previous row, 1sc into each of next 9sc. Turn.
6th row Ch 1, skip first st, 1sc into each of next 9sc, 3sc into center sc of 3sc of previous row, 1sc into each of next 9sc. Fasten off.
Make 2 more leaves in the same way and sew them together as shown.

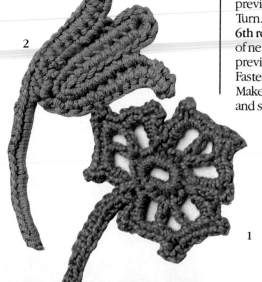

2

1

Picot flower (5)

Make 8ch, join with a sl st to form a ring.
1st round Ch 1, 20sc into ring, sl st to first ch.
2nd round 1sc into same place as sl st * Ch 10, skip 3sc, 1sc into next sc, rep from *, ending with sl st into first sc.
3rd round (Ch 1, 1hdc, 2dc, 1 picot – Ch 3, sl st into first of 3ch – 3tr, 1 picot, 3tr, 1 picot, 2dc, 1hdc, 1sc) into each 10ch loop, sl st to first ch. Fasten off.

Wheel (6)

Make 6ch, join with a sl st to form a ring.
1st round Ch 1, 12sc into ring, sl st to first sc.
2nd round Ch 4, (1dc, ch 1) into each sc, sl st to 3rd of 4ch.
3rd round Ch 1, 3sc into each 1ch sp, sl st to first sc.
4th round * Ch 4, sl st to first ch to form a picot, 1sc into each of next 3sc, rep from * to end, sl st to base of first picot. Fasten off.

Four-leaf clover (7)

Stem Working over a triple cord, work 24sc.
Flower center Work 21sc over cord, join with a sl st to first of these 21sc. Pull the cord to form a ring.
Petal Leave the cord and work into the sc of the ring thus:
1st row (Ch 1, 1sc into next st 4 times. Turn.
2nd row Ch 1, 1sc into first sc, (ch 1, 1sc under next 1ch of first row) 4 times, ch 1, 1sc into same place as last sc. Turn.
3rd row (Ch 1, 1sc under 1ch) 6 times, ch 1, 1sc into same place as last sc. Turn. Work 2 more rows without shaping, then one more row, skipping one st at each end. Fasten off. Work 3 more petals in the same way, skipping 1sc of ring between 2 petals.
From now on work over cord:
Edging Work a row of sc all around outer edges of petals, working (1sc into same place at last st at beg of petal, 1sc into skipped sc on circle, 1sc into same place as first st of next petal) between 2 petals. At end of last petal cont working sc into sts of stem. Fasten off.

Ornate medallions

Whether worked in knitting yarn or crochet cotton, these unusual crochet squares can be used to make beautifully textured fabrics. You can use the medallions to make an entire fabric, as in this beautiful bedspread, or you can combine them with simpler squares for variety.

The basic crochet bedspread

Sizes
Twin bed size measures 71 x 94in.
Double bed size measures 85 x 94in.

Materials
Twin bed size: 68oz of a sport yarn
Double bed size: 75oz of a sport yarn
Size C crochet hook

Gauge
Motif measures approx 13½in square

To save time, take time to check gauge.

Square
Make 8ch. Join with a sl st to form a ring.
1st round Ch 3, 1dc into ring, *(ch 3, 2dc into ring), rep from * 6 more times, ch 3. Join with a sl st to top of first 3ch. 8 2dc groups.
2nd round Sl st to center of next 3ch loop, 1sc into same place as sl st, *(ch 4, 1sc) into next 3ch loop, rep from * 6 more times, ch 4. Join with a sl st to first sc.
3rd round Into each 4ch loop work (1sc, 1hdc, 5dc, 1hdc, 1sc).
4th round *Ch 6, inserting hook from back of work, work 1sc around next sc of 2nd round, rep from * to end.
5th round Into each 6ch loop work (1sc, 1hdc, 7dc, 1hdc, 1sc).
6th round As 4th, working 8ch instead of 6ch.
7th round As 5th, working 9dc instead of 7dc.
8th round As 4th, working 10ch instead of 6ch.
9th round Ch 9, 1dtr into st at base of 9ch, *(ch 1, 1dc into 10ch loop) 3 times into same loop, (ch 1, 1dc into 10ch loop) 3 times into next loop, ch 1, (1dtr, ch 3, 1dtr) into sc between next 2 loops, rep from * to end omitting (1dtr, ch 3, 1dtr) at end of last rep. Join with a sl st to 6th of first 9ch.
10th round Sl st into first 3ch loop, ch 3, (1dc, ch 3, 2dc) into same loop, *1dc into dtr, (1dc into next 1ch sp, 1dc into next dc) 6 times, 1dc into next 1ch sp, 1dc into next dtr, (2dc, ch 3, 2dc) into 3ch sp, rep from * to end omitting (2dc, ch 3, 2dc) at end of last rep. Join with a sl st to top of first 3ch.
11th round Ch 3, *1dc into next dc, (2dc, ch 3, 2dc) into next 3ch sp, 1dc into each of next 18dc, rep from * to end omitting 1dc at end of last rep. Join with a sl st to top of first 3ch.
12th round Ch 3, *1dc into each of next 3dc, (2dc, ch 3, 2dc) into next 3ch sp, 1dc into each of next 20dc, rep from * to end omitting 1dc at end of

---

SPECIAL TECHNIQUE
making a popcorn

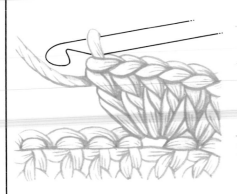
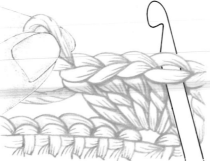
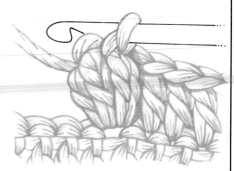

1 With right side of work facing, crochet in pattern to the point where popcorn stitch is to be made. Work five doubles into the next stitch.

2 Withdraw the hook from the working loop and insert it from front to back through the top of the first of the five doubles just made, while holding the working loop with the left hand.

3 Keeping the hook in place, re-insert it into working loop and draw this loop through the first double of the five-double group to make the popcorn stitch. Make sure that the stitches are drawn together neatly to achieve a good shape.

last rep. Join with a sl st to top of first 3ch.

13th round Ch 4, *skip 1dc, 1dc into next dc, ch 1, skip next dc, 1dc into next dc, ch 1, skip next dc, (2dc, ch 3, 2dc) into next 3ch sp, (ch 1, skip next dc, 1dc into next dc) 11 times, ch 1, rep from * to end omitting 1dc and 1ch at end of last rep. Join with a sl st to 3rd of first 4ch.

14th round Sl st into next 1ch sp, ch 4, *(1dc into next sp, ch 1) twice, (2dc, ch 3, 2dc) into next 3ch sp, (ch 1, 1dc into next sp) 12 times, ch 1, rep from * to end omitting 1dc and ch 1 at end of last rep. Join with a sl st to 3rd of first 4ch.

15th round Ch 3, *(1dc into next sp, 1dc into next dc) 3 times, 1dc into next dc, (2dc, ch 3, 2dc) into next 3ch sp, 1dc into each of next 2dc, (1dc into next sp, 1dc into next dc) 12 times, rep from * to end omitting 1dc at end of last rep. Join with a sl st to top of first 3ch.

16th round Ch 3, *work 5dc into next dc, withdraw hook from working loop, insert hook through top of first of these 5dc then back into working loop and draw working loop through first of 5dc – called 1 popcorn – 1pc –, 1dc into each of next 3dc, 1pc into next dc, 1dc into each of next 4dc, (2dc, ch 3, 2dc) into 3ch sp, 1dc into each of next 4dc, (1pc into next dc, 1dc into each of next 3dc) 6 times, rep from * to end omitting 1dc at end of last rep. Join with a sl st to top of first 3ch.

17th round Ch 3, *(1dc into top of next pc, 1dc into each of next 3dc) twice, 1dc into each of next 3dc, (2dc, ch 3, 2dc) into next 3ch sp, 1dc into each of next 6dc, (1dc into top of next pc, 1dc into each of next 3dc) 6 times, rep from * to end omitting 1dc at end of last rep. Join with a sl st to top of first 3ch.

18th round Ch 4, *(skip 1dc, 1dc into next dc, ch 1) 6 times, (2dc, ch 3, 2dc) into 3ch sp, (ch 1, skip 1dc, 1dc into next dc) 16 times, ch 1, rep from * to end omitting 1dc and ch 1 at end of last rep. Join with a sl st to 3rd of first 4ch.

19th round Sl st into next sp, ch 4, *(1dc into next sp, ch 1) 6 times, (2dc, ch 3, 2dc) into next 3ch sp, ch 1, (1dc into next sp, ch 1) 17 times, rep

from * to end omitting 1dc and ch 1 at end of last rep. Join with a sl st to 3rd of first 4ch.

20th round Ch 3, *(1dc into next sp, 1dc into next dc) 7 times, 1dc into next dc, (2dc, ch 3, 2dc) into next 3ch sp, 1dc into next dc, (1dc into next dc, 1dc into next sp) 17 times, rep from * to end. Join with a sl st to top of first 3ch.

21st round Sl st to next dc, ch 3, *1dc into each of next 2dc, (1pc into next dc,

1dc into each of next 3dc), 3 times, 1dc into each of next 2dc, (2dc, ch 3, 2dc) into next 3ch sp, 1dc into each of next 5dc, (1pc into next dc, 1dc into each of next 3dc) 8 times, 1pc into next dc, 1dc into next dc, rep from * to end omitting 1dc at end of last rep. Join with a sl st to top of first 3ch.

22nd round Ch 3, *1dc into each of next 18 sts, (2dc, ch 3, 2dc) into next 3ch sp, 1dc into each of next 41 sts, rep from * to end omitting 1dc at end of last rep. Join with a sl st to top of first 3ch.

23rd round Sl st to next dc, ch 4, *(skip next dc, 1dc into next dc, ch 1) 9 times, (2dc, ch 3, 2dc) into next 3ch sp, ch 1, (skip next dc, 1dc into next dc, ch 1) 22 times, rep from * to end omitting 1dc and ch 1 at end of last rep. Join with a sl st to 3rd of first 4ch. Fasten off.
Make 35 squares in all for twin bed size and 42 squares in all for double bed size.

To finish
Block each square to correct size. Sew squares into strips of five by seven for twin bed size and six by seven for double bed size.

Fringe
Make a fringe along two sides and one end of bedspread: for each clump of fringe cut four pieces of yarn 8in long; knot these four strands into each 1ch sp along edge. Trim evenly as necessary.

Adapting the basic bedspread

Choose any of the medallions featured in the next two pages to make a beautiful bedspread.

Substituting motifs
Substituting one crochet square for another is quite simple: all you need do, if they differ in size, is to make fewer or more squares, depending on the size required for the completed fabric. To calculate the number of squares you will need, make a sample square using the hook and yarn of your choice, measure the size of the finished square and calculate the number needed for the bedspread from this measurement. In some cases the final round of a motif can be repeated, with additional stitches worked on each side of the motif until it is the desired size. If you choose one of these squares as an alternative to the bedspread medallion featured on page 119, you can use this method to make your motif exactly the same size, and so make the same number of squares as are used for the original bedspread.

Pattern Library: Ornate medallions

Diamond cluster motif (1)

Make 6ch. Join with a sl st to form a ring.
1st round Ch 3 to count as first dc, 2dc into ring, (ch 2, 3dc into ring) 3 times, ch 2. Join with a sl st to top of first 3ch. Four blocks of 3dc.
2nd round Ch 3, *leaving last loop of each st on hook, work 5tr into next dc, yo and draw through all loops on hook – called 5tr cluster –, 1dc into next dc, (2dc, ch 2, 2dc) into next 2ch sp, 1dc into next dc, rep from * to end omitting 1dc at end of last rep. Join with a sl st to top of first 3ch.
3rd round Ch 3, *1dc into top of cluster, 1dc into next dc, 5tr cluster into next dc, 1dc into next dc, (2dc, ch 2, 2dc) into next 2ch sp, 1dc into next dc, 5tr cluster into next dc, 1dc into next dc, rep from * to end omitting 1dc at end of last rep. Join with a sl st to top of first 3ch.
4th round Ch 3, *5tr cluster into next dc, 1dc into next dc, 1dc into top of next cluster, 1dc into next dc, 5tr cluster into next dc, 1dc into next dc, (2dc, ch 2, 2dc) into 2ch sp, 1dc into next dc, 5tr cluster into next dc, 1dc into next dc, 1dc into top of next cluster, 1dc into next dc, rep from * to end omitting 1dc at end of last rep. Join with a sl st to top of first 3ch.
5th round Ch 3, *1dc into top of next cluster, 1dc into next dc, 5tr cluster into next dc, 1dc into each of next 5 sts, (2dc, ch 2, 2dc) into next 2ch sp, 1dc into each of next 5 sts, 5tr cluster into next dc, 1dc into next dc, rep from * to end omitting 1dc at end of last rep. Join with a sl st to top of first 3ch.
6th round Ch 3, *5tr cluster into next dc, 1dc into each of next 9 sts, (2dc, ch 2, 2dc) into next 2ch sp, 1dc into each of next 9 sts, rep from * to end omitting 1dc at end of last rep. Join with a sl st to top of first 3ch.
7th round Ch 3, *1dc into each of next 12 sts, (2dc, ch 2, 2dc) into next 2ch sp, 1dc into each of next 11 sts, rep from * to end omitting 1dc at end of last rep. Join with a sl st to top of first 3ch. Fasten off.

Shells and popcorns (2)

Make 6ch. Join with a sl st to form a ring.
1st round Ch 3 to count as first dc, 1dc into ring, (ch 3, 3dc into ring) 3 times, ch 3, 1dc into ring. Join with a sl st to top of first 3ch. Four 3dc blocks.
2nd round Ch 3, *work 5dc into next st, withdraw hook from working loop and insert through top of first of 5dc, insert hook back into working loop and draw through first of 5dc – called 1pc –, 5dc into 3ch sp, 1pc into next dc, 1dc into next dc, rep from * to end omitting 1dc at end of last rep. Join with a sl st to top of 3rd of first 3ch.
3rd round Ch 5, *skip first pc, 1pc into next dc, 1dc into next dc, 3dc into next dc, 1dc into next dc, 1pc into next dc, ch 2, skip 1pc, 1dc into next dc, ch 2, rep from * to end omitting 1dc and 2ch at end of last rep. Join with a sl st to 3rd of first 5ch.
4th round Sl st into next 2ch sp, ch 5, *skip 1pc, 1pc into next dc, 1dc into next dc, 3dc into next dc, 1dc into next dc, 1pc into next dc, ch 2, skip next pc, 1dc into 2ch sp, ch 2, 1dc into next 2ch sp, ch 2, rep from * to end omitting 1dc and 2ch at end of last rep. Join with a sl st to 3rd of first 5ch.
5th round Sl st into next sp, ch 5, *skip 1pc, 1pc into next dc, 1dc into next dc, 3dc into next dc, 1dc into next dc, 1pc into next dc, ch 2, (1dc into next 2ch sp, ch 2) 3 times, rep from * to end omitting 1dc and 2ch at end of last rep. Join with a sl st to 3rd of first 5ch.
6th round Work as 5th, but working section in parentheses 4 times instead of 3.
7th round As 5th, but working section in parentheses 5 times instead of 3. Cont working in this way until motif is required size. Fasten off.

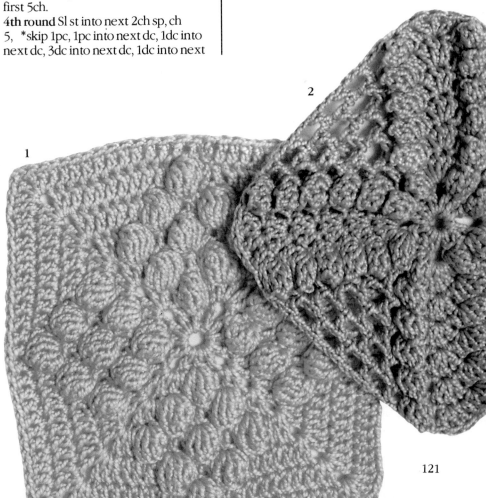

Openwork popcorn motif (3)

Make 8ch. Join with a sl st to form a ring.
1st round Ch 3, leaving last loop of each st on hook work 3tr into ring, yo and draw through all loops on hook – called 3tr cluster –, (ch 3, leaving last loop of each st on hook work 4tr into ring, yo and draw through all loops on hook – called 4tr cluster –, ch 5, 4tr cluster into ring) 3 times, ch 3, 4tr cluster into ring, ch 5. Join with a sl st to top of first cluster. 8 clusters.
2nd round Sl st to 2nd of 3ch, 1sc into same place, *9tr into next 5ch sp, 1sc into 3ch sp, rep from * to end omitting 1sc at end of last rep. Join with a sl st to first sc.
3rd round Ch 3, into st at base of 3ch work (5dc into next st, withdraw hook from working loop and insert into first of 5dc, then back into working loop and draw loop through first of 5dc – called 1pc –), *ch 2, skip 2tr, 1dc into next tr, ch 2, skip 1tr, (2dc, ch 3, 2dc) into next tr, ch 2, skip 1tr, 1dc into next tr, ch 2, 1pc into next sc, rep from * to end omitting 1pc at end of last rep. Join with a sl st to top of first pc.
4th round Ch 3, *(2dc into 2ch sp, 1dc into next dc) twice, 1dc into next dc, (2dc, ch 3, 2dc) into next 3ch sp, 1dc into next dc, (1dc into next dc, 2dc into 2ch sp) twice, 1dc into top of next pc, rep from * to end omitting 1dc at end of last rep. Join with a sl st to top of first 3ch.
5th round Ch 6, 1dc into st at base of 6ch, *skip 2dc, 1dc into each of next 3dc, 1pc into next dc, 1dc into each of next 3dc, (2dc, ch 3, 2dc) into 3ch sp, 1dc into each of next 3dc, 1dc into next dc, 1dc into each of next 3dc, skip 2dc, (1dc, ch 3, 1dc) into next dc, rep from * to end omitting (1dc, ch 3, 1dc) at end of last rep. Join with a sl st to 3rd of first 6ch.
6th round Sl st to 2nd of first 3ch, ch 4, *skip next dc, 1dc into next dc, (ch 1, skip next st, 1dc into next st) 4 times, (2dc, ch 3, 2dc) into 3ch sp, 1dc into next dc, (ch 1, skip next st, 1dc into next st) 4 times, ch 1, 1dc into 2nd of 3ch, ch 1, rep from * to end omitting 1dc and

3

1ch at end of last rep. Join with a sl st to 3rd of first 4ch.
Fasten off.

Embossed motif (4)

Make 6ch. Join with a sl st to form a ring.
1st round Ch 3 to count as first dc, work 15dc into ring. Join with a sl st to top of first 3ch. 16dc.
2nd round Ch 4, (5dc into next dc, ch 1, 1dc into next dc, ch 1) 7 times, 5dc into next dc, ch 1. Join with a sl st to 3rd of first 4ch.
3rd round Ch 4, 1dc into same place as sl st, ch 1, (2dc into each of next 5dc, ch 1, 1dc into next dc, ch 1, 1dc into same place as last dc, ch 1) 7 times, 2dc into each of next 5dc, ch 1. Join with a sl st to 3rd of first 4ch.
4th round Ch 3, 1dc into same place as sl st, ch 1, 2dc into next dc, ch 1, (work 2dc tog 5 times over next 10dc, ch 1, 2dc into next dc, ch 1, 2dc into next dc, ch 1) 7 times, work 2dc tog 5 times over next 10dc, ch 1. Sl st to top of first 3ch.
5th round Ch 4, (1dc into next dc, ch 1) 3 times, *work next 5dc tog, ch 1, (1dc into next dc, ch 1) 4 times, rep from * all around ending with dc worked tog over next 5dc, ch 1. Sl st to 3rd of first 4ch.
6th round Ch 4, *1dc into next dc, ch 1, (2tr, ch 3, 2tr) into next 1ch sp, (ch 1,

1dc into next dc) twice, ch 1, 1hdc into top of next cluster, (ch 1, 1sc into next dc) 4 times, ch 1, 1hdc into top of next cluster, ch 1, 1dc into next dc, ch 1, rep from * to end omitting 1dc and 1ch at end of last rep. Join with a sl st to 3rd of first 4ch.
7th round Ch 3, *1dc into 1ch sp, 1dc into next dc, 1dc into 1ch sp, 1dc into each of next 2tr, (2dc, ch 2, 2dc) into 3ch sp, 1dc into each of next 2tr, (1dc into 1ch sp, 1dc into next dc) twice, 1dc into next 1ch sp, 1dc into next hdc, (1dc into next 1ch sp, 1dc into next sc) 4 times, 1dc into next sp, 1dc into next hdc, 1dc into next sp, 1dc into next dc, rep from * to end omitting 1dc at end of last rep. Join with a sl st to top of first 3ch.
8th round Ch 4, skip next dc, 1dc into next dc, (ch 1, skip next dc, 1dc into next dc) twice, *ch 1, skip next dc, (2dc, ch 2, 2dc) into 2ch sp, (ch 1, skip next dc, 1dc into next dc) 14 times, rep from * to end working (ch 1, skip next dc, 1dc into next dc) 10 times, ch 1 at end of last rep. Join with a sl st to 3rd of first 4ch. Fasten off.

4

122

Chapter 2
Crochet Plus

Crochet plus embroidery

Firm crochet fabrics, especially those worked in single crochet, are ideal backgrounds for embroidery. With a little practice, you will find it remarkably easy to beautify anything from a favorite sweater to a baby's layette like the one shown here.

The basic embroidered set

Size
Coat to fit size B-1
Length 10in
Sleeve seam 5½in
Blanket 30 x 25in

Materials
A knitting worsted yarn
Coat and hat 6oz in main color A
2oz in contrasting color B
Blanket 9oz in main color A
4oz in contrasting color B
Size G crochet hook
Small amounts of embroidery thread in green and two shades of pink

Gauge
18sc and 19 rows to 4in worked on size G hook

To save time, take time to check gauge.

Coat Back
Using A, make 43ch.
Base row (RS) 1sc into 2nd ch from hook, 1sc into each sc to end. Turn. 42sc.
Pattern row Ch 1, skip first sc, 1sc into each sc to end. Turn.
Work even in pat on these 42sc until work measures 9½in. Fasten off.

Edging
With RS facing, skip the turning ch, and join B to first sc at beg of last row worked, ch 1, 1sc into each sc to end of row, *ch 1 to form corner, skip first row end of side edge, 1sc into each row end to next corner, ch 1 to form corner *, 1sc into each ch on lower edge, rep from * to * once more, 1sc into turning ch at beg of last row working in A. Fasten off.

Fronts (alike)
Using A, make 22ch.
Base row (RS) 1sc into 2nd ch from hook, 1sc into each ch to end. Turn. 21sc.
Cont in pat as for back on these 21sc until work measures 9½in. Fasten off.

Edging
Work as for back.

Sleeves (alike)
Using A, make 33ch.
Base row (RS) 1sc into 2nd ch from hook, 1sc into each ch to end. Turn. 32sc.
Cont in pat as for back on these 32sc until work measures 5in. Fasten off.

SPECIAL TECHNIQUE
crochet seaming

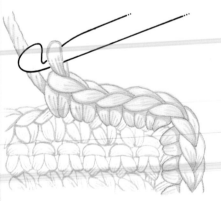

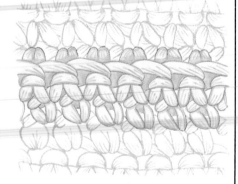

1 First edge the garment pieces with one row of single crochet, working one stitch into each row end at the side edges and into each stitch at the upper and lower edges. Turn corners either by working one chain at each corner, as on the baby's outfit shown here, or by working three single crochets into each of the corner stitches.

2 To join in the pieces, place the edged pieces together with wrong sides facing. Using the same yarn as that used for the edging, join the yarn to the end of the seam. Work one chain and skip the first stitch on the edging. Insert the hook through both edgings under all four loops. Work one single crochet.

3 Continue in this way, joining the edgings by working one single crochet into each pair of stitches on the edging. Seaming a garment in this way produces a raised decorative seam, which looks particularly attractive when worked in a color contrasting with the main fabric.

Edging
Work as for back.

To finish
Using B, join pieces tog with WS facing; using sc, work through both loops of edging of each piece, as follows:

Left shoulder
With back behind left front, join B to 1ch at top corner, ch 1, skip first sc, 1sc into each of next 12sc.
Fasten off.

Right shoulder
With back behind right front, join B to 13th st from top corner, ch 1, skip first sc, 1sc into each of next 11sc, 1sc into 1ch at corner. Fasten off.

Left armhole
With sleeve behind front and back, join B to left side at 16th row and from outer edge of shoulder seam and to 1ch at top corner of sleeve; ch 1, skip first sc, 1sc into each of next 15sc, 1sc into 1ch at top corner of front, 1sc into 1ch at top corner of back, 1sc into each of next 15sc, 1sc into next sc on back and 1ch at top corner of sleeve. Fasten off.

Right armhole
With sleeve behind front and back, join B to back at 16th row end from outer edge of shoulder seam and to 1ch at top corner of sleeve; ch 1, skip first sc, 1sc into each of next 15sc, 1sc into 1ch at top corner of back, 1sc into 1ch at top corner of front, 1sc into each of next 15sc, 1sc into next sc on front and 1ch at top corner of sleeve. Fasten off.

Left side and sleeve seams
With back behind front, join B to 1ch at lower edge of left front and back, ch 1, skip first sc, 1sc into each sc to sleeve, 1sc into each sc on sleeve, ending with 1sc into 1ch at lower corners. Fasten off.

Right side and sleeve seams
With back behind front, join B to 1ch at lower edge of right sleeve, ch 1, 1sc into each sc to front, 1sc into each sc of front and back, ending with 1sc into 1ch at lower corners. Fasten off.

Ties (make 2)
Using B, work a length of ch 7in long. Fasten off.
Sew one end of each tie to front edge 3½in from top corner.
Fold back corners as shown and tack them neatly in place.

Hat
Sides (make 2)
Using A, make 27ch.
Base row (RS) 1sc into 2nd ch from hook, 1sc into each ch to end. 26sc.
Cont in pat as for coat on these 26sc

until work measures 5½in. Fasten off.

Edging
Work as for coat back.

To finish
With WS tog and working through both loops of the edge of each piece, join B to 1ch at top right-hand corners, ch 1, 1sc into each sc to corner, 2sc into 1ch at corner, 1sc into each sc at row ends of sides to corner. 1sc into 1ch at corner. Fasten off.

Ties (make 2)
Using B, work a length of ch 10in long. Fasten off.
Fold corners of hat to RS as shown and tack corners neatly in place.
Sew ties to hat.

Blanket

To make a square
Using A, make 22ch.
Base row (RS) 1sc into 2nd ch from hook, 1sc into each ch to end. Turn. 21sc.
Work pat row as for coat back on these 21sc 21 times.
Fasten off.
Make a total of 30 squares in the same way.

Edging
Work as for coat back.

To finish
Note: Squares are arranged so that blanket is 6 squares long by 5 squares wide. Place alternate squares tog horizontally and vertically, and using B overcast them tog neatly at the edges.

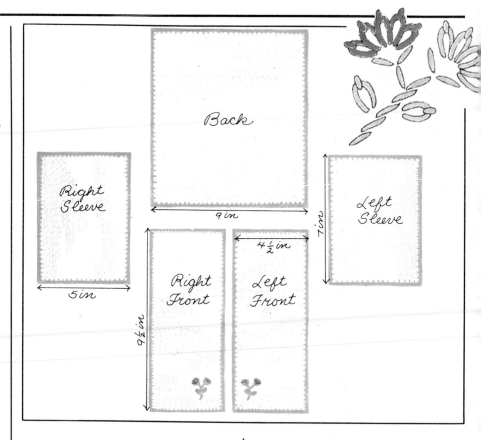

Edging
With RS facing, join B to 1ch at any corner, ch 1, 1sc into each sc to next corner of first square, 1sc into 1ch at corner, * 1sc into 1ch at corner of next square, 1sc into each sc to 1ch at next corner of same square, rep from * around edge of blanket, working 2sc into 1ch at corners of blanket and ending with 1sc into first corner of blanket, join with a sl st to first ch. Fasten off.

Embroidery
The motif above has been embroidered on the coat and blanket, with a slightly smaller version on the hat.
Position the motif at the center of alternate squares on the blanket, reversing the light and dark flowers on alternate rows. Reverse the motif for the left-hand corner of the coat and hat. Work the stem in stem stitch, the upper stem and sepals in straight stitch, the leaves and petals in lazy-daisy.

Adapting the baby's embroidered set

Any simple crochet fabric can be enhanced by adding embroidery.

Embroidery on single crochet
Most of the simpler embroidery stitches can be worked on a firm single crochet fabric in much the same way as when embroidering a woven fabric.
Easy designs can be worked freehand on the fabric, but more complicated motifs are best planned first on paper.

Draw the motif on graph paper so that each square on the paper represents one single crochet. Use different symbols or colors to represent the stitches. There is no need to confine yourself to a plain single crochet fabric as a background for embroidery. Introduce bobbles or holes into the fabric and then outline them with embroidery stitches. Or work a simple embroidery motif and then outline it with surface crochet.

Other variations
Embroidery on other crochet fabrics is less easy, since longer crochet stitches do not provide such a firm base. However, such fabrics can still be decorated – even by those unskilled in embroidery – for an "embroidered" look.
Surface slip stitch produces much the same effect as embroidered chain stitch, and embroidered braid or velvet ribbon can be woven through a double crochet or double mesh fabric to create an interesting effect.

Pattern Library: Embroidered patterns

Sampler (1)
Work alternate rows of double and single crochet. Embroider rows of stitches – here herringbone, threaded stitch and French knots – using contrasting yarns.

Poppies (2)
Thread narrow braid through single crochet and embroider "wheat-ears" on each side using lazy daisy stitch. Work poppies in cross stitch and backstitch, with centers in French knots.

Rainbow (3)
Use the colors of the rainbow to work chain stitch or surface slip stitch arcs onto a single crochet fabric.

Bobble flowers (4)
Work double crochet bobbles in a single crochet fabric. Work stems and leaves in lazy daisy stitch.

Crochet plus quilting

Firm crochet fabrics lend themselves particularly well to quilting with batting. The resulting thick fabric is ideal for winter jackets and coats, such as the vest, bomber jacket and coat shown here.

The basic quilted jackets and coat

Sizes
C-3-4 [C-5-6]
Length: Vest 14½[15¾]in
Bomber jacket: 15 [16] in
Coat
Sleeve seam 16½ [18] in
Bomber jacket 10½ [11½]in
Coat 10 [10¾]in

Note: *Instructions for the larger size are given in square brackets [ ]; where there is only one set of figures it applies to both sizes.*

Materials
A sport yarn
Vest 4oz in main color A and in each of 2 contrasting colors, B and C
Bomber jacket 15oz in main color A and 4oz in contrasting color B
Coat 18 [20]oz
Size E crochet hook
Pair of No. 3 knitting needles
For each garment ⅜ yd of 36in-wide medium-thick polyester batting
Bomber jacket only 16in open-ended zipper
Coat only 6 buttons

Gauge
21hdc and 16 rows to 4in worked on size E hook

To save time, take time to check gauge.

Vest
Body section
*Using A, make 124 [134] ch.
Base row 1hdc into 3rd ch from hook, 1hdc into each ch to end. Turn. 123 [133] sts.
Pattern row Ch 2 to count as first hdc, skip first st, 1hdc into each st to end. Turn.
Rep pat row 5 [6] more times, placing contrasting marker at 62nd [67th] st of first and last row.
Fasten off. * Rep from * to * once more.
Cut a strip of batting measuring ¼in less *all around* than the crochet strips.
Place batting between two strips of crochet so that top, lower edges and markers match.
Using matching yarn, overcast all edges of crochet tog, matching corresponding sts (see page 162) and so enclosing the batting.
Make two padded strips in B and one in C in the same way.

Back yoke
* Using A, make 56 [60] ch.
Work base row as for body section. 55[59] sts.
Work in pat as for body section, placing marker at 28th [29th] st of first and last row.*
Rep from * to * once more.
Sew in batting as for body section. Make one padded strip each in B and C in the same way.

Front yokes (alike)
* Using A, make 26 [28] ch.
Work base row as for body section. 25[27] sts.
Work in pat as for body section, omitting marker.*
Rep from * to * once more.
Sew in batting as for body section. Make one more padded strip in A and two in B in the same way.

Shape neck
* Using C, make 16 [18] ch.
Work base row as for body section. 15[17] sts.
Work in pat as for body section, omitting marker.*
Rep from * to * once more.

SPECIAL TECHNIQUE
working half-double bobbles

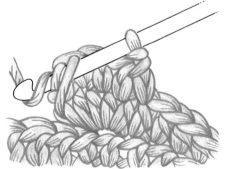

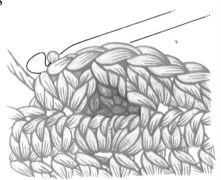

1 *Simple half-double bobbles are worked on alternate strips of the basic coat. With the right side facing, work to the position of the first bobble. Work five half doubles into the next stitch, turn and work one half double into each of the five half doubles.*

2 *Insert the hook into the fifth stitch of the five half doubles just worked. Wind the yarn over the hook and then draw through all loops on the hook to form a bobble.*

3 *The following row is a wrong side row. Work to the position of the bobble. Work one half double into the top of the bobble.*

Sew in batting as for body section. Make one more padded strip in C in the same way.

To finish

Matching corresponding sts (see Know How, page 162), overcast tog four padded strips of body section, making sure that the top of one strip is sewn to the lower edge of the next and so on. Sew tog strips of back and front yokes in the same way.
Join shoulder seams, matching corresponding sts.

Armhole borders (alike)

With RS facing, using knitting needles and C *double,* pick up and K 90 [96] sts across armhole edge.
Work in K1, P1 ribbing for 1in.
Cast off in ribbing.

Neckband

With RS facing, using knitting needles and C *double,* pick up and K 14 sts across right front neck edge, one st in corner, 11 sts up right front neck, one st in corner, 27 [31] sts across back neck, one st in corner, 11 sts down left front neck, one st in corner, 14 sts across left front neck. 81 [85] sts.
Next row (WS) Beg with P1, work in K1, P1 ribbing to end.
Next row Work in K1, P1 ribbing, ending with a K1.
Next row Rib 12, P2 tog, K1, P2 tog, rib 7, P2 tog, K1, P2 tog, rib 23 [27], P2 tog, K1, P2 tog, rib 7, P2 tog, K1, P2 tog, rib 12. 73 [77] sts.
Rib 2 rows.
Next row Rib 11, K2 tog, P1, K2 tog, rib 5, K2 tog, P1, K2 tog, rib 21 [25], K2 tog, P1, K2 tog, rib 5, K2 tog, P1, K2 tog, rib 11. 65 [69] sts.
Rib 1 row.
Bind off in ribbing.

Waistband

With RS facing, using knitting needles and A, pick up and K 123 [133] sts across lower edge of body section.
Work in K1, P1 ribbing for 2in. Bind off in ribbing.

Front bands (alike)

Join top edge of body section to lower edges of yokes, matching corresponding sts and markers. Sew row ends of armhole borders to skipped sts on top of body section.
With RS facing, using crochet hook and A, work 3 rows of sc across front edge. Fasten off.
Using C, work 3 rows of sc across neckband. Fasten off.

Bomber jacket

Body section

Work three padded strips in A and one in B as for Vest body section.

Back and front yokes

Work all strips in A as for Vest yokes.

Sleeves (both alike)

* Using A, make 64 [68] ch.
Work base row as for Vest body section. 63 [67] sts.
Work in pat as for Vest body section, placing marker at 32nd [34th] st of first and last rows.*
Sew in batting as for Vest body section. Make three more padded strips in A and one in B.

To finish

Matching corresponding sts, overcast tog four padded strips of body section as on page 162, making sure that the top of one strip is sewn to the lower edge of the next and so on.
Overcast tog strips of back and front yokes in the same way.
Overcast tog strips of sleeves, as on page 162, in the same way.

Cuffs (alike)

With RS facing, using knitting needles

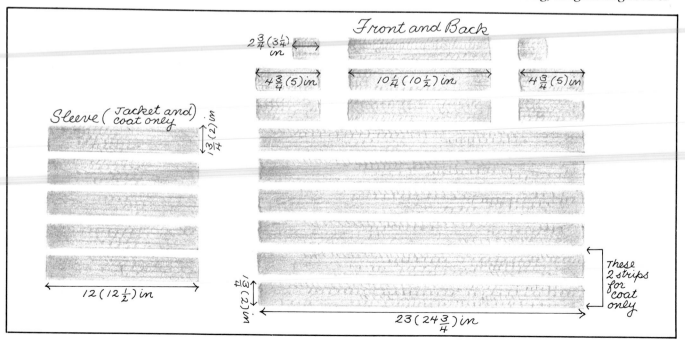

Front and Back

$2\frac{3}{4}(3\frac{1}{4})$ in

$4\frac{3}{4}(5)$ in $10\frac{1}{4}(10\frac{1}{2})$ in $4\frac{3}{4}(5)$ in

Sleeve (*Jacket and coat only*)

$1\frac{3}{4}(2)$ in

$12(12\frac{1}{2})$ in

$1\frac{3}{4}(2)$ in

These 2 strips for coat only

$23(24\frac{3}{4})$ in

and A, pick up and K63 [67] sts across lower edges of sleeve.

Work in K1, P1 ribbing for 2in. Bind off in ribbing.

Join sleeve seams, leaving 5 [6] row ends at top of sleeve unseamed.

Fold cuff to WS. Using matching yarn and herringbone st, sew bound-off edge to edge of padded strips to form double cuff.

Neckband

With RS facing, using knitting needles and A, pick up and K 81 [85] sts as for Vest neckband.

Work in K1, P1 ribbing for 2in. Bind off in ribbing.

Make double neckband as for cuffs.

Waistband

With RS facing, using knitting needles and A, pick up and K 123 [133] sts across lower edge of body section.

Work in K1, P1 ribbing for 5in. Bind off in ribbing.

Make double waistband as for cuffs.

Front bands (alike)

Sew top edge of body section to lower edges of yokes.

With RS facing, using crochet hook and A, work 3 rows of sc evenly across front edge, working into both thicknesses of waistband and neckband. Sew zipper neatly to front bands.

Coat

Body section

Work as for Vest body section from * to * 9 times.

Bobble strips Work as for plain strips, but work bobbles on 4th [5th] row as follows:

Bobble row Ch 2 to count as first hdc, skip first hdc, 1hdc into each of next 5hdc, *5hdc into next hdc, turn, 1hdc into each of 5hdc just worked, turn, insert hook into first of last 5hdc, yo and draw through all loops on hook – bobble formed –, 1hdc into each of next 9 [10] hdc, rep from * to last 7 [6] sts, bobble, 1hdc into each of last 6 [5] sts. Turn.

Make two more bobble strips.

Make three plain padded strips and three padded strips with a bobble strip on RS.

Back yoke

Work as for Vest back yoke from * to * 5 times.

Bobble strips Work as for plain strips, but work bobbles on 4th [5th] row as follows:

Bobble row Ch 2 to count as first hdc, skip first st, 1hdc into next hdc, * bobble, 1hdc into each of next 9hdc, rep from * to last 3[2] sts, bobble, 1hdc into each of last 2 [1] sts. Turn. Make two plain strips and one padded strip with bobble strip on RS.

Right front yoke

Work as for Vest front yokes from * to * 3 times.

Bobble strip Work as for plain strip, but work bobbles on 4th [5th] row as follows:

Bobble row Ch 2 to count as first hdc, skip first st, 1hdc into each of next 5hdc, bobble, 1hdc into each of next 9[10] hdc, bobble, 1hdc into each of next 8[9] sts. Turn.

Make one plain padded strip and one padded strip with a bobble strip on the RS.

Left front yoke

Work as for Vest front yoke from * to * 3 times.

Bobble strip Work as for plain strip, but work bobbles on 4th [5th] row as follows:

Bobble row Ch 2 to count as first hdc, skip first st, 1hdc into each of next 7 [8] sts, bobble, 1hdc into each of next 9 [10] sts, bobble, 1hdc into each of next 6 [5] sts. Turn.

Make one plain padded strip and one padded strip with bobble strip on RS.

Shape neck

Work as for Vest.

Sleeves (alike)

Work as for Bomber jacket sleeves from * to * 16 times.

Bobble strip Work as for plain strips, but work bobbles on 4th [5th] row as follows:

Bobble row Ch 2 to count as first hdc, skip first st, 1hdc into each of next 5 [4] hdc, *bobble, 1hdc into each of next 9 [10] hdc, rep from * 4 times more, bobble, 1hdc into each of next 6 [6] hdc. Turn.

Make three more bobble strips.

Make six plain padded strips and four padded strips with bobble strip on RS.

To finish

Work as for Bomber jacket, noting that there are two extra strips in the length and alternating plain and bobble strips. Join sleeve seams, leaving 5 [6] row ends open at top. Set in sleeves.

Front edgings (alike)

Make 7ch.

Base row 1sc into 2nd ch from hook, 1sc into each ch to end. Turn. 6sc.

Pattern row Ch 1, skip first sc, 1sc into each sc to end. Turn.

Rep pat row until work fits along front edge. Fasten off.

Sew edging in place.

Lower edging

Work 3 rows of sc into lower edge. Fasten off.

Cuff

Work 3 rows of sc into lower edge of sleeve. Fasten off.

Neck edging

Work one row of sc around neck edge, marking 4 corner sc with a contrasting thread. Work 5 more rows of sc, dec 1sc at corners on next and following 2 alternate rows. Fasten off.

Sew buttons to left side, sewing top button on neckband, bottom button 3in from lower edge and rem four buttons evenly spaced in between. Make button loops (see page 164) to correspond on right front.

Adapting the basic quilted jackets and coat

Use these techniques and designs to create warm and stylish garments for the whole family.

The children's garments on page 128 can be varied quite simply by introducing more colors into the design – for example, the vest would look very striking worked in bold primary-colored stripes.

The more experienced crocheter might introduce simple bobble, cluster or jacquard patterns into the stripes.

When making your own designs, keep basic shapes very simple. Avoid shaping armholes and sleeves and use square or slash necklines. Remember, too, that padded crochet is bulky, so allow more ease around the torso and the armholes.

Pattern Library: Padded patterns

Crochet quilting (1)

Quilting can be worked successfully with surface slip stitch. Place thin batting between two pieces of crochet – thicker batting would make it more difficult for the hook to pass through all three layers. Baste along the quilting lines. Work surface slip stitch (see page 155) through all three layers to quilt the fabric.

Note: *It is possible to use surface slip stitch to work more abstract designs.*

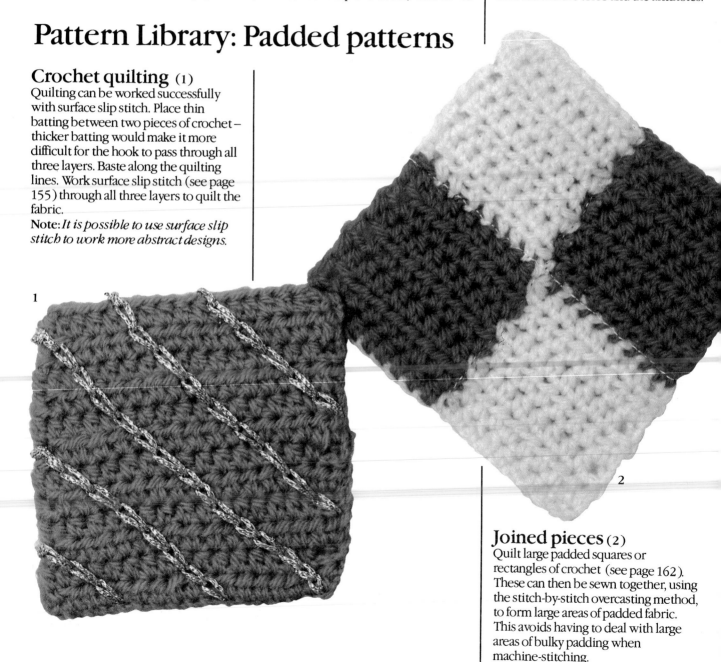

1

2

Joined pieces (2)

Quilt large padded squares or rectangles of crochet (see page 162). These can then be sewn together, using the stitch-by-stitch overcasting method, to form large areas of padded fabric. This avoids having to deal with large areas of bulky padding when machine-stitching.

Filled pockets (3)

Make the required number of ch.
Base row (RS) 1sc into 2nd ch from
hook, 1sc into each st to end. Turn.
* **1st row** (WS) Ch 2 to count as first
hdc, skip first st, inserting hook under
front loop only of each st work in hdc to
end. Turn.
2nd-3rd rows Work in hdc, inserting
hook under both loops of each st as
usual. Fasten off.
With WS facing, turn work
upside-down, return to skipped loops
of last sc row and rejoin yarn to first
unworked loop.
Next row Ch 2 to count as first hdc, skip
first st, 1hdc into each unworked loop
to end. Turn.
Next 2 rows Work in hdc, inserting
hook under both loops of each st as
usual.
Cut a piece of batting slightly smaller all
around than the three rows of crochet
and insert it between the two pieces of
crochet. Fold the first 3 rows up to the
last row worked.
Next row Work a row of sc, inserting the
hook under both loops of the two
edges. Turn. *
Rep from * to * for length required.
Finish the edges by working a row of sc
through both thicknesses of crochet.
Note: *Increase the width of the pockets
by working in double crochet or by
working more rows, but always end
each pocket on a wrong-side row.*

Single-crochet padding (4)

Work small squares in single crochet
and pad as on page 162. Sew them
together to form a really warm and
highly textured fabric.

Backstitch quilting (5)

Quilting by hand, though more
time-consuming, produces as good
results as machine quilting. Baste the
lining, batting and crochet together as
for machine quilting (see page 163).
Then, with right side facing, backstitch
along the basted lines.

Crochet plus appliqué

Spirals – also know as continuous rounds – are the ideal method of working small appliqué motifs which can be sewn to most fabrics. This technique is a very simple way of adding individuality to clothes, as this charming little top illustrates.

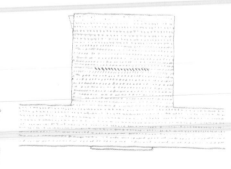

The basic appliquéd top

Sizes
C-3 [C-5:C-7:C10]
Length: 14½[15¾:16¼:17¼] in
Sleeve seam 9 [10½:12¼:13¾] in

Note: *Instructions for larger sizes are in brackets [ ]; where there is only one set of figures it applies to all sizes.*

Materials
8[8:9:9] oz of a sport yarn in main color
Small amounts of sport yarn in yellow, orange green and white
Size C crochet hook

Gauge
20dc and 10 rows to 4in worked on size C hook

To save time, take time to check gauge

Note: *The top is worked in one piece, beginning at the lower edge of the back.*

Main piece
Back
Make 62[67:72:77]ch.
Base row (RS) 1sc into 2nd ch from hook, 1sc into each ch to end. Turn. 61 [66:71:76] sts.
1st-6th rows Ch 1 to count as first sc, skip first st, 1sc into each st to end. Turn.
7th row Ch 3, skip first st, 1dc into each st to end. Turn.
Rep last row until back measures 9½[10¼:10¾:11½]in, ending with a WS row.
Shape sleeve
Using a separate length of yarn, make 45[53:61:69] ch. Fasten off and return to main piece.
Next row Make 47[55:63:71]ch, 1dc into 4th ch from hook, 1dc into each of next 43[51:59:67] ch, 1dc into each of next 61[66:71:76] sts across back, 1dc into first of separate length of ch, 1dc

into each ch to end. Turn.
151[172:193:214] sts.
Work even in dc on these sts until sleeve measures 5[5½:5½:6]in, ending with a WS row.

Shape neck
Using a separate length of yarn, make 39[40:45:48]ch. Fasten off and return to main piece.
Next row Ch 3, skip first st, 1dc into each of next 55[65:73:82] sts, 1dc into first of separate length of ch, 1dc into each ch to end, skip next 39[40:45:48] sts on main piece, 1dc into each st to end. Turn.
151[172:193:214] sts.

SPECIAL TECHNIQUE
"doughboy" pockets

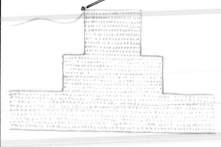
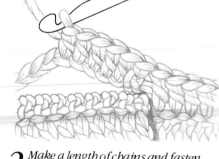

1 After shaping the armholes at the front, work in double crochet for the length given in the pattern, ending with a wrong side row. Fasten off and turn. Skip stitches as instructed at the beginning of the next row and join in yarn to the next stitch. Pattern the center stitches as instructed. End with a wrong side row and fasten off.

2 Make a length of chains and fasten off. With right side facing, return to the stitches skipped in step 1 and rejoin the yarn to the beginning of the row. Pattern across the skipped stitches, place the length of chains behind the pocket and work one double crochet into each chain. Pattern across the stitches skipped at the other edge.

3 Continue in double crochet on these stitches for the stated length, ending with a wrong side row. On the next row join the top of the pocket to the main fabric by working into both the pocket and pocket lining stitches. When the garment is completed, sew the top edge of the pocket lining to the wrong side of the front.

Front and sleeve

Work even in dc on these sts until sleeve measures 10¼[11:11:11¼] in, ending with a WS row.
Fasten off and turn.

Shape front

With RS facing, skip first 45 [53:61:69] sts; rejoin yarn to next st.
Next row Ch 3, skip first st at base of 3ch, 1dc into each of next 60 [65:70:75] sts, turn. 61 [66:71:76] sts.
Work even in dc on these sts until front measures 3¼[3½:4:4½]in from armhole, ending with a WS row. Fasten off and turn.

Pocket

With RS facing, skip first 13 [14:15:16] sts; rejoin yarn to next st.
Next row Ch 3, skip first st at base of 3ch, 1dc into each of next 34 [37:40:43] sts. Turn. 35 [38:41:44] sts.
Work even in dc on these sts until pocket measures 5 [5½:5½:6] in, ending with a WS row. Fasten off.

Pocket lining

Using a separate length of yarn, make 35 [38:41:44]ch. Fasten off and return to main piece. With RS facing, return to sts skipped at beg of pocket and rejoin yarn to beg of row.
Next row Ch 3, skip first st at base of 3ch, 1dc into each of next 12[13:14:15] sts, place separate length of ch behind pocket, 1dc into first of separate length of ch, 1dc into each ch to end, skip pocket, 1dc into each of last 13 [14:15:16] sts on main piece. Turn. 61 [66:71:76] sts.
Work even in dc on these sts until pocket lining measures 5 [5½:5½:6] in, ending with a WS row.

Join pocket

Next row Ch1 to count as first sc, skip first st, 1sc into each of next 12[13:14:15] sts, bring last row of pocket up in front of last row of pocket lining, 1sc into first st on pocket and next st on pocket lining, 1sc into each of next 34[37:40:43] sts on pocket and pocket lining, 1sc into each of last 13[14:15:16] sts on pocket lining, working through 2 sts tog. Turn. 61[66:71:76] sts.
Cont in sc on these sts for 6 more rows. Fasten off.

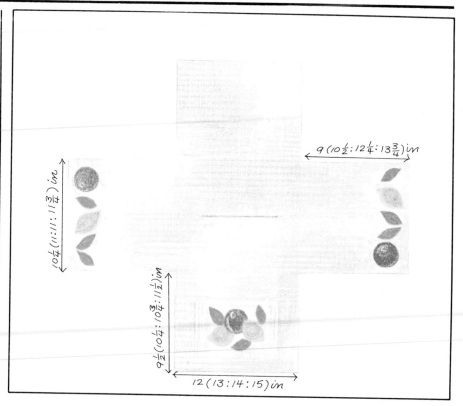

9 (10½:12¼:13¾) in
10¼ (11:11:11¾) in
9½ (10¼:10¾:11½) in
12 (13:14:15) in

To finish

Press or block the work, according to yarn used.

Pocket edges (both alike)

With RS facing work a row of sc into side edge of pocket, working 2sc into each dc row end.
Work 4 more rows of sc.
Fasten off.
Sew sc row ends neatly to RS of front.
Sew top of pocket lining to WS of front.
Join sleeve and side seams, leaving 2¼[2¾:2¾:3] in open at bottom of each side seam to form slits.

Neck edging

With RS facing work one round of sc into neck edge, working 1sc into each st and joining last to first st with a sl st. Fasten off.

Cuff edgings (both alike)

With RS facing work one round of sc into cuff edge, working 2sc into each dc row end and joining last to first st with a sl st. Fasten off.

Lower edging

With RS facing join yarn to top of RH slit.

Next row Ch 1, 2sc into each row end to corner, 3sc into corner, 1sc, into each st on last row of front, 3sc into corner, 2sc into each row end to top of LH slit, 2sc into each row end to corner, 3sc into corner, 1sc into each st on base row of back, 3sc into corner, 2sc into each row end to top of RH slit, sl st to first ch. Fasten off.

Oranges (make 3)

Using orange, make 4ch, sl st to first ch to form a ring.
1st round 8sc into ring.
2nd round 2sc into each of next 8sc. 16sc.
3rd round (2sc into next sc, 1sc into next sc) 8 times. 24sc.
4th round (2sc into next sc, 1sc into each of next 2sc) 8 times. 32sc.
5th round (2sc into next sc, 1sc into each of next 3sc) 8 times. 40sc.
Cont to inc 8sc on each round in this way until orange measures 2¼in in diameter, sl st to next sc. Fasten off.
Make two more oranges in the same way, working a "highlight" of 18sc in yellow on the 5th round of one orange.

Lemons (make 4)

Using yellow work as for oranges until work measures 1¾in in diameter.

Next round * 1 sc into next st, 1dc into next st, 2tr into next st, 1dc into next st *, 1sc into each st to opposite side of circle, rep from * to * once more, 1sc into each st to end. Fasten off.

Make three more lemons in the same way, working a "highlight" of 10sc in white on the 5th round of one lemon.

Leaves (make 9)

Using green, make 8ch.

1st round 1sc into 2nd ch from hook, 1sc into each of next 5ch, 3sc into last ch, 1sc into rem loop of each of next 6ch.

2nd round Ch 3, skip next ch, * 1sc into next sc, 1hdc into next sc, 1dc into each of next 3sc, 1hdc into next sc, 1sc, into next sc *, 1sc into next sc, rep from * to * once more, sl st to first ch. Fasten off.

Make eight more leaves in same way.

To apply motifs

Using green, embroider one cross stitch on each orange to represent the stalk. Press or block each motif.

Sew three leaves, two lemons (including lemon with a white highlight) and highlighted orange to the front pocket. Sew one orange, one lemon and three leaves to each sleeve.

Adapting the basic appliquéd top

Any of the spiral fruits and vegetables in the Pattern Library could be sewn onto the basic top. Use nature's colors for authenticity, choosing different shades to suggest, for example, the bloom on fruit or natural highlights and shadows. When sewing on the spirals, use matching yarn – split if necessary – and slip-stitches, worked just under the edge.

Spiral shapes can be worked quite freely in single crochet, with other stitches, introduced to alter the shape; for example, the lemons on the basic top are formed by working doubles and triples at opposite points on the spiral. You may need to experiment to obtain a convincing shape. Having a picture or the object itself in front of you while you work is a great help, especially when matching colors.

Pattern Library: Spiral patterns

Apple

Use red or green as the main color, introducing brown, yellow, white or pink as desired.

Work as for Orange on page 136 until work measures approx 2in in diameter.

Next 2 rounds 1sc into each sc to opposite side of circle, sl st into next st, 1sc into each sc to end.

Next round 1sc into each sc to opposite side of circle, sl st into next sl st. Fasten off.

Stalk Either embroider the stalk in stem stitch or join brown yarn to indentation on apple, work 4ch, sl st into each ch, sl st into joining on apple. Fasten off.

Calyx Using brown, work a cross stitch on the opposite indentation to the stalk.

Leaf Work as given for leaf of Orange on this page, using one or two shades of green as desired.

Lime

Use green as the main color, introducing yellow and white as desired. Work as for Lemon as instructed above.

Mushroom

Use beige for stalk and cap and brown for first row of cap.

Stalk Make 7ch.

1st round 1sc into 2nd ch from hook, 1sc into each of next 4ch, 3sc into last ch, 1sc into each of next 5 single loops on opposite side of ch, 3sc into turning ch.

Next round 1 sc into each sc to end, working 3sc at each point. Fasten off.

Cap Join yarn ½in from top of stalk.

Next row Ch 3, skip st at base of joining, 1dc into each sc to opposite side of stalk, sl st into side of last dc worked, sl st into next sc on stalk. Turn.

Next row 1sc into each st to end, sl st into side of last dc, sl st into next sc on stalk. Turn.

Next row. Skip first sl st, sl st into first st, 2sc into each st to last 2 sts, sl st into next st. Turn.

Rep last row twice more. Fasten off.

Pear

Use green or yellow as the main color, introducing yellow, white or red as desired. Work as for Orange on page 136 until work measures approx 1½in in diameter.

Next round Ch 10, 1sc into 2nd ch from hook, 1sc into each of next 8ch, 1sc into each sc on circle, 1sc into each of next 9 single loops on opposite side of ch, 3sc into last st.

Next round 1sc into each sc to 3sc worked on last round, 1sc into next sc, 3sc into next sc, 1sc into each of next 2sc, work in hdc to within 4 sts of ring, work in dc to end.

Rep last round once more, working hdc and dc into other edge of top. Fasten off.

Stalk and calyx Work as for Apple, working stalk into top of pear and calyx into opposite edge.

Leaf Work as for leaf of Orange, on page 137.

Tomato

Use red as main color, highlighting work with pink or white, as desired. Work as for Orange on page 136 until work measures approx 1½in in diameter. Fasten off.

Stalk Using green, make 5ch.

1st row Sl st into 2nd ch from hook, 3sc into next ch, sl st into each of last 2ch. Fasten off.

Rejoin yarn to center of 3sc worked on last row, make 3ch, 1sc into 2nd ch from hook, 1sc into last ch, sl st into joining. Fasten off.

Cherries

Use red as main color, introducing pink or white for highlights.

Work as for Orange on page 140 until work measures approx 1in in diameter. Fasten off.

Leaf Work as for leaf of Orange, on page 137.

Stalk Join green to edge of Cherry, ch for the required length, sl st into each ch, sl st into edge of Cherry at joining. Fasten off.

Chapter 3
Edgings and Trimmings

Picot and shell edgings

Pointed shell edging (1)

Worked on a base row of single crochet over a multiple of 3 stitches either directly onto the main fabric or as a separate edging.

Picot row (RS) Ch 1, skip first sc, skip one st, (1sc, 1hdc, 1dc, 1tr, ch 2, sl st into top of tr, 1dc, 1hdc, 1sc) into next sc – called shell –, * skip 2sc, 1 shell into next sc, rep from * to end, working 1sc into edge stitch.

Lace shell edging (2)

Worked on a base row of single crochet with a number of stitches divisible by 13 plus 5, either directly on to your fabric or as a separate edging.

1st row (RS) Ch 1, skip first sc, 1sc into each of next 9sc, ch 3, sl st into first of these 3ch – called picot –, * 1sc into each of next 13sc, 1 picot, rep from * last rep with 9sc working last sc into turning ch. Turn.

2nd row Ch 2, skip first st, skip next st 1dc into next st, ch 1 skip one st, 1sc into next st, * ch 4, skip 3sts, 1sc into next sc before picot, ch 5, 1sc into sc after picot, ch 4, skip 3 sts, 1sc into next sc, ch 1, skip one st, 1dc into next st, ch 1, skip one st, 1sc into next sc, rep from * to end, 1 sc into turning ch. Turn.

3rd row * Ch 3, 1sc into next dc, ch3, 1sc into next 4ch sp, 10dc into next 5ch sp, 1sc into next 4ch sp, rep from * to end, ch 3, 1sc into next dc, ch 2, 1sc into turning ch.

Looped picot edging (3)

Worked on a base row of single crochet with any number of stitches, either directly onto main fabric or as a separate edging.

Picot row (RS) Sl st into first st, * ch 4, sl st into first of these ch – called picot –, sl st into next st, rep from * to end.

4

5

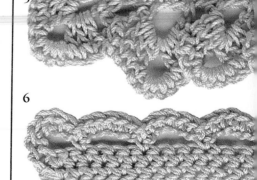

6

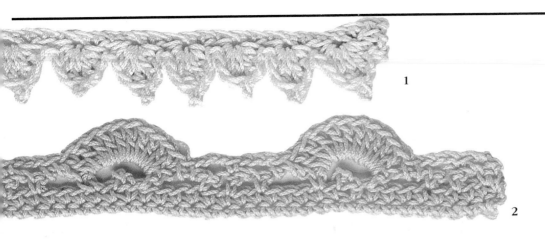

1

2

3

Irish picot edging (4)

Work at least one or more base rows of single crochet with a multiple of 3 sts, either directly onto your fabric or as a separate edging.

Picot row (RS) Ch 1, skip first sc, 1sc into each of next 2sc, * ch 4, remove hook and insert into first of ch just worked, pick up 4th chain and draw through first ch, 1sc into each of next 3sc, rep from * to end.

Ruffled edging (5)

Worked on a base row of single crochet with a multiple of 4 plus 3 stitches either directly onto the main fabric or as a separate edging.

1st row Ch 5, skip 2 sts, 1sc into next st, * ch 5, skip one st, 1sc into next st, rep from * to end , working last sc into turning ch. Turn.

2nd row (RS) Ch 3, 2dc into first 5ch loop, ch 3, 3dc into same loop, * ch 2, sl st into next 5ch loop, ch 2, (3dc, ch 3, 3dc) into next loop, rep from * to end.

3rd row Ch 1, skip first sc, 1sc into each dc and sl st and 5sc into each 3ch sp to end.

Buttonhole edging (6)

Worked on a base row of single crochet with a multiple of 4 plus 1 sts, either directly onto the main fabric or as a separate edging.

1st row (RS) Ch 1, skip first sc, 1sc into each sc to end, 1sc into turning ch. Break off yarn and return to beg of row.

2nd row (RS) As first. Break off yarn and return to beg of row.

3rd row (RS) Ch 1, skip first sc, * ch 6, skip 3sc, 1sc into next sc, rep from * to end, working last sc into last st. Turn.

4th row Ch 1, skip first st, * 1 sl st into top loop of each of next 6ch, 1sl st into next sc, rep from * to end.

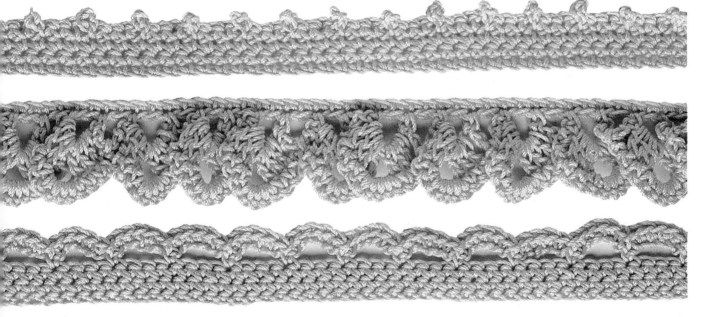

Panels

Large flower panel (1)

Make 28ch.

Base row 1dc into 6th ch from hook, (ch 1, skip next ch, 1dc into next ch) 11 times. Turn.

1st row (RS) Ch 4, skip first dc, 1dc into next dc, (ch 1, 1dc into next dc) 3 times, ch 4, skip next dc, 1tr into next dc, ch 4, skip next dc, 1dc into next dc, (ch 1, 1dc into next dc) 3 times, ch 1, 1dc into last sp. Turn.

2nd row Ch 4, skip first dc, 1dc into next dc, (ch 1, 1dc into next dc) twice, ch 4, 1sc into next 4ch sp, 1sc into next tr, 1sc into next 4ch sp, ch 4, skip next dc, 1dc into next dc, (ch 1, 1dc into next dc) twice, ch 1, 1dc into last sp. Turn.

3rd row Ch 4, skip first dc, 1dc into next dc, ch 1, 1dc into next dc, ch 5, 1dc into next 4ch sp, 1dc into each of next 3sc, 1dc into next 4ch sp, ch 5, skip next dc, (1dc into next dc, ch 1) twice, 1dc into last sp. Turn.

4th row Ch 4, skip first dc, (1dc into next dc, ch 1) twice, 1dc into next 5ch sp, ch 5, skip next dc, 1sc into each of next 3dc, ch 5, 1dc into next 5ch sp, (ch 1, 1dc into next dc) twice, ch 1, 1dc into last sp. Turn.

5th row Ch 4, skip first dc, (1dc into next dc, ch 1) 3 times, 1dc into next 5ch sp, ch 3, 1tr into center sc of next 3sc, ch 3, 1dc into next 5ch sp, ch 1, (1dc into next dc, ch 1) 3 times, 1dc into last sp. Turn.

6th row Ch 4, skip first dc, (1dc into next dc, ch 1) 4 times, 1dc into next 3ch sp, ch 1, 1dc into next tr, ch 1, 1dc into next 3ch sp, ch 1, (1dc into next dc, ch 1) 4 times, 1dc into last sp. Turn.

7th row Ch 4, skip first dc, (1dc into next dc, ch 1) 11 times, 1dc into last sp. Turn.

8th row As 7th row.

First-8th rows form pat. Rep them for length required.

1

Ribbon coronet panel (2)

Make 35ch.

Base row Skip first 3ch, (1dc into next ch, ch 3, skip next 2ch, 1sc into next ch, ch 3, skip next 2ch, 1dc into next ch, ch 5, skip next 5ch) twice, 1dc into next ch, ch 3, skip next 2ch, 1sc into next ch, ch 3, skip next 2ch, 1dc into each of last 2ch. Turn.

1st row (RS) Ch 3, skip first dc, 1dc into next dc, (ch 5, 7dc into next 5ch sp) twice, ch 5, 1dc into next dc, 1dc into top of 3ch. Turn.

2nd row Ch 3, skip first dc, 1dc into next dc, (ch 3, 1sc into next 5ch sp, ch 3, 1dc into first dc of group, ch 5, 1dc into last dc of group) twice, ch 3, 1sc into next 5ch loop, ch 3, 1dc into next dc, 1dc into top of 3ch. Turn.

First and 2nd rows form pat. Rep them for length required. Thread ribbon as shown.

2

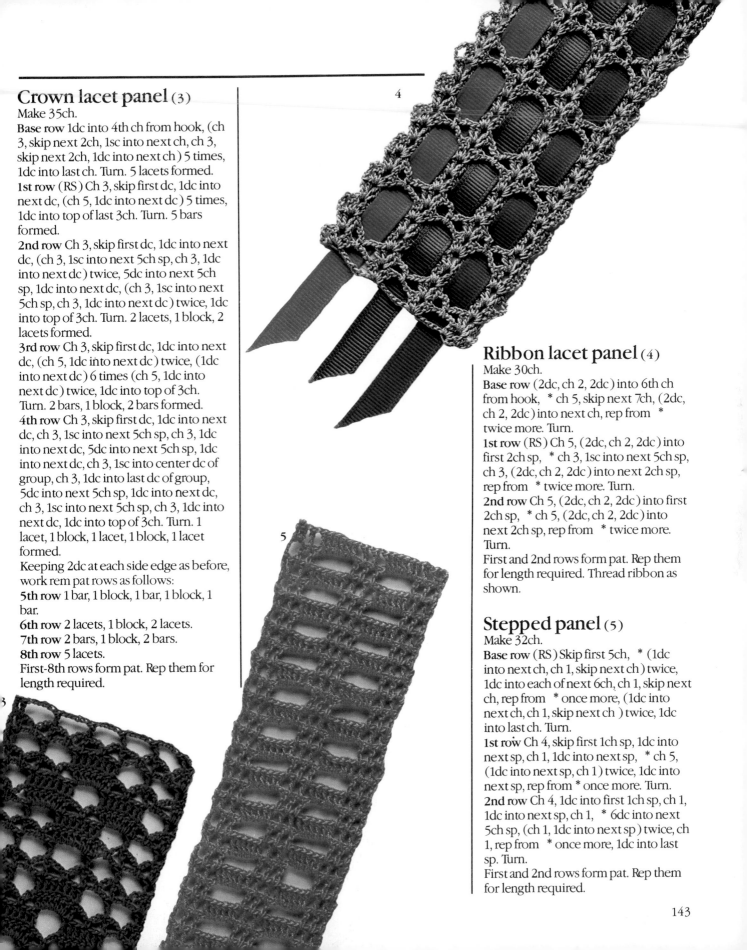

Crown lacet panel (3)

Make 35ch.

Base row 1dc into 4th ch from hook, (ch 3, skip next 2ch, 1sc into next ch, ch 3, skip next 2ch, 1dc into next ch) 5 times, 1dc into last ch. Turn. 5 lacets formed.

1st row (RS) Ch 3, skip first dc, 1dc into next dc, (ch 5, 1dc into next dc) 5 times, 1dc into top of last 3ch. Turn. 5 bars formed.

2nd row Ch 3, skip first dc, 1dc into next dc, (ch 3, 1sc into next 5ch sp, ch 3, 1dc into next dc) twice, 5dc into next 5ch sp, 1dc into next dc, (ch 3, 1sc into next 5ch sp, ch 3, 1dc into next dc) twice, 1dc into top of 3ch. Turn. 2 lacets, 1 block, 2 lacets formed.

3rd row Ch 3, skip first dc, 1dc into next dc, (ch 5, 1dc into next dc) twice, (1dc into next dc) 6 times (ch 5, 1dc into next dc) twice, 1dc into top of 3ch. Turn. 2 bars, 1 block, 2 bars formed.

4th row Ch 3, skip first dc, 1dc into next dc, ch 3, 1sc into next 5ch sp, ch 3, 1dc into next dc, 5dc into next 5ch sp, 1dc into next dc, ch 3, 1sc into center dc of group, ch 3, 1dc into last dc of group, 5dc into next 5ch sp, 1dc into next dc, ch 3, 1sc into next 5ch sp, ch 3, 1dc into next dc, 1dc into top of 3ch. Turn. 1 lacet, 1 block, 1 lacet, 1 block, 1 lacet formed.

Keeping 2dc at each side edge as before, work rem pat rows as follows:

5th row 1 bar, 1 block, 1 bar, 1 block, 1 bar.

6th row 2 lacets, 1 block, 2 lacets.

7th row 2 bars, 1 block, 2 bars.

8th row 5 lacets.

First-8th rows form pat. Rep them for length required.

Ribbon lacet panel (4)

Make 30ch.

Base row (2dc, ch 2, 2dc) into 6th ch from hook, * ch 5, skip next 7ch, (2dc, ch 2, 2dc) into next ch, rep from * twice more. Turn.

1st row (RS) Ch 5, (2dc, ch 2, 2dc) into first 2ch sp, * ch 3, 1sc into next 5ch sp, ch 3, (2dc, ch 2, 2dc) into next 2ch sp, rep from * twice more. Turn.

2nd row Ch 5, (2dc, ch 2, 2dc) into first 2ch sp, * ch 5, (2dc, ch 2, 2dc) into next 2ch sp, rep from * twice more. Turn.

First and 2nd rows form pat. Rep them for length required. Thread ribbon as shown.

Stepped panel (5)

Make 32ch.

Base row (RS) Skip first 5ch, * (1dc into next ch, ch 1, skip next ch) twice, 1dc into each of next 6ch, ch 1, skip next ch, rep from * once more, (1dc into next ch, ch 1, skip next ch) twice, 1dc into last ch. Turn.

1st row Ch 4, skip first 1ch sp, 1dc into next sp, ch 1, 1dc into next sp, * ch 5, (1dc into next sp, ch 1) twice, 1dc into next sp, rep from * once more. Turn.

2nd row Ch 4, 1dc into first 1ch sp, ch 1, 1dc into next sp, ch 1, * 6dc into next 5ch sp, (ch 1, 1dc into next sp) twice, ch 1, rep from * once more, 1dc into last sp. Turn.

First and 2nd rows form pat. Rep them for length required.

Buttons

Two-color unfilled button

Use 2 colors, A and B. Using A, make 3ch.

1st round Ch 1, 7sc into ring, join with a sl st to first ch.

2nd round Working from *left to right* ch 1, skip first sc, 1sc into front loop only of each st to end, join with a sl st to first ch. Fasten off.

3rd round Join in B. Working from right to left ch 1, skip first sc, 2sc into back loop only of each st to end, join with a sl st to first ch.

4th round As 2nd round.

5th round Ch 1, skip first sc, 1sc into back loop only of each st to end, join with a sl st to first ch.

6th round Ch 1, skip first sc, * 1sc, dec 1sc over next 2 sts, rep from * to end, join with a sl st to first ch.

7th round Ch 1, skip first sc, * dec 1sc over next 2 sts, rep from * twice, 1sc into next sc. Fasten off.

Drawstring glitter button

Make 3ch. Work as first and 2nd rounds of Drawstring button.

3rd round Ch 1, skip first sc, 1sc into each st to end, join with a sl st to first ch.

4th round Ch 1, skip first sc, * dec 1sc over next 2 sts, 1sc, rep from * to end, join with a sl st to first ch. Fasten off, leaving 10in of yarn. Weave yarn through each st of 4th round and complete as Drawstring button.

Two-color unfilled button   Drawstring glitter button   Two-color ball button

Drawstring button

Make 3ch, sl st to first ch to form a ring.

1st round Ch 3, 11dc into ring, join with a sl st to 3rd of first 3ch.

2nd round Ch 1, skip first dc, 1sc into each st to end, join with a sl st to first ch.

3rd round As 2nd round.

Fasten off, leaving 10in of yarn. Weave yarn through each st of 3rd round. Fill button with small amount of yarn and draw up yarn end to secure it.

Two-color ball button

Use 2 colors, A and B. Using A, make 4ch, sl st to first ch to form a ring.

1st round Ch 3, 9dc into ring, join with a sl st to 3rd of first 3ch. Fasten off.

2nd round Using B, ch 1, skip first dc, * 1sc into circle, 1sc into next dc, rep from * to end, 1sc into ring, join with sl st to first ch.

3rd round Ch 1, skip first sc, 1sc into each st to end, join with a sl st to first ch.

4th round Ch 1, skip first sc, * dec 1sc over next 2 sts, rep from * 3 times, 1sc into next sc, join with a sl st to first ch. Fasten off leaving 10in of yarn. Weave yarn through 4th round and complete as Drawstring button.

Cluster button

Before beginning, wind off a small ball of yarn for padding. Make 5ch, sl st to first ch to form a ring.

1st round Ch 4, leaving last loop of each st on hook, work 2tr into ring, yo, draw through 3 loops on hook, (leaving last loop of each st on hook, 3tr into ring, yo, draw through 4 loops on hook) 7 times, join with a sl st to 4th of first 4 ch.

2nd round Ch 1, (dec 1sc over next 2 sts) 4 times, inserting small ball of yarn as button closes. Fasten off tightly.

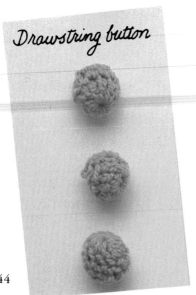

Drawstring button

Cluster button

Chapter 4
Know~How

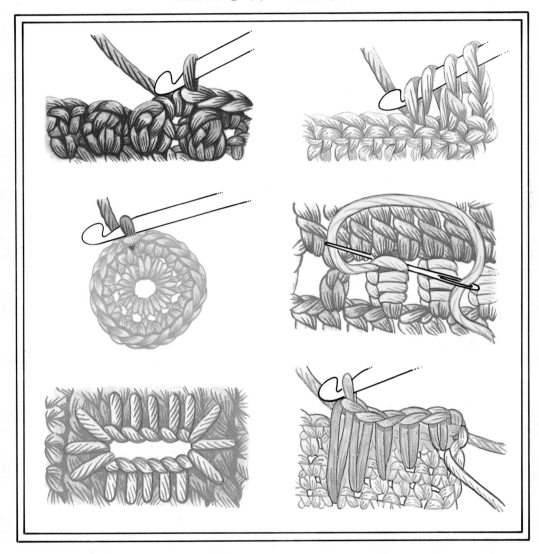

Basic stitches and techniques

Foundation chain (ch)

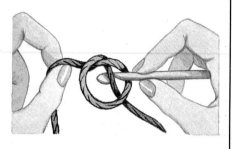

1 Make a slip loop and place it over the hook. Hold the hook in your right hand as if you were holding a pencil.

2 Thread the yarn as shown between the fingers of the left hand so that it will flow freely and evenly.

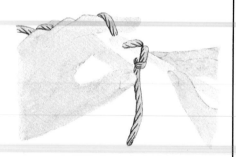

3 Take the yarn over the hook and draw through the loop to make the first chain. After making a few chains, move up your finger and thumb to just below the hook.

Slip stitch (sl st)

1 To work slip stitch along a foundation chain, insert the hook from front to back under the top two loops of the second chain from the hook. Take the yarn counter-clockwise over the hook and draw it through the chain and the loop on the hook — one loops remains and one slip stitch has been worked. Continue in this way to the end.

2 Slip stitch is often used when shaping. When the required number of slip stitches has been worked, slip stitch into the next stitch, work the turning chain to count as the first stitch (here we show two, for a half double fabric) and continue in pattern.

3 Slip stitch is also used when working in rounds to join the last stitch of the round to the first. After the last stitch has been worked, insert the hook into the top of the turning chain, which counts as the first stitch, and work a slip stitch.

Single crochet (sc)

1 To work the base row, skip the first of the foundation chains and insert the hook from front to back under the top two loops of the second chain from the hook. Take the yarn over the hook and draw through a loop — two loops on the hook.

2 Take the yarn over the hook and draw it through the two loops on the hook — one loop remains and one single crochet has been worked. Work one single crochet into the next and every foundation chain, then turn the work so that the hook is once more at the beginning.

3 To begin the next row, work one turning chain to count as the first stitch. Skip the last stitch of the previous row and work one single crochet into every following stitch, working the last single crochet into the turning chain of the previous row. Repeat as often as desired to make a single crochet fabric.

Half double crochet (hdc)

1 To work the base row, take the yarn over the hook and insert the hook from front to back under the top two loops of the third chain from the hook. Take the yarn over the hook and draw through a loop — three loops on the hook.

2 Take the yarn over the hook and draw through all three loops — one loop remains and one half double has been worked. Take the yarn over the hook and work a half double as before into the next chain. Continue in this way to the last chain. Turn the work.

3 Work two chains to count as the first half double. Skip the first half double of the previous row and work into the next stitch.

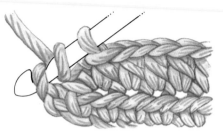

4 Work one half double into each half double to the turning chain. Then work one half double into the top of the turning chain and turn.

Double crochet (dc)

1 Make a chain the length needed. Take the yarn counter-clockwise over the hook. Skip the first three chains and insert the hook from front to back under the top two loops of the fourth chain from the hook. (The three chains skipped at the beginning should be counted as the first double crochet.)

2 Take the yarn counter-clockwise over the hook and draw yarn through the chain — three loops on the hook.

3 Take the yarn counter-clockwise over the hook. Draw the yarn through the first two loops on the hook — two loops remain on the hook.

4 Take the yarn counter-clockwise over the hook. Draw the yarn through the remaining two loops on the hook — one double crochet has been worked and one loop only remains on the hook.

147

Triple (tr)

1 To work the base row, take the yarn counter-clockwise over the hook twice and insert the hook from front to back under the top two loops of the fifth chain from the hook. Take the yarn once over the hook, through the chain and draw yarn over it through the first two loops on the hook — three loops remain on the hook.

2 Take the yarn over the hook and draw it through the first two loops on the hook — two loops remain. Take the yarn over the hook and draw it through the remaining two loops on the hook — one loop remains and one triple has been worked. Continue working triples in this way into the next and each chain to the end. Turn.

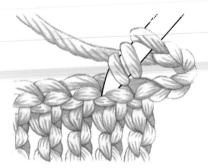

3 At the beginning of the next and every following row, work four turning chains to count as the first triple. At the end of each row work the last triple into the top of the four turning chains.

Double triple and triple triple (dtr and tr tr)

These long stitches are usually worked as part of a more intricate stitch pattern.

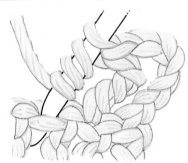

1 Begin a double triple row with five turning chains. Yarn over hook three times and insert the hook into the next stitch. Yarn over hook and draw through a loop — five loops on hook. * Yarn over hook and draw through first two loops on hook *, repeat from * to * three more times until there is one loop left on the hook. One double triple has been completed.

2 Triple triple is worked in the same way except that each row begins with six turning chains and the yarn is wound four times around the hook. Insert the hook into the next stitch and work from * to * five times, when one loop will remain.

Fastening off

Work the last stitch of the last row in the usual way. Cut the yarn to approximately 5 in. Take the yarn over the hook and draw through the loop on the hook to fasten off.

Joining in new yarn

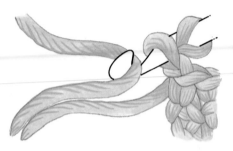

Always join in new yarn at the end of a row. Insert hook into turning chain, yarn over hook and draw through a loop — two loops on hook. Cut off old yarn to 5 in. Complete stitch using the new yarn.

148

Using two colors

1 To change colors on any crochet fabric, work the stitch (double shown above) as usual until there are two loops on the hook. Drop the old color and draw the new color through two loops on hook.

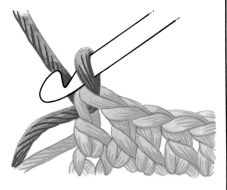

2 When working in stripes, change color as in step 1 on the last stitch of a row, drawing the new color through the last two loops on the hook. Work the turning chain in the new color.

3 Use separate balls of yarn when working large areas in one color. However, when working only a few stitches in each color, carry the color not in use loosely on the wrong side at the base of the row, working over it with the other color.

Increasing

1 To increase one stitch in a single crochei, half double or double crochet fabric, simply work two stitches into the top of one stitch of the previous row. Although increases are usually worked at the edges of the fabric, they can, if desired, be worked into any stitch of the row.

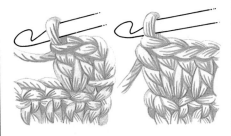

2 It may be possible (depending on the pattern) to achieve a neater edge when increasing by working all the extra stitches one stitch in from each edge. At the beginning of the row, work the turning chains and skip the first stitch, work two stitches into the next stitch; at the end of the row, work to within the last two stitches (including the turning chains) and work two stitches into the next stitch and one stitch into the top of the turning chains.

3 Occasionally it may be necessary to increase two or more stitches into one stitch of the previous row. To increase two stitches into one stitch, simply work three stitches all into one stitch (i.e. two increased stitches plus the original stitch).

Decreasing

Decreases can be worked into any stitches but are usually worked near the edges – if possible one stitch in from it.

1 To decrease one single crochet stitch, insert the hook into the next stitch, yarn over book and draw through a loop — two loops on the hook; insert the hook into the next stitch, yarn over book and draw through a loop — three loops on the hook; yarn over and draw through three loops — one single crochet decreased.

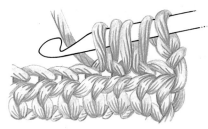

2 To decrease one half double crochet stitch, take the yarn over the hook, insert the hook into the next stitch, yarn over book and draw through a loop — three loops on the hook; yarn over book, insert the hook into the next stitch and work as before until five loops remain; yarn over book and draw through all five loops — one half double decreased.

3 To decrease one double crochet, take the yarn over the hook, insert the hook into the next stitch, yarn over book and draw through a loop — three loops on the hook; yarn over book and draw through the first two loops — two loops on the hook. Work the next stitch as before until three loops remain, yarn over book and draw through all three loops — one double crochet decreased.

Berry stitch

1 **With the** wrong *side facing, work to the position of the berry stitch. Wind the yarn counter-clockwise around the hook and insert the hook into the next stitch. Wind the yarn around the hook and draw through a loop* loosely. *Wind the yarn around the hook and draw through the first loop on the hook — three loops remain on the hook.*

2 *Wind the yarn around the hook and insert the hook into the same stitch as in step 1. Wind the yarn around the hook and draw through a loose loop as before — five loops on the hook. Wind the yarn around the hook and draw through the first four loops on the hook — two loops remain.*

3 *Draw the yarn through the remaining two loops — one loop remains and one berry stitch has been formed. When working an all-over berry stitch fabric, keep the work even by slip stitching into the next stitch and by working, on the following right-side row, a slip stitch into the top of each berry and a single crochet into the top of each slip stitch.*

Bullion stitches

Bullion stitches are tiny bobbles which are usually combined with other stitches to form a variety of textured patterns.

1 *To work a small bullion stitch, make any number of chains plus three turning chains. Wind the yarn three times only around the shank of the hook.*

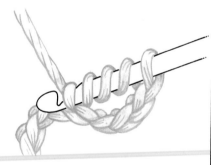

2 *Securing the loops on the hook with the third finger of the left hand, insert the hook into the fourth chain from the hook. Wind the yarn around the hook and draw through a loop — five loops are now on the hook.*

3 *Keeping the working yarn taut, wind it around the hook and draw through all loops on the hook to form a smooth, even roll. It may be difficult at first to draw through all loops in one movement; if so, you can either draw the hook through loops one at a time or lift loops off the hook with your fingers.*

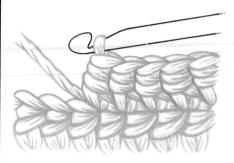

4 *Continue in this way, working a bullion stitch into each chain. On following rows work into the two top horizontal loops of each stitch.*

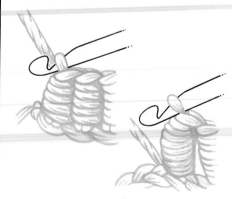

5 *Larger bullion stitches — which require more turning chains — are worked by winding the yarn more times around the hook. The stitches on the left were formed from five loops and the stitches on the right from ten. Using a larger hook than usual will make it easier to draw the hook through the greater number of loops.*

Rice stitches

Rice stitches are worked in much the same way as bullion stitches. Again, practice is necessary for good results.

1 To work small rice stitch, make an odd number of chains plus three turning chains. Wind the yarn three times around the hook.

2 Insert the hook into the fourth chain from the hook and draw a loop through the chain and through the four loops on the hook to complete the first rice stitch.

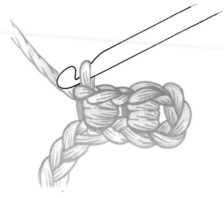

3 Work one chain, skip the next foundation chain and work a rice stitch into the next stitch. Continue in this way to the end. On following rows work rice stitch into the chain spaces, working one chain after each individual stitch.

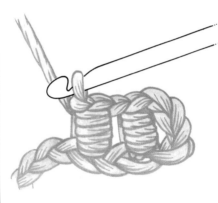

4 Larger stitches can be worked by winding the yarn more times around the hook. Again, using a larger hook and winding the yarn around the shank will make it easier to draw the hook through the loops. Try to keep an even tension at the same time.

Graduated-stitch patterns

It is easily possible in crochet to work stitches of different heights – "graduated stitches" – in the same row. This characteristic of crochet can be used to create interesting wave-like patterns.

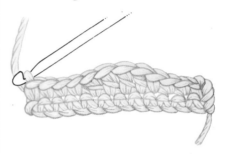

1 A simple pattern, based on a combination of single and double crochet, illustrates this technique very well. After a base row of single crochet, begin the first row with four single crochets followed by four doubles. Work these single and double crochets alternately along the row to produce a series of tall and short stitches.

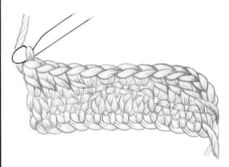

2 On the next row, to prevent the fabric from wrinkling, compensate for the unevenness of the previous row by working tall stitches into the short stitches and vice versa. So work doubles into the single crochets and single crochets into the doubles.
Note: When working these patterns, emphasize the wavy appearance by using contrasting yarns.

Elongated stitches

Zigzag effects can be created easily by working single crochet stitches of varying lengths over a single crochet fabric in a contrasting color.

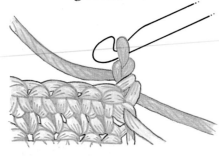

1 Work the required number of single crochet rows in the first color. Drop this color and join in a contrasting color. Make one chain and skip the first stitch.

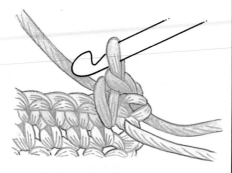

2 Skip the last row in the first color and insert the hook into the preceding row one stitch to the left. Work a single crochet as usual, extending the yarn so that the fabric is not pulled out of shape.

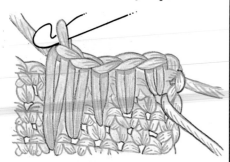

3 Insert the hook one row below and one stitch to the left of the last point. Work a single crochet as usual. Continue in this way until the slope is the desired length.

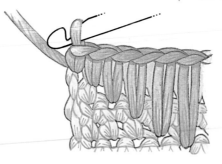

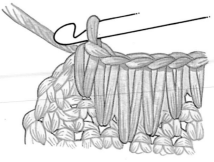

4 Work the second side of the zigzag in the same way, still working one stitch to the left but one row higher each time. Complete the pattern by working one single crochet into the last row in the first color, then work one single crochet into the turning chains.

5 When shaping an elongated-stitch fabric, work the decreasing or increasing in the ordinary single crochet rows. Then adjust the zigzag pattern to fit.

Working afghan squares in rounds

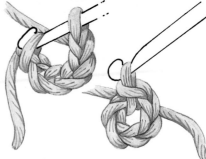

1 Make a small number of chains — usually between four and six — and join them into a ring with a slip stitch; insert hook in first chain, yarn over hook, and draw through chain and through loop on hook.

2 On the first round, work four groups of doubles (here there are four stitches in each group) into the ring, separating the groups with two chains. Fasten off.

3 To begin the next round, join in the new color to the next chain space and work three chains to count as the first double. On this and following rounds, work two double groups separated by chain spaces at each corner, and one group of doubles into each chain space along the sides.

Working in continuous rounds

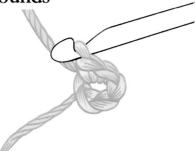

1 Many patterns and motifs are worked in continuous rounds of crochet. At the beginning of the first and following round, omit the one chain that is normal when working rounds of single crochet.

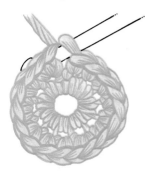

2 To end a round, work one single crochet into the last stitch. Do not join the first and last stitch with a slip stitch as usual, but simply begin the next round by working one single crochet into the first stitch of the round.

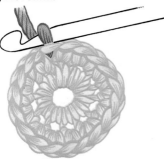

3 To change color when working continuous rounds, work the last single crochet in the old color. Insert hook into first stitch of round and draw through new color. Continue in pattern, working into same place as joining, using the new color and working over the end of the old color.

Lacets

Lacets are two-row patterns, formed from a combination of V-shaped *lacets* and chain *bars*.

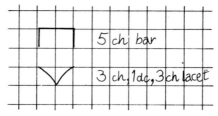

1 Patterns may be formed entirely from lacets, but often the lacets are combined with filet spaces and blocks; in this case filet charts are used. The symbols are given in the diagram above, which also shows the number of chains in the lacet and bar.

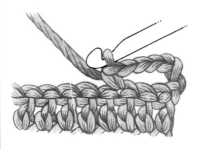

2 Begin with the lacet row. Make six chains to count as the first double crochet and three chains. Skip the first three stitches and work one single crochet into the next stitch. Make three chains, skip the next two stitches and work one double crochet into the next stitch.

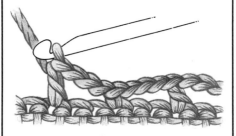

3 Make three chains, skip the next two stitches and work one single crochet into the next stitch. Make three chains, skip the next two stitches and work one double into the next stitch. This step forms the lacet and is repeated to the end.

4 Work the bar on the next row. Begin with eight chains to count as the first double and five chains. Skip the first double and work one double into the next double. * Work five chains to form the next bar and work one double into the next double. Repeat from *

5 To work a lacet over a bar, work the doubles into the doubles of the bar row and work the single crochets into the third of five chains of each bar.

Irish crochet

Working over a cord

To give a raised effect, Irish motifs may be worked over a cord. For the cord use either three or four strands of cotton twisted together or a thicker cotton in the same color. When the motif is finished, cut the cord close to the stitches.

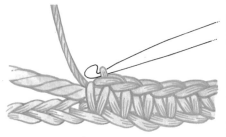

1 Having worked the foundation chain, hold the cord at the back of the work in the left hand. Work into the chain and over the cord at the same time.

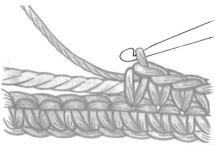

2 At the end of the row, turn and work the next row over the cord, still holding the cord at the back of the work.

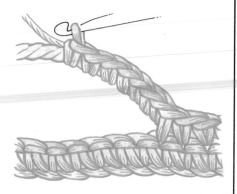

3 To work over the cord alone, hold it away from the main body of the crochet, and work along the cord, pushing the stitches together to cover the cord.

Traditional method of working Irish crochet

For the basic outline of the garment, choose a fairly simple dressmaking pattern without elaborate shaping. Make the pattern in a medium-weight interfacing, omitting shoulder seams and cutting away seam or hem allowances on the front, neck and lower edges. Ignore facings and do not seam or set in the sleeves, if any.

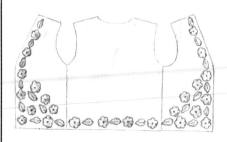

1 Lay the seamed pattern pieces out flat and arrange the motifs on the interfacing as you wish. Pin and baste the motifs firmly to the interfacing.

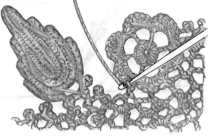

2 Using a matching yarn, fill in the spaces between the pattern motifs with picot mesh. Join in the mesh to the edge of the motifs as you work using single crochet or slip stitch. Do not worry if the mesh seems irregular. This is unavoidable and adds to the beauty of the lace.

3 Remove the work from the interfacing and, after blocking (see below), join in shoulder and sleeve seams and set in sleeves. Work a narrow picot edging along the neck, front and lower edges, or work a separate edging and sew it to the mesh.

Embroidery on crochet

A good way of varying simple crochet fabrics is by embroidering them. For beginners a single crochet fabric, worked with a firm tension in knitting worsted yarn on a size F hook, is the ideal fabric. Other stitches, such as doubles, can also be decorated, but working the embroidery on the looser fabric produced is more difficult. Use a crochet cotton for the fabric, to make it relatively strong. Use embroidery floss or other lightweight thread for the embroidery.

Embroidery on single crochet

1 Thread the embroidery yarn — knitting worsted is probably easiest for beginners — into a large-eyed tapestry needle. When working embroidery to cover an area secure the yarn by threading it through the center of a few stitches on the right side of fabric. Work over the end of yarn when embroidering.

2 To secure the yarn when working running stitch or stem stitch, work a small backstitch on the wrong side of the crochet fabric, making sure that the fabric is not pulled out of shape and that the backstitch is invisible on the right side.

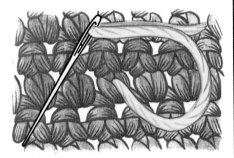

3 When working the embroidery, try to insert the needle through the center of the stitches. Working between rows or stitches could easily pull the crochet out of shape, so forming a hole.

4 Never pull the embroidery yarn too tightly through the crochet, as this could pucker the fabric. Holding the yarn with the thumb and forefinger of the left hand while you draw it through the fabric should help you to keep the tension loose. To fasten off the embroidery yarn, take it to the back of the work and run it through the embroidery stitches. Cut off the end close to the stitches.

Embroidery on double crochet

1 When working an all-over or free-hand embroidery design on double crochet or mesh fabrics, insert the needle through the center of the stitches as for single crochet.

2 Outline filet motifs with satin stitch. Work the embroidery stitches very loosely, holding the yarn as in step 4 above to avoid puckering the filet and inserting the needle into the top of each double.

3 Decorate a double and chain space fabric by working buttonhole stitch loosely around the doubles.

Surface slip stitch

This resembles embroidered chain stitch, but is worked with a crochet hook.

1 Use either one or two strands of yarn, depending on how raised you want the crochet to be. Hold the yarn at the back (wrong side) of the work and insert the hook from front to back into the foundation chain and draw through a loop to the front.

2 Insert the hook from front to back into the first row. Wind the yarn around the hook and draw through a loop to the front of the work to form the first slip stitch and to secure the yarn firmly.

3 Continue in this way up the fabric. You can work either a straight line or zigzags or curves. Your instructions will tell you to work into, for example, "one row above one stitch to the right" or the pattern will be shown in chart form.

Jacquard patterns

Working from charts

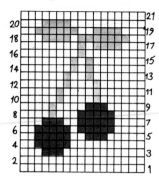

1 Odd-numbered rows are shown on the right-hand side of the chart and even-numbered rows on the left. Read odd-numbered rows from right to left and even-numbered rows from left to right.

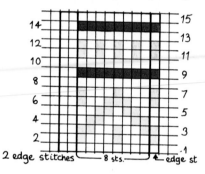

2 edge stitches ← 8 sts. → edge st

2 On "Fair Isle" charts the stitches shown within the bold lines are repeated across the row, while those outside these lines are worked at the beginning and end of the rows only.

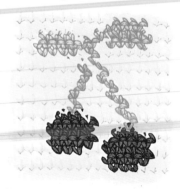

3 Patterns may sometimes instruct you to "reverse the chart" to produce a mirror image; the illustration above is a mirror image of the chart in step 1. This is done simply by reading the odd-numbered rows from left to right and the even-numbered rows from right to left.

Stranding yarn

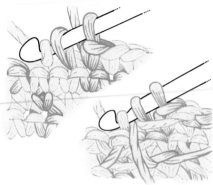

1 When working jacquard patterns, change colors as shown on page 149. In repeating patterns, as in step 2 of "Working from charts," strand the yarn not in use loosely at the back of the work on right-side rows (above left). On wrong-side rows strand the yarn at the front of work (above right).

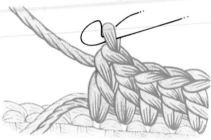

2 It is possible to work over the yarn not in use (see page 149) to produce a double fabric. This technique can also be used when introducing a new ball of yarn. Work over the ends as shown to avoid darning in ends when the work is completed.

Working large motifs

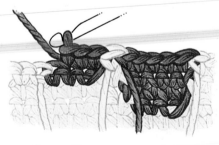

1 When working individual motifs, such as the cherries in step 1 of "Working from charts," do not waste yarn by stranding. Instead, use a separate ball of yarn for each section of color. To

prevent tangles, use yard-long pieces of yarn. Although these will tangle, they are fairly short and so it is easy to pull each length free as required.

2 Change colors as usual, but leave the old color hanging on the wrong side of the work, ready for the return row. If necessary, however, strand across a few stitches — for example, across the cherry stems.

Charting motifs

1 Work a gauge sample in your yarn; for best results work in single crochet. Draw a graph showing the number of stitches and rows required to make the motif the desired size; each square represents one stitch. Sketch the motif on the graph. Using suitable colors, block in the shape. Where more than half of a square falls within the outline, color it in; where less than half, leave it blank.

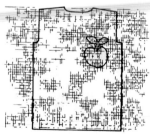

2 To position a motif, draw the outline of the garment on graph paper. Place the motif as required on the graph and follow this chart when making the garment.

Picture jacquard

As a base for the design use an existing pattern for a garment worked in single crochet.

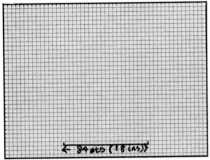

1 Use large sheets of graph paper and a sharp pencil. Count the number of single crochets on the front across the first row after the waistband (on a pullover, the same as for the back) plus any increasing.

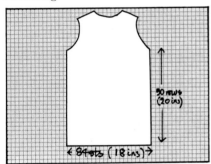

2 Count off and mark the number of rows to the armhole shaping. If the pattern is not specific, multiply the number of rows to 4 in as given under "Gauge" by the length in inches to the armholes, then divide by 4. Then draw in any armhole, neck and shoulder shaping.

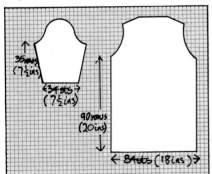

3 If you want to extend the pattern across the back and sleeves, draw these outlines in the same way.

Charting the picture

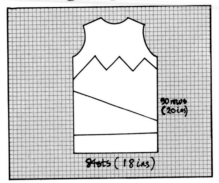

1 Because single crochet — which is best for picture jacquard — often has the same number of stitches and rows to 4 in, a picture can be drawn directly on the graph. If the stitch is not square, take this into account when transferring the picture.

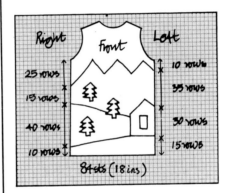

2 Next add finer detail. The amount of this depends on the thickness of the yarn: the finer the yarn, the more detail is possible. Whatever the yarn, however, very fine details, such as those used on the winter sweater on page 52, are best embroidered.

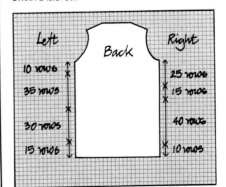

3 If you want to continue the picture on the back, it must match precisely at

the side seams. Count the number of rows to the first outline on both edges of the front and mark the corresponding squares at each edge on the back. Continue marking other corresponding outlines in the same way.

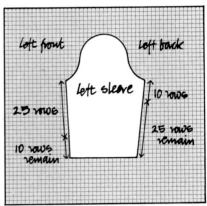

4 To extend the picture onto the left sleeve, count the number of rows on the front from the beginning of the left armhole shaping down to the first outline. Mark the same number of rows on the front edge of the left sleeve from the beginning of the shaping. Draw in the outlines on the back edge of the left sleeve in the same way. Mark outlines on the right sleeve to correspond with the outlines on the right armhole edges of both the front and the back.

5 Finally, color within the outlines to provide a guide to follow when making the sweater. Use natural colors and introduce areas of textured yarn as appropriate (see page 57).
When working the jacquard, don't waste yarn by stranding; instead use bobbins. Introduce each new color neatly when completing the last stitch in the old color (see Special Technique, page 54).

Left-handed crochet

Because right-handed people are in the majority most instructions and tools are designed with them in mind. Crochet patterns are no exception, since it would be very costly to print two sets of instructions. Some left-handed people can learn right-handed crochet and, with practice, they become as proficient as the naturally right-handed. If you find this impossible, don't be discouraged; it is perfectly possible to crochet with the left hand.

Beginning

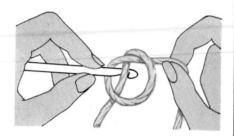

1 Hold the hook lightly but firmly in your left hand. Make a slip knot on the hook and pull the short end of yarn to tighten the loop.

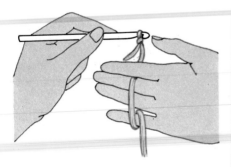

2 To maintain even tension, wind the working yarn around the fingers of your right hand: loop the yarn around your little finger, across your palm and behind your first finger. Pull the yarn gently so that it lies firmly around your fingers.

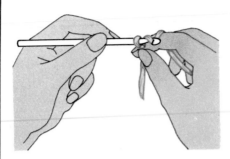

3 To work the foundation chain: hold the short end of yarn in your right hand to secure the loop. Take the hook under the taut working yarn and catch the yarn with the hook. Draw the yarn through the loop on the hook to form the first chain. Continue in this way.

Basic stitches

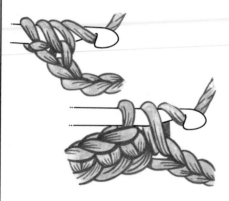

1 Although left-handers crochet from left to right, the instructions for basic stitches in this "Know-how" section can usually be used by left- or right-handed people, though the illustrations are "right-handed." The illustrations above show the first two steps of single crochet as worked by a left-handed person.

2 The drawings in step 1 are the same as those on page 146, but they have been reversed and so are "left-handed." To reverse other drawings in this book, simply hold a mirror at the side of the drawing at a right angle to the page. The resulting mirror image will be left-handed.

Following patterns

Practice the basic crochet stitches until you are ready to tackle a pattern. For your first attempt choose a simple garment in a basic stitch.

Many crochet patterns do not mention left or right. When they do, read "left" for "right" and vice versa. With practice and common sense you will learn when to apply this rule.

Interesting textures and motifs

Working around the stem

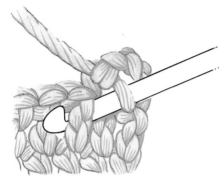

1 To work a double crochet from the front — known as "1dc front" — around the stem of a stitch, take the yarn over the hook, and insert the hook from front to back into the space between two stitches. Bring the hook to the front of the work between the second and the next stitch. Complete the stitch in the usual way.

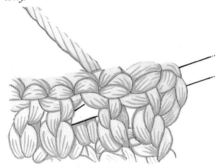

2 Work a double from the back — known as a "1dc back" — around the stem of a stitch in the same way, but insert the hook between stitches from back to front and then from front to back.

3 A neat crochet ribbing pattern can be formed by working doubles around the stem from the front and back alternately along the row.

Working between stitches

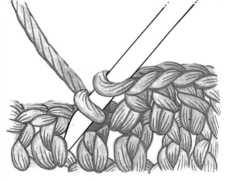

Take the yarn over the hook and insert the hook from front to back into the space between two stitches beneath the small connecting loop at the top of the stitch. Complete the stitch in the usual way.

Working into a single loop

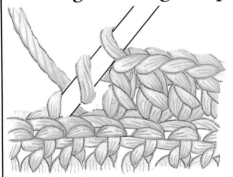

1 To work a double crochet into the back loop of a stitch, take the yarn over the hook and insert the hook into the back loop of the two loops lying at the top of the stitch.
Complete the stitch in the usual way.

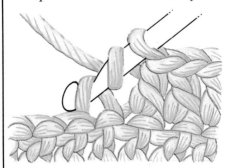

2 A double crochet worked into the front loop of a stitch is formed in the same way, except that the hook is inserted into the front loop of the two loops lying at the top of the stitch.

Triple bobbles

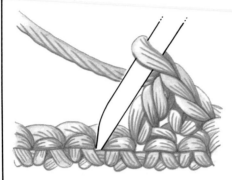

1 Small bobbles can be worked on a single crochet fabric by bending triples in half. With the wrong side facing, work a triple in the usual way. Work a single crochet into the next stitch, bending the triple in half to form a small bobble on the front of the work. If the bobble seems flat after it has been bent in half, push it through to the right side of the work with the fingers.

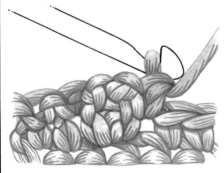

2 Larger bobbles may be formed by working two or more triples into the next stitch, but leaving the last loop of each triple stitch on the hook. Take the yarn over the hook and draw through all loops. Secure the bobbles as in step 1. (Wrong side is shown above.)

Working filet crochet

Filet charts

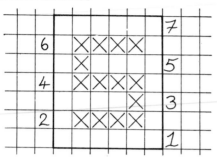

1 Filet crochet is usually worked by following graphed charts, in which blocks of double crochet and spaces, formed by working chains across a given number of stitches, are shown as crosses and blank squares respectively. In the chart above, each blank square represents a two-chain space plus a connecting double, and each cross represents two doubles plus a connecting double.

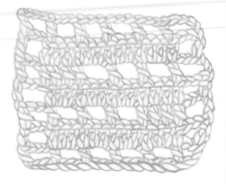

2 The sample above has been worked following the chart in step 1. Read the odd-numbered rows from right to left and the even-numbered rows from left to right.

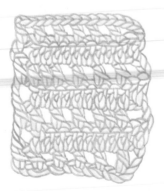

3 Sometimes filet patterns are worked so that each space is formed from one chain plus a connecting double and each block is formed from one double plus one connecting double, thus producing a narrower fabric. The same chart can thus be interpreted in different ways. The sample above has been worked from the chart in step 1.

Mesh background

1 Make a multiple of three chains plus two extra. Work one double crochet into the eighth chain from the hook. * Make two chains. Skip the next two foundation chains and work one double into the next foundation chain. Continue from * to the last foundation chain.

2 On following rows, begin by working five chains to count as the first double and two-chain space. Work one double into the next double. * Work two chains and then one double into the next double. Continue from * to the end, working the last double into the turning chain.

Beginning with a block

1 To begin a piece of filet with a block of doubles, make enough foundation chains for the spaces and blocks on the first row. Work two more chains and then work one double into the fourth chain from the hook; the first three chains count as the first double. Complete the first block by working one double into each of the next two foundation chains.

2 On following rows, to begin with a block work three chains to count as the first double. Skip the first double and work one double into each of the next three doubles.

Working a block above a space

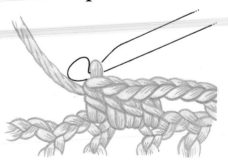

Work one double into the next connecting double. Then work two doubles into the space, followed by one double into the next connecting double.

Working a space above a block

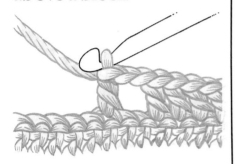

Work one double into the next connecting double. Work two chains, skip the next two doubles and work one double into the next double.

Shaping filet crochet

The methods of shaping given here are for a two-double, two-chain mesh; for a wider or denser mesh, work more or fewer chains at the beginning or end of the rows.

Increasing a space

1 To increase a space at the end of a row, work seven chains at the beginning of the previous row. Skip the first chain from the hook and slip stitch into each of the next three chains. (The remaining three chains count as the first double of the row.)

2 Pattern to the end and turn. Work to the end of the increase row, working the last double into the turning chains. Make two chains and work one double into the first slip stitch as shown to form the new space.

3 To increase a space at the beginning of a row, work seven chains at the end of the previous row. Turn. Begin the increase row by working one double into the first stitch to form the new space.

4 To increase two spaces at either end of a row, work ten chains at the beginning or end of the previous row, as appropriate. At the beginning of the row below the increase, slip stitch into the second to seventh chain from the hook. Work two chains and one double into the top of the second double of the previous row. When increasing over chains made at the end of a row, work one double into the eighth chain from the hook, make two chains, and work one double into the first double of the previous row.

Increasing a block

1 To increase at the end of a row, follow step 1 of "Increasing a space." Pattern to the end of the row and turn. Work to the end of the row, working one double into the turning chains. Work one double into each of the additional slip stitches to form the new block. To increase two blocks, work ten chains as in either of the two methods in step 4 of "Increasing a space."

2 To increase a block at the beginning of a row, work five chains at the end of the previous row and turn. Work one double into the fourth chain from the hook (the first three chains count as the first double). Work one double into the next chain and one double into the first double of the previous row to form the new block. Work ten chains as before to increase two blocks.

Decreasing a space

1 At the beginning of a row, work one chain and skip the first double. Slip stitch into each of the next two chains and into the next double. Work five chains to count as the first double and two-chain space. Work one double into the next double and pattern to end. Decrease two spaces by slip stitching over an extra two chains and a double.

161

Padded work

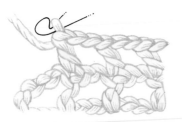

2 At the end of a row, lea.. the last space unworked. To decrease two spaces, skip an extra space.

Decreasing a block

1 At the beginning of a row, make one chain and skip the first double. Slip stitch into each of the next three doubles to decrease one block. Begin the row with five chains to count as the first double and two-chain space. Decrease two blocks by slip stitching across two blocks of the previous row.

2 To decrease at the end of a row, pattern to the last four doubles, work one double into the next double. Turn, leaving the remaining doubles unworked. Decrease two blocks by leaving six doubles unworked.

By padding or quilting with synthetic batting you can add more texture and warmth to your designs.

Simple padding

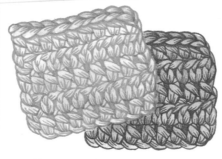

1 Almost any shape can be padded, but rectangular pieces are best. Work two pieces of crochet with the same number of stitches and rows. The right-side piece could be decorated, though any fancy stitches should be closely textured to conceal the batting.

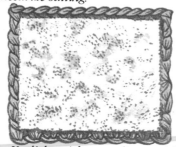

2 Use lightweight or medium-weight batting. Cut it ¼in smaller all around than the crochet. Place the batting on the wrong side of one piece of crochet and place the wrong side of the other piece on top. Pin through all three layers to hold them together.

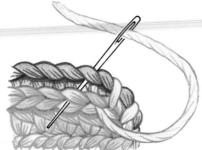

3 Either join the pieces with single crochet (see page 124) or work a stitch-by-stitch overcast seam. For the latter, secure the yarn at the corner.

Holding the two edges together, insert the needle under corresponding top single loops of the both pieces and draw the yarn through.

4 Continue in this way to the end. This method produces a neat seam, which is almost invisible on the right side.

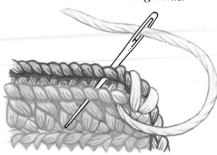

5 To join the padded pieces, place them together with right sides facing. Use stitch-by-stitch overcasting as before, inserting the needle under the loops seamed in steps 3 and 4.

Quilting
Quilting crochet is easier if you use your pattern as a guide — geometric designs are simplest.

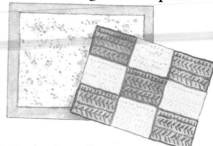

1 Cut batting to the same size as the crochet. Cut out lining approximately ½in larger all around than the crochet to provide a seam allowance. Place the batting on the wrong side of the lining and then place the wrong side of the crochet on top of the batting.

Finishing techniques

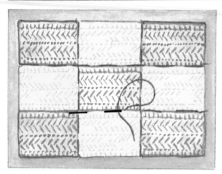

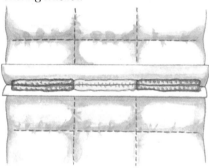

2 *Using contrasting sewing thread, baste through all three layers along the quilting lines. Stitch along quilting lines. Experiment to find the best stitch length and foot pressure. Remove the basting stitches.*

3 *To seam quilted crochet, place the quilted pieces together with right sides facing. Machine stitch approximately⅝in from the edge, catching the edge of the crochet. Trim the lining seam allowance on one side only.*

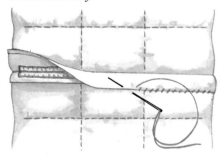

4 *Turn under the raw edge of the other lining seam allowance; slipstitch it to the lining on the other side, as shown, to hide the raw edges. Bind the outer raw edges either with strips of crochet or with bias strips of lining fabric.*

Buttonholes

Buttonholes keep their shape best when worked in fabrics made of firm, close-textured stitches such as single crochet. They can be worked either in the main fabric or in a separate band.

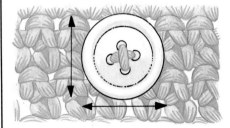

1 *Before beginning, place the button on the crochet. Count the number of rows or stitches covered by the diameter of the button, then subtract one. This will give a rough idea of the number of chains or rows needed to form the buttonhole; but check as you work to make sure this is correct.*

2 *Crochet buttonholes should look very neat, but they will keep their shape better if reinforced with buttonhole stitch. Use a tapestry needle and matching yarn to work the stitches.*

Horizontal buttonholes

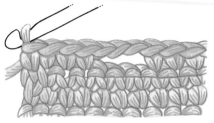

1 *Beginning at the edge nearest to the buttonhole, work to the position of the buttonhole. Make the number of chains needed to form the buttonhole. Skip the same number of stitches and work into the next stitch.*

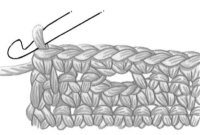

2 *On the return row, work one stitch into each chain of the previous row. Work to the end of the row. One horizontal buttonhole has been formed.*

Vertical buttonholes

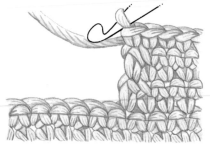

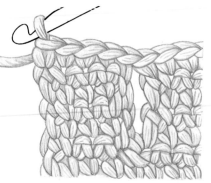

1 Beginning at the edge nearest the buttonhole, work to the position of the buttonhole. Turn, leaving the remaining stitches unworked. Work the number of rows needed for the buttonhole, ending at the buttonhole edge.

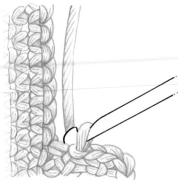

2 Do not turn. Slip stitch down the edge of the buttonhole, working the last slip stitch into the same place as the first stitch on the side of the buttonhole.

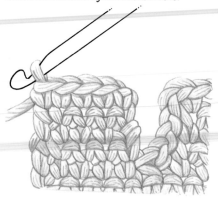

3 Skip one stitch and work into each of the stitches left unworked in step 1. Pattern on these stitches until the second edge of the buttonhole is the same number of rows as the first, ending at the side edge.

4 Turn and work to the buttonhole. Work one stitch into the edge stitch on the other side of the buttonhole to join in the two sides together. Pattern to the end of the row. Count the stitches to make sure none have been accidentally skipped. Turn and continue in pattern, working over the top stitches of the buttonhole very carefully. Repeat steps 1 through 4 for each buttonhole.

Button loops

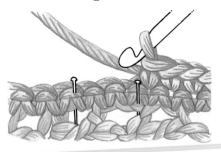

1 With the wrong side facing, work one row of single crochet into the side edge of the work. Mark the position of the loops with pins. Turn and work to the first pin.

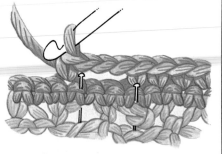

2 Make enough chains to slip easily, but not loosely, over the button. Skip the same number of stitches. Work a single crochet into the next stitch. Continue in this way until all loops have been worked.

Making a twisted cord

1 A twisted cord can be made of various numbers of strands, to produce different thicknesses of cord. The number is usually specified in the pattern. Take the required number of strands, cut to three times the length of the finished cord, and knot each end.

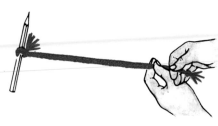

2 Fasten one end of the cord around a door handle, or knot it over a pencil and anchor in a convenient place. Holding the strands taut, rotate them until they are tightly twisted.

3 Fold the strands in half at the center and knot the ends together. Holding the knot, give the cord a sharp shake and even out the twists by smoothing the cord from the knotted end. Re-knot at the fold and cut both ends to make neat tassels.

Working an invisible seam

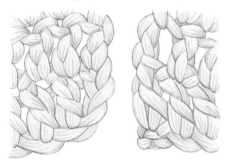

1 This flat seam is ideal for baby clothes and other delicate garments, especially those made of lace, since it does not produce a hard ridge. It also has the advantage of enabling patterns to be matched easily. First place the pieces edge to edge, right side upward, matching patterns.

2 Using a matching yarn (here a contrasting color is used for clarity) and a tapestry needle, secure the yarn to one lower edge. Take the needle over to the other side edge and pass it under one stitch.

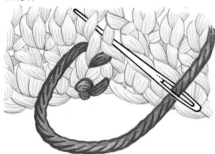

3 Take the needle back to the first side edge and under the next stitch. Pull the yarn through firmly to make the stitch invisible, but not so tightly that the fabric puckers.
Continue catching one stitch on each edge until the seam is complete.

Picking up stitches

Picking up stitches is a technique used more often in knitted than in crocheted garments, but it is required wherever knitted ribbing is added to a crocheted fabric edge. The pattern will specify the size needles to be used and the number of stitches to be picked up. The instructions are written: "Pick up and K [knit]" followed by the number of stitches.

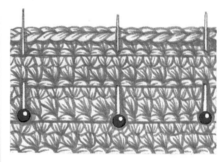

1 To ensure that the stitches are picked up evenly, divide the edge into equal sections and mark the sections with pins.

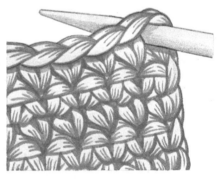

2 Divide the number of sections into the number of stitches specified in the pattern and start picking up an equal number of stitches per section. Insert the tip of the needle into a row end on vertical edges or into a stitch on horizontal edges.

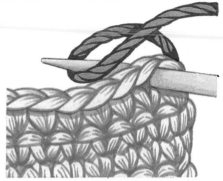

3 With the yarn at the back of the work, take it under and over the point of the needle, and draw a loop through.

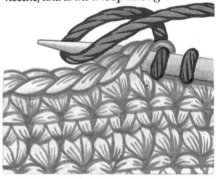

4 Insert the tip of the needle into the next stitch or row end. Take the yarn under and over the point of the needle and draw a loop through. Continue in this way until the correct number of stitches have been picked up.

INDEX

Crochet hook sizes

American sizes		Metric sizes
14		0.60mm
13		–
12		0.75mm
11		–
10		1.00mm
9		–
8	steel	1.25mm
7		1.50mm
6		–
5		–
4		1.75mm
3		–
2		–
1		–
0		2.00mm
B		2.50mm
C		3.00mm
D		–
E		3.50mm
F		4.00mm
G		4.50mm
H		5.00mm
–		5.50mm
I		6.00mm
J		6.50mm
K		700mm
10		–
11		8.00mm
12	wood	–
13		9.00mm
15		10.00mm
16		–

Note: American hook sizes vary slightly according to the manufacturer.

Sizes

The garments in this book are sized according to the system set forth by the National Bureau of Standards. This table gives the chest measurement (and, in the case of babies, also the weight and age) for each size. More detailed information is given in the introduction and measurement diagram for each pattern.

Babies

size	B-1	B-2	B-3
chest	to 18in	to 20in	to 22in
weight	5-10lbs	11-18lbs	19-24lbs
age	newborn	6 months	12 months

Children

size	C-2	C-3	C-4	C-5	C-6	C-7
chest	21in	22in	23in	24in	25in	26in

size	C-8	C-10	C-12	C-14	C-16
chest	27in	28in	30in	32in	34in

Misses

size	6	8	10	12
bust	30½in	31½in	32½in	34in

size	14	16	18	
bust	36in	38in	40in	

Men

size	34	36	38	40
chest	34in	36in	38in	40in

size	42	44	46	48
chest	42in	44in	46in	48in

Note: at C-14 a girl's size may change to a Misses' 6 or 8.
at C-16 a boy's size may change to a Man's 34.